WELCOME

A MEMOIR BY

KRISTI VANDERZON, KINDRA
GILLETTE, AND KACIE MOLINA

TO THE
JOURNEY

ADVENTURE TO BOLIVIA

To our amazing, fun, and beautiful mother on her 49th Birthday! We love you so much and adore all of the wonderful memories of our many adventures together. We also want to dedicate this book to our grandma, Carol Ellen Stevens, whose unconditional care and support through our many crazy life adventures will always be in our hearts. Thank you for being our role models of motherhood, love, beauty, grace, and faith!

Your daughters,

Kindra and Kacie

Welcome To The Journey

Adventure to Bolivia

Kristi VanderZon, Kindra Gillette, and Kacie Molina

TABLE OF CONTENTS

FOREWORD

I am so excited to finally share this story with you all! I have experienced so many different cultures, ideas, and religions over my young life that I used to deem ordinary. At the ripe young age of 22 and moving to the modern lifestyle, I have begun to realize how fascinating my life has been. Although I have previously considered myself to be uninterested in writing, I recently started sharing my stories via a blog and found out I really enjoy writing! I have been rewarded by people sharing their unique experiences with me and reminiscing about the "good old days" that my stories remind them of. But let's get back to the introduction.

I'm the youngest of the family this story is about. There's David, my dad, Kristi, my mom, Kindra, my older sister, and then there's me, Kacie. My sister and I are collaborating on this project together. It's been fun reminiscing and reliving our adventures. It's been bringing us closer even though we now live many miles away and live different lifestyles. I feel blessed to still have such a close and loving relationship with my sister despite all the lifestyle changes and different opinions we hold. We want to surprise mom with this book of her email entries, Kindra's journal, and some thoughts from me tucked in. So, surprise, mom! Happy 49th birthday and we love you so much!

Our family has been on many adventures that someday I would like to record and publish in more books. For the sake of staying focused on our biggest and most exciting adventure to date, I will be brief in introducing how the experience came about. When I was born back in 1998, my family lived in the big city of Milwaukee, WI. My dad, David, was a big city firefighter. One of those super amazing humans who jumped into fires to rescue people and put the fires out. Just your everyday hero, facing the danger and helping anyway. Kristi was a stay-at-home mom and made every day of Kindra and I's life a fun learning adventure. Library expeditions, playdates, lots of outside time, delicious home-cooked snacks and meals, and all that topped off with lots of love and joy!

I spent my first 6 years in the city of Milwaukee before we moved to the beautiful north woods of Michigan and started our homesteading adventures. From there, we met and joined a local Charity church (a more liberal group of Christians that branched from the traditional Amish church). We romped around on horseback, raised goats, and had a grand time. We built homes and moved, met new people, and eventually found our way to Tennessee to join a horse and buggy Amish community and church. While living there, we learned about Bolivia through the missionary stories of fellow community members and friends. We decided we wanted to go try life in the jungle. My parents are the type to tackle any adventure, big or small. This one was definitely the former :)

This is the tale of our adventure to Bolivia and our life while we lived there. Thank you for taking the time to read this book and share in the adventure with us. Welcome to the Journey

I could only squeeze a fraction of the pictures I wanted to share in this book, so here's the link to our website where you can check out extra pictures and videos!
https://welcometothejourney.us/

If you would like to hear more adventures from before or after our Bolivia trip, feel free to drop us a line and let us know here. Mom has over 10 years of daily journal entries that recorded our life in the Amish and homesteading. I'm sure before she shares them she'd love to hear some encouragement from her readers!
https://welcometothejourney.us/?page_id=7

If you have any questions feel free to post them here and I will do my best to personally answer them!

https://welcometothejourney.us/?page_id=16

INTRODUCTION

This book is a collection of journals and emails from our journey to Bolivia. Although our names are real, for the rest of the people who appear in this book, their names are changed to protect their privacy. They all exist, and everything in this book is pure truth and non-fiction.

Since this book is written by all three of us girls, I will be sure to note who wrote what sections so you can stay connected with each of our thoughts and experiences throughout the trip.

I, Kacie Molina, am the youngest of the two VanderZon daughters in the story. I'm now married, hence the name change. I am compiling this book, and when you see my writing, it will look like this:

"Author Note From Kacie Molina:

I was too young to enjoy journaling, so much of my writing will fill in the story gaps. I am also writing the forward and the epilogue."

My sister, Kindra Gillette, the eldest of the two VanderZon daughters in this story, is also now married. When you see Kindra's writing, it will look like this:

"Kindra's Journal   Date: 00/00/0000

Kindra faithfully journaled every day in a beautiful leather-bound journal. She has immaculate handwriting. Since I can't include the original journal pages, I hope this font gives a bit of the handwritten journal feels."

Our dear mother, Kristi VanderZon, was and continues to be kind, caring, and ever making us laugh. Mom has always been a fantastic writer, and I'm so glad she will finally have a book to her name! When you see Kristi's writing, it will look like this:

"Trip summary by Kristi VanderZon   Date: 00/00/0000

Kristi would write summaries of our trip experiences and email them to our friends and family to update them on our progress. mom would pick out pictures to share, and those will be included just like they were in the emails."

There are only 3 of us authoring this book, although we are a family of four, and this book contains four main characters. Our dad, David VanderZon, does not seem to enjoy writing. As the designated driver, dad was kept busy behind our Land Cruiser's steering wheel for most of the trip. Thank you, dad, for driving so diligently and keeping us safe even on the crazy and dangerous roads. I never fully appreciated the effort and concentration driving a vehicle takes until I got a license and drove something other than a horse and buggy. In a third-world environment where driving rules are constantly changing, and the signs are all in a language you can't understand, it must have made driving even more intense. Way to go, dad!

Some of the ideas expressed are from a strict religious view and, as such, may sound harsh. I left them in the book because our view of the world at that time was very different, as seen through the Amish lens. You get the good, the amazing, and ugly in this book. Life is not always pretty, but it's the ups and downs that make for a full experience.

CHAPTER 1

WHY FLY WHEN YOU CAN DRIVE?

Life on the farm was lovely. We all worked together gardening and farming. We made our living off of taking our organic vegetables to the farmer's market in Nashville, TN. Heirloom tomatoes were our specialty, and our customers loved them! Every week they would come to visit our Pilgrims Produce booth and stock up on the beauties. Chemical-free, nutrient-rich was how we maintained our garden. Simple and nutritious.

Kindra and I had a pony named Scout that we would hitch to a little cart and run errands around the community with. He was no ordinary pony, changing color every spring and fall. Whenever he shed and got his new layer of fur the following season, his color would change. That's all just to say Scout was an exceptional pony.

We trained one of our goats to pull a cart for the smaller tasks and take me on rides. And, just because it was a fun challenge training a goat to do the job of a horse. Who wouldn't want to ride around on a milk crate throne pulled by their favorite goat?!?

We had a great rhythm in our life. Weekdays were filled with gardening, animal chores, homeschooling, sewing, baking, quilt knottings, sorghum pressings, work bees, and adventuring around the hills of Tennessee with our pony. Saturdays were market days, and we all looked forward to picking and packing the beautiful produce we worked so hard to tend. It was fun to see our customer's faces light up as they rushed over to our booth to get their share of yummy organic produce.

We knew our regular customers by name and shared lots of laughter and wonderful conversations with each and every one of them. I even got to experience a brief moment of exciting "fame" when my recipe for zucchini bars was published on one of the local chef's blogs. That was tremendous excitement for me! We would trade produce with other booths for cheesecakes, meat, buttermilk, caramel corn, lemonade, and more.

Once we got home, we would open up our little cash till and count all the profits from the day. It was so rewarding to watch the cash pile up in exchange for the labor of our hands. Sundays were church days, and since there was a hill in between the 2 parts of our community, each side would take turns crossing the hill to go to church.

We lived on the Cane Creek side, which could have been called the "main" side. Russell Creek was on the other side of the hill, tucked back into a rustic holler. Both church houses were special places, quiet aside from the occasional sound of a horse whinnying or snorting. It was quite a sight to see all the horses and buggies tied to hitching posts and trees. We varied our methods of transportation depending on the weather and our moods. Sometimes walking, sometimes biking, and my favorite method of taking the buggy.

Men and women entered through different doors and sat on different sides of the church. Singing was rustic and monotone. Unlike the Charity churches, where they would sing harmony, the Amish prefer to sing in unison. There was no air conditioning, and let me tell you, you missed it on those super hot southern days. The pew in front of you held all the hymn books and fans. These fans were truly the best thing ever! The faint breeze they blew on your face was quite rejuvenating during the long services by the elders and brethren.

After church, it was customary to either go over to a family's house for dinner or invite one over to your house. I enjoyed playing with the children and getting to know the other families. The food was always delicious, and the company was edifying. Sunday nights were filled with popcorn, smoothies, and hymn singings.

On one of these particular evenings, when we were visiting with our friends Roland and Leonna, they told us about the time they lived in Bolivia. How Leonna grew up in Bolivia that they had a house sitting down there vacant. Most of her family, including her parents and some siblings, still lived in the jungle near Ixiamas, Bolivia. The more stories they told us, the more we were intrigued. Eventually, Leonna's brother visited from Bolivia and filled our heads with even more tales of Bolivia. I think it was a simultaneous desire to travel that swept over all four of us at the same time.

We were never ones to follow the rules or be told what to do. As much as we appreciated the community, we realized it was time for us to move on and find some more freedom. Usually, you would need to get permission and blessing from the church to make such a big move, but we just up and decided to go. Although some community members shunned us, some were still very accepting and supportive of our family and journey.

Ironically, in my homeschool studies, my Christian history curriculum of the year was on Central and South America. As the summer continued and our plans got real and progressed, we stumbled across a chapter discussing the Pan-American Highway, the road that connects Alaska to Argentina. That is, all except for a small but very perilous section of Panama called the Darien Gap. It connects Panama to Columbia but has no roads to actually make the crossing. As soon as we saw it was possible to drive, we started scheming.

We researched and bought an 84 Toyota Land Cruiser, a beautiful royal blue, and got it expedition ready. It was so exciting as we packed and planned. We each got a plastic tote and a travelers-style large backpack to condense all of our precious belongings into. This precious little space had to include room for clothes and other necessities. To make this real estate even more precious, the backpacks had to be practically packed and easy to use during travel.

I was particularly attached to my baby dolls at the time and had 5 of them. They all had names and birthdays. In order of "oldest" to "youngest" their names were Caleb, Regula, Gideon, Maranatha, and baby Timothy (who we called Timoteo since we were learning Spanish). They were precious to me, so despite them taking up most of the tiny space I had to pack, I brought them all along.

We sat around the living room at night listening to Pimsleur Spanish learning CDs. We would *"Eschuche y repito"* (*listen and repeat)* many phrases like *"Cuanto cuesta una cerveza"* *(how much does a beer cost)* and *"Como te llamas"* *(what is your name)*. We learned some extra Spanish from a Christian Spanish children's curriculum. All the songs for the kids helped cement the new language in our minds. We ordered an English-Spanish dictionary to learn as we traveled. Our language skills, or lack thereof, caused lots of laughter and fun our entire trip.

There were definitely some tough decisions and sacrifices to be made. One particularly hard one for me was parting from our beloved animals and finding new homes for them. Most of them we'd had since we lived in Michigan, and some of them were born on our farm and raised by Kindra and me. Scout the pony, all of our chickens which were too many to name, and the goats. Buttercup was the wise matriarch of the herd and was my sister's milker. Lily May was Buttercup's baby who grew up to be my milker, and she was the goat we trained to pull the cart. They were both such good girls. We also had three of their kids: Bluebell, Lupine, and Tula June, who we had to sell. The easiest to part with was Molasses the Billy. He was stinky but a good and friendly billy. Some old Tennessee hillbilly saw our ad for him and, while he proudly walked away with his purchase, triumphantly hollered out, "He ain't kin to no one around here!" Apparently, finding a new bloodline from Michigan to add to his goat herd was a treasure. I'm glad Molasses went somewhere where he was probably treated like a king.

Another complicated part of our departure was the news that our precious grandma was diagnosed with terminal cancer. We got this news shortly before our departure date. It was super hard on all of us, but especially mom. The heartache never went away, and we miss grandma so much. She was such a kind-hearted and beautiful person inside and out. She was thoughtful and took tender loving care of all her children, grandchildren, and great-grandchildren alike. There was nothing like going to grandpa and grandma's house. With a warm and inviting scent to the house, lots of love and acceptance, and a fun-filled backyard with a creek we grandchildren would fish in. Grandma was a home keeper and an inspiration to all who knew her. A true Proverbs 31 woman: "An excellent wife who can find? She is far more precious than jewels." We miss her greatly, and life will never be the same without her. With heavy hearts, we set out not knowing if we would ever see her again.

When our day of departure finally arrived, we said tearful goodbyes to all of our friends. We were blessed with lots of delicious food for the road and some Spanish Christian literature to pass out on our travels. With excitement and just a twinge of uncertainty, we left behind the life we had known for something totally new and uncharted. Rolling away from our small community and entering the vast and uncertain world, the journey was underway, and there was no turning back.

Author: Kristi VanderZon   **Date: 7/26/2010**

All Packed Up!

Well, for all our family and friends who have been waiting to hear if we're really going to head south to Bolivia, the time has finally arrived! Lord willing, we will pull out early tomorrow morning on this pilgrimage. We've packed, repacked, and gone over the Land Cruiser more times than we can count. We've got the two dogs, Walter & Biddy, and we're all eager to begin our trip. We look forward to what the Lord has for us as we travel. We'll be in touch as often as we can. We appreciate all your prayers! Trusting in Him... The VanderZons

CHAPTER 2

THE STATES

Author: Kacie Molina

The roof rack was loaded and the dogs were in the back panting from the hot Tennessee weather. As we claimed our seats and shut the doors, feelings of sadness, excitement, and the great unknown filled us all. We had many a stop to make on our way out, including picking up the dog's passports and a quick stop at the library for an internet connection to research.

Dad was our faithful driver. Mom was the co-pilot, which included navigating, reading books out loud to us, passing out snacks, and bringing her cheerful, uplifting presence. Kindra sat behind dad, graceful and grown-up. She helped keep an eye on the road and massage the weary driver as needed. I sat behind mom, playing with my favorite puzzle, the Rubik's cube, and amusing myself with the scenery. The dogs Walter and Biddy had a platform in the back of the Land Cruiser that dad built for them. They had a great view and had a very annoying habit of drooling all over Kindra's and my head as they excitedly awaited every new bend in the road.

Kindra's Journal   7/27/2010

All right, I have a whole empty journal in front of me, and I'm excited to write. We packed up the Land Cruiser around 7:00 this morning, then went and had our breakfast with the family who's farm we lived on and have grown quite close with.

On our way out, we stopped at many of our friend's houses to drop off various things and say goodbye to everyone. Saying goodbye to Joseph and his family was the hardest of all! We gathered up the wet clothes we had left there last night while dad and Joseph aired up the tires and strapped the watermelon that Joseph insisted we take to the top.

After we had all gathered and shared counsels with each other, we knelt for prayer together. Seeing Joseph and dad cry and be so sad was almost too much to watch. It made me sad too!

Here we are out on the road and our 1984 Toyota fj60 Land cruiser. The dogs occupied the platform dad built for them right behind Kacie and my seat. This, however, causes a dilemma as, when the dogs are hot, they pant and fling their doggy drool all over me and the stack of pillows between Kacie and me. I'm sure it will perfect our patience!

Dad and mom occupy the front seats, of course. Although dad implicitly explained his desire for clutter-free foot room for mom, she still seems to have an ever-growing pile of things in front of her. And to add to the amazingness of this, every time I clean the pile up for her, it only seems to increase. All of this said was to illustrate my point of dad's patience with us girls. It has really blessed me to see him so surrendered to follow whatever God's plan seems to be for us each day.

We left our Cane Creek community at noon and traveled little more than 157 miles. He still seems to be entirely at rest with it all. Praise God for his tender mercies! We traveled most of our miles today on the Natchez Trace highway. It's gorgeous, and I really enjoy the open woods and fields, along with no billboards or advertisements.

In the big city of Tupelo, we had to stop at Walmart. It was a long hot stop because we had to return the steering wheel lock, get a cap for our one burner stove, and try to fix the air conditioning, which is hardly working.

Around 6:00 p.m., we stopped at a campground on Davis lake. It was really beautiful, and we could see the big lake right from our site. After we set up our tent, we went to cool off in the lake. This was easier said than done, however, because the water was warmer than bathwater. We all took showers to rinse off the lake water, then went back and had our supper.

After we settled into the tent, mom read us two more chapters of Palace Beautiful, which was very interesting. Reading would not have been possible, but thanks to our camping friend John who gave us a lovely lantern, we have light in our tent! Praise the Lord! John told us he'd be praying for us and wished us God's blessing. We'll try to keep in touch through email with him. It's much cooler now! Good night :-)

Author Note From Kacie Molina:

We started on the Natchez Trace Hwy that runs 440 miles from Nashville, TN to Natchez, MS. Since it is a historical parkway, there were many sights to see along the way. It's always nice to stretch your legs and let the dogs out for a bit on long travel days, and these historical sights were perfect! We got to learn so much history and see so many beautiful places (yay, unschooling for allowing us to adventure and learn in such a natural way!). I think one of my favorite stops was a cypress swamp with boardwalks in MS. We got to stay at some fun campgrounds and get immersed in the local southern food and culture along the way. After the Natchez Trace Hwy, it was onwards to Texas.

Kacie and Kindra with the dogs on the Natchez Trace HWY

Kindra's Journal   7/28/2010

Slept quite well last night and woke up on my own at an early hour. Walked down to the bathhouse then came back and packed up sleeping bags, backpacks, and clothes that never seem to dry. Took the dogs for a walk with Kacie to the creek while mom and dad took down the tent.

I cut up the melon Joseph Yoder gave us with dad's Leatherman knife, which was quite the task since the watermelon was giant. I'm sure that was the first Joseph watermelon to be part of a thousand-mile expedition!

We were on the road by 9:00, then stopped around noon at a cypress swamp that had a boardwalk through it. I thought it was fascinating! The cypress and tupelo trees are very tall and thick at the base. They grow out of water that is so smooth and covered with this light green colored, how would I describe it.. slime type substance. It was quite a sight!

Dad stopped at a hardware store and got some supplies because we needed to repack the vehicle. The Land Cruiser has a bad wobble on every bump we hit, making the vehicle sway sideways. It's scary when the swaying gets bad because it's not just a little sway; it goes way back and forth! Dad said, "I don't know if I've ever gripped the steering wheel so tight".

Cypress Swamp

Poor mom is crying because we were playing my cousin Alaina's CD and listening to the song she wrote for grandma. I know it's hard on her as we speed south and away from grandma, knowing that she will have chemotherapy on Friday. It makes me cry on mom's behalf because I can't imagine mom having to go through that.

We pulled off the road around 4:30 p.m. to set up camp. There was an alligator head at the camp office almost two feet long, and we asked where the alligator was from. They said from the lake right there. We were all in sober awe as they pointed out the window right to the very water we wanted to swim in! Can you imagine? The alligator they shot was over 11 ft long.

It was thundering when we arrived at our campsite, so we quickly set up our tent and put sleeping bags, mats, and pillows in there for Kacie to distribute. Afterward, we got our Berkey water filter going and had a supper of dried apricots, almonds, and bread with honey.

Dad started unpacking the roof rack and started putting our heavy totes with books and things in the back of the land cruiser. He thought if he could get the bulk of the weight lower down on the vehicle, it would sway less. I really hope it helps!

I set up laundry lines to hang the ever-present wet clothes on. That baler twine I packed and thought I wouldn't be needed until way further down the road, was very graciously welcomed into my lineup of bungee cords. My makeshift clothesline worked really well. I wish I would have packed more baler twine though.

After we finished packing everything back into the Land Cruiser, we went to take showers. Our only tent camping neighbor is a Land Cruiser fan and is visiting with us while admiring the Land Cruiser. It was a good day with a high of 90 degrees. Very hot with lots of sunshine. I must be sure to keep track of temperature to share with our family and friends!

Kindra's Journal   7/29/2010

Slept pretty well despite having to pull off a tick in the middle of the night. There are many ticks down here, and we're all bitten up by some seemingly invisible bug.

After living on nuts and fruit for two days, we were all ravenous this morning. So much so that dad and I weren't feeling very well anymore, and I was getting a headache.

Our Land Cruiser fan from the campground told us that historic downtown Natchez was beautiful with lots of old buildings, so we went there to find a place to get breakfast. After packing up camp, which took a lot longer since it was our first day with the tarp on top of the vehicle. We had our Bible reading, then headed out for Natchez.

Natchez was indeed an old-time town, and we stopped at a visitor center where we read some fascinating slave history. We found a place to get breakfast, but despite the friendliness of the people, it took them an hour to make our food. With full bellies, we finally headed south. I was disappointed with the selay, but dad did well with the setback.

This afternoon we finally found a post office to mail out some letters. In one of the towns that we passed through, we saw a little boy meticulously grooming his pony in front of an auto shop. They made a super cute sight!

We set up our camp at Sam Houston State Park, then took a boardwalk with the dogs. Just us girls and mom went while dad stayed behind to look at maps. Mom and Kacie took the dogs, which were on their leashes, down on this little platform that didn't have railings.

Now, this swamp that we were walking through was covered in grass and green slime. Biddy thought it was solid ground. To her surprise, after launching off of the platform, she splashed into the water! I was not paying attention to what Mom and Kacie were doing until I heard a splash, and Mom started screaming for help. I dashed down the stairs to the platform where mom was hanging over the edge. Biddy was writhing around as water splashed everywhere. I grabbed hold of Mom with one hand and Biddy's collar with the other. With a heave, I managed to get the sopping wet dog up onto the platform just as dad arrived on the scene; bless his heart! He ran so incredibly fast that his flip-flops went flying right off.

We went into town for a few things then did some hiking back in the campground. Dad decided on a loop that runs next to the river and the swamp. We took showers, but my towel has been so damp for days that it smelled terrible. We're sleeping without the rain fly tonight. Life is good!

Kindra's Journal   7/30/2010

High of 100 degrees and very humid! As you can see by the sticker here, we made it to the Texas welcome center this morning. Our drive to Galveston was fun because we got to drive right along the Gulf of Mexico for a while and then take a ferry boat over to Galveston City.

There are lots of signs written in Spanish and English, how exciting! I love trying to read it, and I'm happy when I actually figure out the words. After we waited an hour in the scorching sun, we got on the ferry. We saw many big ships and fishing boats from the top of the ship. It was worth the long wait.

After getting gas, we went to the laundromat, where it was almost all Spanish-speaking people. I had fun trying out some Spanish on an older lady from Guatemala. We sat on the laundromat's steps for an hour with the dogs, and it was hot.

Before we left our campsite this morning, Kacie and I had fun feeding a deer some bread right out of our tent. That was special! After the laundromat, we found the library. I was so thrilled with this discovery. That was our next stop, and just dad and I ran in. Yes, I literally had to run to keep up with him.

Finally, I thought, I can email my cousin Alaina. My hopes were very high as I patiently waited for dad to finish up on the computer. In anticipation, I planned what I would write to her. Just then, dad turned to me and said, "why don't you just write to Alaina another time. It's not super important, is it?" Oh, the definition of disappointment! I answered cheerfully, which was very difficult, and replied, "Sure, that's fine". It was a trial for me to get through, but I had victory through Jesus the Lord.

We arrived at our campground around 5:30. It was an area on the Colorado River. There were few sights available to camp in. Unfortunately, the site we chose was, unbeknownst to us, in the party section. As soon as we set up our tent, the neighbors started to play terrible music loudly and use the world's worst language ever heard! Dad was not happy about the whole scenario and went to look at the other more expensive area to see if there was an empty site. There was. Praise the Lord!

While mom and dad went back to take down the tent, we girls took the dogs down to the Colorado River and played with them. It was a lovely river. After we played on the playground swings, we headed back to camp. Mom and Dad went off to take showers. We had a sincere prayer time for grandma because she had her first chemotherapy today.

Kindra's Journal   7/31/2010

Hello again! Today had a high temperature of 100 degrees again. It makes me smile when I record the temperatures for the day because it makes me think of Cindy Owens at the Franklin Farmers Market. She was one of our faithful customers and our friend. She wanted me to record the temperatures of the places we travel through, so she can decide what climate she likes the best when she reads this. Our Farmer's Market friends were always so kind, and we got a few emails from them yesterday.

We stopped at Walmart for a few things, including tennis balls for exercising the dogs. Of all days, this has been our most productive traveling day. Praise the Lord!

I haven't seen so much expansive land without any trees before. Well, there are a few trees, but it's just so flat. You can see so far and the vegetation consists of little shrubs and other small vegetation. There are lots of palm trees on the coast and they are pretty to look at. It is so hot, incredible hotness and even the breeze is hot. There seems to be no shade.

Since we only have three more American stamps and it's our last day in the states, mom wants to write Grandpa and Grandma, and I'll write to our friends in Tennessee.

We arrived at Boca Chica Beach after stopping at a border station to ask their advice about crossing into Mexico tomorrow. There one piece of advice about going to Mexico was "Don't do it". We enjoyed the waves out in the ocean waters and had tons of fun. We were amazed to be one of the few gringos on the beach.

Mom spotted a tortoise while we were sitting on the pier. It was so cute! Drove the Land Cruiser around some sandy roads, then found a flat spot to set up camp. On our way back from the pier, we got to help some people unhook a stingray. Dad held it while we girls petted it. It was very slimy and sticky.

Here we are, extremely sticky and sandy and being covered in more sand. I soon realized that talking about my infirmities wasn't well-received since we were all sticky, grimy, and miserable. We all tried to quietly bear our infirmities for the moment and go to bed. As the sand-swept through the tent and covered me, my pillow, and now gritty blanket, I thought about the trip. What will it be like? Is something bad going to happen to us? I know God loves and cares.

CHAPTER 3

MEXICO

Kindra's Journal 8/01/2010

Today had a high of 95 degrees.

Here we are, speeding towards the border, covered in sticky saltwater mist but happy. First, however, we need to find a windshield wiper because poor mom busted the passenger side wiper when she threw Kacie's backpack onto the hood. I've been praying that the Lord will have his hand in this because dad says they're hard to find.

I'm a little nervous about the whole Mexico thing, but as we charged through the sand to pack up this morning, I thought of all our friends back in Michigan and Tennessee who are praying for us! It made me feel so much better. I feel like it is God's will for us to go, so I am going to set out in faith. More later on the whole border crossing experience...

Hallelujah, praise the Lord! We are across the border and well on our way. What an experience! We arrived at the border at 10:00 and got our passports stamped, then waited in line for one and a half hours to get our vehicle permit. When we were waiting in line, a nice Christian lady gave us such excellent advice and was very helpful. She even found a money changer for us and made sure the exchange rate was fair. Bless her! We also met a nice man named Tim from Barton Creek, Belize.

Almost everything was in Spanish, and everyone spoke Spanish! After we thought we were all done, we went to leave, and the workers wanted to inspect all of the things we had in the *vehiculo* (vehicle). Oh, I can't believe I just wrote that in Spanish!

After seeing the communication barrier, they settled on an itemized list with individualized prices for everything. Then they wanted to see in the roof rack and under the back platform, both of which involved a considerable amount of unplanned effort and delay. I was just thankful that they didn't look in my tote. We finally left the border at 1:30. Right after we pulled out of the border station and jostled over numerous *topès* (speed bumps), we were welcomed into Matamoros by a swarm of interesting people.

We had no sooner locked the doors when a team of men ran out to the Land Cruiser, squirted some fluid from a water bottle onto the windshield, then proceeded to scrub and squeegee until the glass was spotless. With a bow of satisfaction, they stepped up to the window for some pay. The audience of vehicles had many stunt masters at the first stoplight and took us by surprise. We quickly figured out how to drive on the different road system and immediately started using our little green translating book.

We soon found out what checkpoints are. I don't know if I breathed a breath the whole first checkpoint! Official guards came out clad head to toe in full camouflage uniforms. They had helmets strapped on under their chins, bulletproof vests, long sleeve shirts, pants, big boots, and serious big black machine guns hanging from their shoulders.

They told us to pull off the main way and hand over dad's passport. While the soldier walked off with it, we were left to wonder. I was getting a little worried, but of course, after a few minutes, they brought it back and we were on our way. The military men have the ability to maintain an icy stare; it's a strange look. They drive around buses with two massive machine guns mounted on the roof and soldiers riding up on the roof to man the guns in case of use.

Our first bathroom experience was at a Pemex gas station. It was three pesos per person, and as soon as we girls finished and left the stalls, the "gestapo" rushed in to check all the stalls looking for who knows what. We gave him a Good and Evil comic book, and I think he liked it. You'll hear me mention these Good and Evil books a lot. Someone donated a big box of them in Spanish for us to distribute on our trip.

We are spending the night at the hotel, Rio Soto de Marine. It's a nice hotel by Mexican standards, but I wouldn't be so thrilled by American standards! I'm sure happy for a hot shower; it felt great.

We went to the restaurant Tampico for dinner, which was on the dinkier end of things like the hotel. Ordering food in Spanish was much easier than getting a hotel. When we got back, we took the dogs for a walk then smuggled them into our room.

Mom forgot about the whole Mexico food poisoning thing and, in an attempt to make sure we all avoided getting sick, mixed us up some activated charcoal. She used hotel water for all of us girls, which seemed worse than taking no medicine at all! She felt terrible about it.

Earlier at the restaurant, we thought not to drink the water, so we all ordered bottled drinks. We thought we were doing well until dad squeezed a lime into his beverage, and Kacie and I both poured our cokes in the glasses that came with them! Wow, we sure broke lots of rules!

Kacie gave the young man at the hotel desk a Good and Evil book. I later found him on the couch in the lobby reading it. After I gave my new language skills some thought, I said *"le gusta la libro?"* (do you like the book), and he answered with an *"ah bueno"* (ah, good) and a thumbs up. It was rewarding to see him enjoying it!

The hotel had a computer for the dwellers to use, so we took the opportunity to do a group email. I thought it strange how the computer said all of our words were spelled wrong because they were in English, haha. Also, all of the computer settings were in Spanish, which made it both difficult and interesting to operate.

I finally got to email Alaina. Although I never pictured myself communicating via email, it's tough to find a post office here. So, email is not a bad way to go!

It's late, and we're in our room for the night. Dad just shuttled the dogs into our room through the glass sliding doors. Just before it got dark, we walked the dogs up and down the main street in front of the hotel. This was a little nerve-wracking for me but a great experience nonetheless.

All of the brightly colored little beer shacks and food stands were lit up, and the people seemed to be enjoying themselves. They are very friendly even though we have a significant language barrier. We made friends with the hotel workers. I miss everyone back home so much. God is good.

Author Note From Kacie Molina:

I usually won't include the same day from 2 people's perspectives, but since this was a big, momentous day, I thought you would enjoy both.

Author: Kristi VanderZon   08/01/2010

Hello all dear family and friends that are praying for us,

Today we finally crossed that great divide of the Mexican border. Last night we put our tent up at a beautiful beach outside of Brownsville, TX. On the Gulf of Mexico by the Rio Grande. Saw a stingray reeled in by a neighboring fisherman and enjoyed a night listening to the waves.

In contrast to that peace and quiet, we spent over three hours at customs, waiting to cross the border. Met a few amigos in line who shared some helpful information on our travel route. They only searched a few of our totes and most of our time was spent waiting in line.

Coming into Matamoros was indeed an initiation of sorts. At the first red light, two men were washing our window, and another was breathing fire. They each wanted a peso. The police were wasting no time pulling people over, but we made it through. Before we stopped for the night, we went through four Mexican military checkpoints. There's no question there's a war going on here. David seems to attract the wrong kind of attention with his bushy beard.

As one guard tried to communicate, they're looking for the Taliban. Yes, they were serious and had fortified bunkers of sandbags or bricks. Although it was intimidating with all the machine guns and uniforms, they were kind and let us go on our way.

Tonight finds us in the tiny town of Soto de Marine, in a comfortable hotel where we feel almost at home with goats, sheep, chickens, and no shortage of dogs roaming around outside our door.

We enjoyed a fine Mexican meal at a little restaurant down the street. After hardly eating all day, we're praising the Lord for his goodness, protection, and food. It's a blessing to have you all out there praying and thinking of us.

Dad and Mom, Our hearts and thoughts are with you every moment as mom is beginning treatment. We love you!

Thanks all, and please continue praying for us!

Love, David, Kristi, Kindra, and Kacie

Kindra's Journal   8/02/2010

High of 90 degrees today.

Good morning, we're still alive and feeling pretty good. After last evening's hotel water accident, I went straight to taking some natural medicine to try to combat any potentially harmful bacteria that may have been in the water. However, my combination of activated charcoal, MMS, and oregano oil, followed later by some green superfood powder, left my stomach feeling a bit off. Hopefully, it'll kill whatever was in the water.

We hurriedly packed our things and left the keys with the man whom we gave the book to last evening. He thanked me and then gave me a folded-up piece of paper. I quickly brought it to the rest of the family. It was addressed "To my foreign friendlies". How sweet and funny. He told us his name was Lewis and that he will take excellent care of the book. He loved to read the Bible, and his parents would enjoy the book too. Then he signed the letter "His servant Lewis, the steward at the Hotel Rey". How encouraging!

The roads are very rough this morning on the way out of town, but we're all impressed with the *topès*. What an ingenious idea! They are very effective at controlling the speed of traffic.

All of the people seem very industrious. Almost everywhere you go, someone is mopping, sweeping, cleaning windows, spraying sanitizing spray, or hosing down parking lots.

As we traveled on, we passed the Tropic of Cancer. Strange name, but it was marked on the map.

We're finally seeing what real Mexican housing is like. Some have thatch roofs with sticks tied neatly together to form the walls, while others are cement-style buildings painted with bright contrasting colors and have metal roofs. Most of them have tidy little yards out front and the occasional horse tied up by their necks next to the highway.

We've seen lots of cowboys on their horses and donkeys along the road in the little towns we pass. I found it interesting when one of the cowboys reminded me of one of our close friends in the community just by the way he rode his horse! I really do miss all our friends back in the states. It's pretty scenery with mountains in the distance. It's so hard to write right now; these roads are terrible and bumpy. The Lord is merciful to his children!

Here we are cruising through Tampico. All I know about this city is from a video clip for tourists that we watched this morning. All it showed were women with pretty dresses, horses, beaches, and friendly Mexicans. Well, let me tell you, it was not so! We were doing well sticking to route 180, although the driving is horn-honking crazy with people pushing and darting everywhere.

We got through another window washing rush at a stoplight and were impressed with the impeccable job they did. As we were driving through a bunch of jostling traffic, a man in a green uniform stepped into the middle of the road right in front of us. He waved us into the lane closest to the curb but let us keep going. How odd, we thought. We were grateful he didn't stop us. But, not more than three blocks down, two other men in green uniforms stepped out into the road and sternly waved us in front of their police car.

There was no mistaking or ignoring it was us they wanted. Alright, I thought. The gringos they've been waiting for have finally arrived. The car was dead quiet, and I think I've come into a funny understanding of the verse "And the violent take it by force" (Mathew 11:12). I immediately started to pray for dad, for the two men approaching the window, for us girls, and for wisdom and guidance.

The first one to approach the window was a light-complexioned burly man with a very short haircut. He had his gun halfway out of its holster by the time he reached the vehicle. His sidekick, however, was the opposite of him. He had much darker-colored skin but the same short haircut and bulletproof vest as his partner. Both were holding their guns and had the ability not to crack a smile. This, I thought, was very scary, but I was able to trust in God.

Immediately they demanded papers along with insurance. Then, dad followed them around to the back of the Land Cruiser. Dad was doing very well and being friendly to them, but I didn't know what the tall man would do to him. While we girls sat in the vehicle, the darker man kept busy talking to us about America. Well, that's as much as we could understand in our broken Spanish. I turned around and looked at the back window to see the big light-colored man using his finger to write numbers in the grime on the glass.

Meanwhile, his partner in crime wanted passports, papers, and permits for the dogs. As we kept shaking our heads to motion "no" and giving him a confused look, he seemed to lose interest. Sadly, his interest was piqued at every *señorita* who passed by the scene. Finally, dad reappeared, saying, "okay, he started out demanding a 6,000 peso fine, and now he is all right with 200 pesos".

Right then, the darker man came up and was telling me in Spanish, "you know what I'm saying. Tell your dad we will let you go if you pay the ticket". At that point, dad said, "don't act like you know what he's saying." Because I didn't want to lie, I just shook my head no and looked confused. Then dad got a bright idea and turned to the cops saying, "Señor, you take us to Alamo with your lights on" and made signs with his hands like lights on top of the police car. The man got excited and said, "yes, if we paid."

Dad then told me to give him a Good and Evil and tell him we prayed for him today and we love him. So I did, and guess what he said? "For love, I will let you go". Again he thanked us for the book and shook hands with dad, and off we went. That was so scary. Praise the Lord we are safe! We serve a God who works miracles, and I know he can put who he wants us to meet in our paths and take out the ones he would rather us avoid. After that experience, we were very thankful to Eric Coltman for the travel tips he gave us and how well those tips worked!

We were traveling on a four-lane highway that actually contained six to eight lanes depending on how many people decided to pass at the same time. We were trying so hard to stay on the right road and follow the signs, but there were fewer and fewer signs until we didn't have any more to follow! The road kept getting skinnier until it turned into a one-lane, one-way street. The sidewalks were packed with people, such as I've never seen before. So many people were busily going to the hundreds of stores that lined the streets. Mom, bless her heart, desperately tried to find where we were on the map, but none of the street signs matched up with our newly purchased map from the Pemex station. Suddenly all of the cars in front of us started to turn off. We were left the only vehicle on the almost abandoned street. This was a terrible situation. Even dad said, "I don't have any idea what to do. I just have to keep driving".

Suddenly, the road came to a tee, and there was a Pemex station amidst all the abandoned buildings. Praise God, for he preserves the stranger! There was a Spanish-speaking man there who gave us perfect directions out of the city. God answers prayer.

Found a hotel for the evening after searching in vain for some Mennonite missionaries in a little town called El Idolo. The hotel was fascinating because it had lots of trees trimmed into different shapes, such as houses, circles, spirals, boxes, and hearts. Had a pleasant walk with the dogs. Praise God!

Kindra's Journal   8/03/2010

Cool with a high of 75 degrees

We started the first hour of our journey buying bananas and getting stopped by some Federales. This pullover went well, and we gave the officers a book. Drove some super windy road up into the mountains. Travel was very slow.

There were so many road workers with their pickaxes and shovels fixing the road, which was in very poor condition. The mountains are beautiful, and we saw many people herding sheep, horses, and cattle along the green hills. I love seeing it! The temperature was perfect.

We had finally reached our destination city of Tlaxcala. Though we weren't far from our host family, the Barajas, there was no way to find them. We had their phone number but no phone to call it. Somehow we made it down this little street and saw a payphone, so we stopped to use it. People stare at you as if they've never seen a gringo before. I'm sure some of them hadn't.

We dialed the number of the Barajas, and someone answered. However, we later learned that at this point, the person on the other end forgot all of their English. This presented quite a problem because Dad seemed to have forgotten all of his Spanish, so mom got the idea to get someone to talk for us.

Mom and I spotted someone that seemed like a good candidate. We bumbled with our growing Spanish skills, *"Perdon señor. Por favor hablar a nuestro amigo por telephono"* (Excuse me, sir, can you please talk to our friend on the phone). Would you believe what he said? "Sure"! What a relief. Yes, the man spoke a little English and after a few minutes on the phone hung up and said, "stay right here, don't move. He'll be here in 15 minutes". What joyous words!

I had no idea who "he" was, but I couldn't wait for him to get there. And, sure enough, about 15 minutes later, he arrived on a motorcycle. The man got off, pulled off his helmet, and shook all of our hands. "Hello, my name is Marco Felipe, son of Danielle Baraja. Welcome to Tlaxcala. Let's go home." Ah, you need to have been on the journey standing right there with us to appreciate this as much as we did!

Marco Felipe waived for us to make a u-turn right in a road that wasn't even big enough to turn around in one go. Just as dad said he doesn't know how he's going to do it, Marco Felipe pulled out right into the traffic, stopping it for us. We praised the Lord as we followed our new found brother in Christ on his motorcycle back through a maze of streets to the Barajas home. Mom summed up the situation into a fitting description that "he's like a night and shining armor". That's truly what it felt like!

We pulled up into a parking lot surrounded by four-story-high apartments, eight dwellings per building. As we followed Tony to his apartment, a neighbor lady asked a string of questions about the gringos in Spanish. We met the rest of the Baraja family in their apartment.

The parents Danielle and Patricia, along with their children Danny, Marco Felipe, Jeremiah, and Arielli. All of them are incredibly kind! Sang songs and played guitars late into the night. Great fellowship despite the language barrier! I'm so tired.

Kindra's Journal   8/04/2010

Woke up this morning, and all was quiet. Last night I slept on all four of our camping mats with the rest of our family on the bed. It was so very comfortable!

Enjoyed breakfast with the family around 8:30, then washed our clothes and hung them up on the roof to dry. On my way back down to the apartment, I stopped and looked over the edge to see where the happy Spanish music was coming from. The sound was from the housetop of a Mexican who, with his big sombrero, was busy up on a ladder painting his house a bright yellow. It was fun hanging laundry out on the roof. Earlier in the morning, Jeremiah took us up to the very top of the building. The climb up the ladder was well worth the view of Tlaxcala.

Danny and Tony took us into town to run some errands. We needed to go to a pharmacy, post office, and bank. We all got in the "Combe", their old Volkswagen bus that is very common around here and headed out. Tony stopped at a fantastic viewpoint and historical sight. We stood at the top of a 300 step stairway with a water fountain that flowed from top to bottom and enjoyed the view. Then they took us to El Centro and past the plaza.

They found a very tiny parking space, pretty much one in a million. The streets were packed with people! After securing the "Combe" we took to the streets. It's incredible how good it feels to have friends to lead the way and guide you. Danny and Tony in front strolled on in their casual manner, with Kacie and me behind them, and Mom and dad behind us. We walked on and on, staying right behind our guides. We made all our stops successfully.

At the post office, the stamps cost over a dollar, and at the pharmacy, the inhaler medicine dad needed cost half the price it does in the states. Give a little, take a little, I guess. Last of all and most difficult was finding a bank to change our dollars into pesos! Finally, after our fourth failed attempt, Danny took off running down the street and came back saying he found a place to do it. Dad just needed to give him our dollars, and he would exchange them for us. I never thought it would be so challenging to change your money into local currency.

We greatly appreciated our Spanish-speaking brothers in Christ helping us out like that! Made our way back to the "Combe" where Biddy went crazy when

Danny tried to open the door for us. Danny found it very entertaining! Dad went and bought everyone a coke, and then we headed for home.

We enjoyed a meal at the Barajas together. While dad looked at the Land Cruiser, Kacie and I had a delightful time playing the guitar and dulcimer with Jeremiah and Arieli. They love the dulcimer, and I enjoyed hearing Jeremiah play the guitar.

We left for the Moreno's around 6:15 in the "Combe" and after a maze of *topès* and brick roads, we finally arrived at the Morenos. They were thrilled to see us, and after making introductions, they ran to get a picture of Josue, their son who was in DF (the capital). It was clear that he was very special to them!

We had a great time sharing testimonies and singing, followed by Bible reading and preaching. Even though it was in a different language, I thought it was a spirit-filled meeting by what little I could understand. Afterward, we took pictures with everyone there and enjoyed some coffee with sweet bread before we all left.

It was pretty cold as we piled back into the "Combe". Just as we were pulling away, Gabby came out to wave goodbye. We bobbled back to the Baraja's apartment, and by the time we emailed and wrote letters, it was past midnight.

Kindra's Journal   08/05/2010

Today had a high of 70

Got up and enjoyed a time of fellowship as we shared breakfast and sang songs. It was so special. Said goodbyes to all but Danny and Marco Felipe, who led us to the highway on the same motorcycle we followed into their house. Almost every street dog we passed, Danny would turn around and point to it and smile. The dogs were the source of much laughter over the past few days.

Finally, we came to the sign for Puebla. Marco Felipe pulled over, and we all got out. It seemed way too soon to have to say goodbye. Dad asked Marco Felipe to pray, so we all stood in a little circle, and even though the prayer was in Spanish, I found I understood quite a bit more than I did when we got there. Having Tony and Danny help us translate was huge! We said bye to them and headed out. It was so sad to leave them there. We all felt like we left our hearts there.

We got lost in Oaxaca, but the Lord directed a man to give us directions once again. Although they were in Spanish, they worked! On our way out, dad made his first stoplight purchase of some tasty churros.

Today was our first day that we had a problem finding a place to stay for the night. It was getting dark, raining, and all of the hotels were either closed or abandoned. We just kept driving and praying that the Lord would provide a place, and of course, he eventually did. Praise him!

I didn't care for how many Catholic pictures were on the walls, but I was just glad to be there. We walked the dogs down the street and happened upon a taco stand. We bought some since we hadn't eaten since breakfast. Walter and Biddy were thrilled to be out of the car.

There was a big median in the road with benches, so we ate there in front of the hotel with the dogs. We tried to look unconcerned. We were super friendly to every person we saw and hope the kindness strategy pays off to help us stay safe here. All was well until a shady-looking pickup truck slowed way down, and a mean-looking man stared at us with a seemingly sinister look on his face. We all thought it best to head to our room.

Upon arriving in our room, we all said nothing. Everyone knew the situation wasn't good. Finally, someone suggested we pray, so we knelt for prayer and lifted up our petition to our father. Abba father, who loves us and has so faithfully led us safely through our lives. Why, if we ask in the name of Jesus would he disappoint us now?

I couldn't make it through without crying, and let me tell you, it takes something substantial to bring that out in me. When we started to pray about Tlaxcala and thought about what we had just left this very morning, it was too much. Leaving our little haven of rest and being pushed out into the streets with signs I can't read, police everywhere, bad /uncoordinated maps, and speaking a foreign language all adds up! It takes so much to hold all of your emotions from the day together. Tired, lost, scared, lonely, uncertain, and happy. Then, when you stop for the night and let your guard down, it all comes out.

We're all sleeping in our clothes tonight because we're a little unsure. I know God will not let us down. He preserves The stranger.

Kindra's Journal   8/06/2010

Low of 60, high of 90

Job 33:14 was the verse of the day as we saw it spray-painted on the side of a massive culvert on the side of the road. It goes, "For God speaketh once, yea twice, yet man perceiveth it not". I surely want to make sure that we don't miss God's voice on anything on this trip. We all survived the night despite our lack of sleep. Mom later informed me that she slept with her hands cupped to illustrate being held within Christ, and Christ in God. Bless her!

We were on our way into the mountains, where we observed many different dwellings, waterfalls, and footpaths. Being in the clouds and on the steepest, curviest roads I've seen was so beautiful.

Stopped in a little roadside town to shop, where we received a very warm welcome. We bought some sweet bread and plantains since we hadn't eaten yet today, and our appetites were nagging us. Some charming old ladies got us to buy some of their really pretty knitted items.

Finally arrived at Brian and Linda Mast's after traveling 5 hours and only going 100 miles today. Enjoyed supper with them, and then we all got in their pickup truck to get water from the river where everyone was bathing! I couldn't believe there were people with no clothes on. Went to Carl and Karen Habegger's to spend the night. Had a pleasant time exchanging travel and adventure stories. Very hot!

Kindra's Journal   8/07/2010

90 plus degrees and humid!

I got up and took a lovely cold shower. Then we all enjoyed a time of devotion together with the Habegger's about what to add to our faith from Second Peter, chapter one. After unpacking the vehicle and doing a load of laundry, we headed for the beach!

On our way there, we were shocked to see gringos, many of them parading the streets of the little beach villages. White people are a rare and homelike sight nowadays. The water was beautiful and refreshing with huge waves. Of course, Walter was the star of the day.

I doubt I'll ever forget those towering waves and white bubbly foam. We all enjoyed waiting for enormous waves to come and carry us away up onto the shore, then being pulled quickly back out by another wave. One poor man had the misfortune of having his swim trunks ripped right off his body because of the mighty current.

After we got back, we showered in the cement shower house, then headed to Brian Mast's for supper. This morning we had tortillas for breakfast. I couldn't help but roll them up the way the Baraja's had shown us. We need to pray that the Lord will make his will plainly known. Dad says he's lonely too.

Well, my face is so sunburnt it feels hotter than ablaze. I've got a headache. Will we ever make it to Bolivia?

Kindra's Journal   8/08/2010

85 degrees and humid

Woke up and had breakfast at Carl and Karen's, then headed out for church way back in the boonies. We rode to the town of Tonameca where we met up with Lee Rudolph's family, rearranged rides and vehicles, then headed for their house. I've never seen roads so rough and rutted. Despite the local's hard work to fill in the holes, it was quite a ride!

We arrived at the lean-to church area with benches and enjoyed the view of surrounding hillsides. When I asked to use the outhouse, Linda made it clear that it wasn't to be used unless absolutely necessary. She pointed out a tiny thatched-roof down the hill, so I meandered down there. I discovered the door/open side of the building, and aside from the bucket of ash and toilet paper can, it was spotless. There was no toilet but instead a raw hole in the middle of the floor. It works fine, certainly better than the mountain rest stop from the other day!

I did my best to understand the preaching but also took time to note the area. To the right of us was an open summer kitchen with a waist-high cooking pit, a broken chair table, and various utensils hanging by strings on walls. Three very skinny dogs guarded the doorway. Multiple chickens sprawled out on the dirt floor, apparently unconcerned with the dogs. At one point, I heard a noise and looked over at the broken chair next to me. I saw a chicken very much enjoying, or seemingly enjoying, the constant drone of Spanish that proceeded from the box that served as a pulpit.

We enjoyed our afternoon meal at Lee and Karen's house, then headed back to Nato's and threw the dogs their balls in the river. Natives are continually amazed at Walter's antics and Biddy's jumping abilities. Went back to the lean-to for a night meeting. I really enjoyed seeing the native's homes with the thatch and cement walls. It was fascinating. Nato let us take his little one-year-old, Abigail, to church with us. I just loved holding her. She is so cute!

We bought two cold coconuts on the way home and then cleaned out the Land Cruiser for our departure in the morning. Enjoyed our evening with Carl and Karen, looking at pictures till 10:00. I think after three evenings, we finally broke their sober personalities.

My face is burning up from the sunburn! My face felt so swollen and hot this morning, just such a terrible burn. If Christ is my all and all, it doesn't matter where we are!

Kindra's Journal   8/09/2010

90 degrees and very hot!

Mom was very sick last night and didn't sleep well. We had an excellent devotion time and breakfast before we packed the Land Cruiser with its poor broken roof. Mom finally took a shower and came outside. Dad and I walked the dogs down to the store and got her a coke. According to Roland's advice, it's supposed to be the ticket to recovery.

Our host family went to their Spanish lessons this morning, and we babysat their little daughter for them. Dad called Eric Coltman this morning, and they said, please come and stay! Praise the Lord. It's so good to know you're not a burden to people.

The other day when we were at the beach, I forgot to take the money out of the secret pocket in my dress! Although it was soaking wet, it was still there. This morning, I was trying to discreetly dry it on the Land Cruiser's tailgate, which was scalding hot. As I was methodically flipping it, dad had a humorous thought and said, "it looks like you are cooking money". Funny man! It's now all successfully tucked back into my apron waistband.

It's 11:15, and dad says that we'll head out as soon as Carl and Karen get back. I wonder what the road holds for us today? Rumors have been heard about mountains between here and Tuxtla. I sure hope that's true.

Well, here we are in a little hotel that only costs 300 pesos, about $26 US dollars, but the price is fitting. The town appears to be a little rough, and there's a prison just down the road. And let me tell you, it doesn't look very hard to escape!

We didn't travel very far today because we started out after 1:00, but we drove till 6:45. There were lots of roads with "very dangerous curves" signs that say it all.

We had our lunch around 2:30 at a mountain restaurant. The place was perched on the side of a mountain. Upon looking over the waist-high brick wall, you could see a beautiful rushing river down in the cavern. You could also see what appeared to be a multi-generational flock of colorful ducks, chickens, and guinea hens. Inside the restaurant were two parrots in cages. The more charming of the two was named Charlotte. On the opposite side of the wall, there was a miniature chicken coop containing three half-grown chicks.

Upon noting mom's illness as she rested in the hammock near our table, The friendly owner brought her a brown piece of bark with instructions to boil it for tea. God provided yet again. I will continue to trust in him. He hasn't failed me yet. I appreciate all of the prayers from our friends and family.

Kindra's Journal   8/10/2010

Woke up around 6 this morning and made the coffee that we randomly found for sale outside of a gas station. It was surprisingly tasty. God seems to have gifted us with it because when we pulled into the Pemex station, a big bag of coffee was sitting on top of the stack of oil. It was good Mexican coffee, and the entire gigantic bag only cost 5 US dollars.

We were on the road by 8, thanks to our new way of staying at hotels. Instead of unpacking our packs from the top of the Land Cruiser, we just slept in our clothes. I enjoyed taking the opportunity of extra time to catch up on bible reading, journaling, and letter writing.

The Federales pulled us off at one of their checkpoints. The officer did a fascinating sound effect complete with charades of buckling in oneself with the seatbelt, which resulted in dad quickly complying. We gave him a Good and Evil book and a track from the Barajas.

Our supply of Pesos was running low today. We didn't want to stop and eat at a restaurant even though we hadn't eaten anything aside from the obligatory and unappetizing granola and sunflower seeds. We wouldn't have much to spare out of our roughly 600 pesos by our calculations of toll fees and gas prices.

It was 1:30, and I hadn't seen a single banana vendor yet, so we stopped at a Pemex station and bought some juice and nuts. While we were there, a whole busload of European travelers piled in, and the station was packed. My relieved feeling of, "Hey, we're not the only gringos anymore" soon faded. I realized the majority of the group just bustled about and cared very little about the native peoples. They didn't wear the typical friendly smile we try to always portray, especially since we crossed the border into an unknown land. For instance, upon passing by a worksite, dad gave a wave to the workers, and they got huge smiles on their faces while they waved really high in the air!

Over our many road hours, since we entered Mexico, all of us have been very impressed by the road maintenance crews we so often see. Our first sign that a roadwork crew is not too far ahead is a man diligently waving his red flag way up above his head, then way back down, up again, and down. Many of the workers have towels draped over their heads to keep the sun off of their faces. The work they accomplish often amazes me. Rock walls, fencing over cliffs, and rock retention walls are just a few of the interesting projects they do. A shovel, wheelbarrow, and pickaxe are the most common tools they seem to work with down here.

We saw a man riding a wild horse who reminded us all of one of our close friends from the community in Tennessee. I know he was Mexican, but I think we all agreed it was the eyes that were the most similar.

We managed once again to get lost and took some terrible side roads because of highway construction. Still, it wasn't terrifying this time because we ended up in an industrial part of town rather than the center of the city, which we try to avoid like the plague.

From Tuxtla, we headed quickly up into the mountains where we could see quaint little towns down below. The fog became thicker as we ascended into and above the clouds. We reached our destination, San Cristóbal de Las Casas, around 4:00. The directions were easy to follow, and we found the Coltman's house without a problem. Praise the Lord!

Keegan Coltman gave us a warm welcome as he paused from his upcoming wedding preparations for his friend. He showed us around the Mansion type house that we will be staying in. After we took the dogs for a walk, Kacie and I played on the trampoline until late into the night.

Kindra's Journal   8/11/2010

90 degrees in the lowlands and a blessed 65 degrees in the mountains...

We woke up this morning and enjoyed practicing some Spanish with Sylvia, the maid while helping her make breakfast. I then worked on laundry and read my Bible.

Keegan asked me to count all of the white chairs on the property and then deliver the total sum to his wife, Julie. Julie is planning a bridal shower for Steven and Gracie this weekend. She was clad in pajama pants and a sweater, sitting at her computer when I found her. We've come at a hectic time and are mostly left to our own demise. It's pretty amazing here!

This afternoon around 2:00, we all piled back into the Land Cruiser along with Keegan, who graciously came along to show us around. Our primary mission on this trip into town was to get a plan to fix the vehicle. Our first stop was at Diego's auto shop, where many brothers of the church are employed.

From there, we went to a hardware store, suspension shop, and numerous tire stores. Drove by the *Andedor*, a section of the city for only foot traffic, and then another auto repair shop on our way home. All of this business took about three hours, then we went home and dropped off the dogs.

Then, without Keegan or the dogs and armed with our English/Spanish dictionary, we set off on our own to drop off the cruiser for it to get the springs repaired. Upon our arrival at the Chassis De Oro auto shop, dad called me over to help him talk. Yay! My favorite job on the entire trip has been translating.

So within 15 minutes, we had the vehicle parked, the man paid, a receipt in our hand, and we were waiting in the drizzly rain for a taxi.

This was our first time taking a taxi, so it was a fun challenge for us. However, in less than a minute, we climbed into a cab and headed for Moxviquil. Our driver talked on his radio speaker for a while, saying who knows what. When people babble in a language you don't understand, your mind tends to wander and imagine what they're saying.

When he dropped us off at the reserve, our troubles began as we soon discovered all of the doors and gates to the compound were locked! Dad tried many different things, but ultimately, he climbed the blue gate and weaselled through between the bars above it.

I wrote some emails for friends this evening before we went over to Keegan and Julie's for supper. Allice played the piano for Steven to practice his wedding song. It sounded great. Keegan showed us some really neat maps and pictures of Indian tribes and villages in the area. One of the biggest challenges of the day was Keegan and Julie's little girls. I'm just trying to let the experience cultivate a love for children like the love Jesus had for all. Today was a good day. What will tomorrow hold?

Kindra's Journal   8/12/2010

It wasn't a good night's sleep because my covers kept falling off, so I was cold, and the wedding party arrived at midnight with lots of noise! Despite all that, we pulled our act together. We got a taxi to take us to the Zocalo, where we attempted to exchange some money.

This was not very easy because after waiting in line to exchange our money, they finally said that the actual passport isn't what they wanted, but a copy of it. We walked down a few blocks to the street of copy stores, made one copy, and then walked back to the bank. We finally made the transaction. However, that bank could only exchange $300 US Dollars, so we had to go to another bank because we needed more Pesos than that.

We arrived at the second bank only to find that we were to repeat the same process. Go get a copy, stand in line, sign various documents, and count Pesos. I smiled to myself as I thought of Dan's story of the Panama Canal we had just read this morning. Amazing similarities. Dad said, "where is Dan when you need him?" How true.

We got to walk around on the Andedor for a while and bought a shirt for mom. One of the Indian ladies came up to me and then, in the whiniest voice, begged me for a Peso. It's so hard to get them to stop! You pretty well have to not look and just walk away. I tell them that their offerings are very nice, but I just don't need what they are offering.

We needed to get lunch, so we stopped at a street vendor who was selling tacos. Now, if you could paint a picture of where people say not to eat, this would have been it! I believe they broke almost every food safety rule as we began to observe the situation. After ordering our tacos, we noticed that the little pot of fresh vegetables and salsa for you to put on your plates had people just sitting on it like a table. The scooping utensils had been touched by who knows how many people, and the stand owner lady was just wiping off the dirty plates and stacking them back on the clean pile! Not to mention, all things considered, I highly doubt those vegetables were washed. The food was pretty good, and we're all still alive.

After our meal, we walked through the marketplace. We enjoyed looking at all the different sweaters, wrap skirts, shirts, and hammocks. I enjoyed observing all the different ways of Indian dress because the people here are from tribes much different than you find further north in Mexico.

The men dressed much the same, but the women wear high collared silk embroidered shirts and long thick furry black skirts held up by a wide piece of material that they wrap around their waist. Many of the women have their long black hair braided and pulled together with colorful ribbons. It is pretty modest but very different from the clothing styles I'm used to seeing.

We got a taxi that took us back to Chassis de Oro to pick up the Land Cruiser. I was really impressed with the new springs in the back, very nice.

Later that afternoon, we headed out to a nature park called Arcotete for a woods walk. After paying 10 pesos for parking the new and improved Land Cruiser, we headed down a neat little stone trail that led to a river. We could see way up into an enormous cave hollowed out by the river flowing through it. The cave was very spacious, with about 50 ft to 60 ft from the river to the top of the cave!

From there, we hiked up a steep hill to some lookouts of the river. We then hiked along a trail following the river. At the top of another steep hill, we came across a clearing where a man was hard at work in his field using a hoe to rake up sticks into piles for burning. We saw some pretty tiny flowers with lots of white petals and a beautiful blue in the middle. Dad enjoyed sitting down for a while and tossing the dogs their new favorite sticks. On our way back, we took a tour through the cave that the river flowed through. It was spectacular!

We met a friendly family at the park who took their picture with us. There was an elegant swinging bridge we got to cross over. We met some people who gave us advice on Guatemala.

Had supper at Keegan's. I really enjoyed the view from their windows that overlooked the city at night because it's all lit up.

Kindra's Journal   8/13/2010

Today I would describe the weather as extremely comfortable and cool.

After breakfast, I went along with dad to Diego's shop to fix the Land Cruiser. Of course, I really enjoyed this because I did a little interpreting for dad. After we dropped off the vehicles, dad decided to try walking home.

It was enjoyable being able to slow down and really observe the people. Aside from the many students on the streets, there were car washes, weld shops, and other stores. Dad and I especially enjoyed looking at a little cooking grill a man had made from cut-off rebar and an old tire rim. The graffiti on the street was also quite impressive; it included parrot's faces, lions, and many other things that were painted exceptionally well!

Behind the compound is the most peaceful nature reserve that has lots of trails to walk. We took the dogs on a 1 3/4 mile hike that was all the way up a steep hill. The woods are different but beautiful, and we were rewarded at the top with a surprise sinkhole cave. The cave had rock all around it and went very far down. The way down was much faster.

We took a taxi to the Andedor, walked to the block where you can exchange money, and stopped at a grocery store for milk. When dad and I were looking at coffee, some young man came up and said to dad, "*amigo*" (friend), followed by the famous question "*de donde viene*" (where are you from)? While I helped dad carry on his conversation, I noticed the man had a Christian t-shirt on. The man was so nice. I wished I would have asked him more about his Christianity.

While dad and Kacie went to exchange dollars, mom and I found a bench in the plaza and sat down. For the whole 30 minutes, dad was in the bank, we were swarmed by mobs of Indian women who whined and pleaded for us to buy their things. I thought I had the perfect answer when I figured out that dad had all the pesos, but when I told them they thought we were lying, oops!

After we got home, Kacie and I played on the trampoline, and Kacie helped me perfect my backflip. Some Mexican came to buy the tires off the Land Cruiser. The whole tire thing is quite the situation because it's supposed to be at Diego's shop by 9:00, yet it sits tireless in front of Keegan's shop! Dad and Keegan ran around till almost 9:00 p.m. trying to find rims for the tires, but their efforts were in vain.

We fried bananas for supper. I got an email from Alaina, so I wrote her back and wrote to Grandpa and Grandma as well. I miss writing paper letters, though. The fireworks are going off almost constantly here. Took a bath and felt great! "Praise the Lord, oh my soul, and forget not all His benefits!"

Kindra's Journal   8/14/2010

Okay, today was pretty uneventful, mostly spent looking for tires and rims. It looks like we'll be here for a while because even finding the rims in the states is complex.

The Eric Coltman household was a buzz of activity as the bride and groom's friends prepared for the wedding shower of Steven and Gracie. When dad and Keegan left the compound to look for rims this morning, dad said that Keegan was worried about Julie having too much to do, so she needed us girls to help.

So, off I went to ask her what I could do and was sent to find two long white tables and set them up. After that task was complete, I returned to the house to ask if I could be used for anything else. The house seemed to be in a state of relaxation, as most people were just taking a coffee break. They assured me they would come and find me if necessary. Then, just as I was almost safely on the other side of the door, I heard, "Kiiiiiindraaaaa, you could sew some curtains for us".

After I measured the windows and jotted down their desires on how the curtain should look, I was hard at work. While Mom and Kacie struggled to cut them out relatively straight with a tape measure, I cruised along on the sewing machine. We made three total, but that equaled six because they are double layered. Brown with white eyelets that looked really nice.

We went for a walk this afternoon back behind the compound and way up the mountain again, except this time we went up on the Sendero trail. The flowers are beautiful! Purple and yellow, fuzzy red, viny, and tiny flowers were in quite an abundance.

This evening we headed for the Zocalo to walk around and get supper. This plan worked out quite well because just as the bridal shower guests arrived, we were leaving. While we were waiting for our supper at a street-side restaurant, two little children, a boy and girl, came up with baskets full of little painted clay animals. They were so persistent that we found ourselves with piles of tiny animals in front of us on the table! The little children named each of them in Spanish as they took them out of the basket. Another little boy came up asking for a tortilla, but the waitress quickly shooed them all out. We walked through almost every part of the market, looking at all of the sweaters, shirts, wraps, and trinkets.

When we made our way back to the Zocalo, we were watching a native Indian pow-wow when a dirty, tiny, ragged little boy came out saying, "I wanna peso". He was so small! Bless dad's heart, though, because he sent Kacie to get the little niño a peso. We sat for a while in the plaza just to watch the goings-on. The young people seem to go about without any supervision, except for the police here, who are all shined up. The police dress in all black with black machine guns.

Despite the growing darkness, we continued to peruse from the east to the west of the Andedor. We stopped at the grocery store to buy some beans, juice, milk, and yogurt. Still, with time to burn before the bridal parties were over, we walked on down the Andedor to see the arched gate passage. It was pretty massive.

We seem to be quite a spectacle here as we see so many people staring, laughing at us, or calling us *gringos*. Sometimes dad will give a half-hearted laugh and say, "*Sì gringos*". What a good sport!

After looking at a few clothing stores for skirts, we began looking for a taxi. When walking on the Andedor, you need to be careful because most people, including us, are looking around at the many sites. It would be easy to have a crash with oncoming people traffic. We eventually found a taxi and began heading back to Moxviquil around 8:00 p.m. Despite the day's slowness, it was very enjoyable. We all found it fun to be out at night. Praise ye the Lord.

Kindra's Journal   8/15/2010

High of 75 degrees

Alright, I suppose for the ones of you reading this journal, it might be getting repetitive as we haven't been on the road lately. So I'm going to keep this page short. I made some repairs and added pockets to our dresses. I read a double portion of my daily Bible reading along with having a family bible study.

After lunch, mom, dad, and Kacie ventured down to Colonia Ojo de Agua to buy tortillas and the ever mysterious " *Pollo Asada,* "which turned out to be very delicious! *(Note from Kacie: Pollo Asada is a Mexican seasoned and grilled chicken that is pretty much the equivalent of a rotisserie chicken in the US)*

Dad has been meticulous about not letting an email slip in unnoticed, haha! He and mom picked apart and laughed away one of the emails that I had received. The things you find amusing when you're bored never cease to amaze me.

We finally completed the Sendero loop in the Moxviquil reserve behind the house. We discovered yet another cave that also went way back in. The one and a half mile loop is such serious terrain, very steep up and down.

Kacie finally convinced me to put on the authentic Indian shirt and skirt and show Mom and dad. I liked how the silkiness felt in the shirt. Biddy does not like the turtles that are in a tote. She avoids them whenever possible.

Eric Coltman and his family are arriving from the US tomorrow. We had hoped they could bring us the rims, but how will we get them now?

Kindra's Journal   8/16/2010

Not a very busy day. However, we made it down to the Andedor again. Allice had stopped by and told us that we could sign up for a language lesson at 11:00, so we got a taxi and headed that way. We talked to the receptionist at El Punto Laguna school, Eduardo. We decided to set up a lesson for tomorrow at 9:00.

We went to the indoor artisans market to look for a skirt for mom and Kacie because they both need one more. After walking for a while, we finally spied several skirts and purchased one for mom. We happened upon some extremely cheap restaurants, so we stopped and got something to eat. The food was different than we were used to but delicious.

We got approached by so many beggars today that dad resolved, starting tomorrow, he would bring pesos to hand out. We took a relaxing hike. Received an email from the Barajas family in Tlaxcala, MX that ended in "with patience possess ye your souls". Dad got a little YouTube happy and spent a good amount of time watching them.

Author: Kindra   Gillette 8/17/2010

Cold and Rainy

Woke up at 6:00 a.m., had breakfast, and then got ready for our Spanish lesson. On the way, our cab driver was listening to preaching on the radio. He gave us a flyer for a Puerto Rican preacher who is preaching here in Mexico on Sunday.

Enjoyed our Spanish lesson from 9:00 to 12:00. I think we learned some pretty helpful phrases and verb charts.

We took a pleasant walk with the dogs. We decided to hike somewhere other than Moxviquil today after the unsettling conversation we had with a poor Mexican at the beginning of our hike. He kept saying, be careful, robbers, your rich clothing, and many more, be carefuls. I like to think he wasn't quite right, but I know that God can send angels to guard us in many different forms.

Mom and dad spent a lot of time this afternoon on Spanish verbs. Biddy got in a fight this evening with Shadow, a resident dog here inside the house. Biddy got cut up pretty good. We walked down to Ojo de Agua to buy tortillas and *Pollo Asada* for supper.

Passed Manuel, one of the hired helpers here, on his way home. Dad wants to go see where Salvador and Manuel live. That would be amazing! I've been pretty sick with a cold for two days now.

Kindra's Journal   8/18/2010

Cold and drizzly. Definitely sweater weather.

I live! This morning I experienced the worst sickness ever in my life, without a doubt. I perceived its cause was taking four times the amount of MMS necessary to combat my cold. I honestly didn't know how I would make it through. Now, if I could look back and hear myself say that, I would think to tell myself to toughen up a little bit.

Of course, you make it, but when mom found me sprawled on my back on the bathroom floor that was made of bare cold concrete, that's truly pretty bad. Well, let me spare you the details because I will certainly never forget them. I went through my ups and downs as far as my illness today, but the rest of the family was quite productive.

With the help of his newly found welder friend, Dad made a support to fix the Land Cruiser roof. Mom moved us out of Eric's house and into the building across the yard, which is under construction. We girls swept and wiped up the shavings and sawdust, and now I feel quite at home!

Took a cab to the Andedor for groceries and pizza. We just couldn't eat any more tortillas and beans. We saw our Spanish teacher from yesterday, Eduardo, and his Israeli friends who asked us to take their picture. Admired dad's fresh additions on the Land Cruiser.

Kindra's Journal   8/19/2010

Cold, overcast, and rainy

I spent most of my day still sick, lying on the floor in the half-finished house we're staying in. Dad spent most of his time with his new friend Isaiah Coltman getting some tires for the rims that arrived on top of Eric's van the night before. The rims finally arrived!

In the afternoon, we girls went over to meet the rest of Eric's family, including his 16-year-old Indian daughter, who has cerebral palsy. Their Indian daughter still wears her native dress and is very talented at playing the piano with her amputated arm. It was so precious to see her playing her single noted hymns and Isaiah singing the words to them.

As we were eating our supper of beans, rice, and tortillas, dad suddenly remembered that we had wanted to see the Zapatistas movie that started at 8:00. We hurriedly got our coats on and waited out in the rainy darkness for an empty cab. Eventually, we arrived at El Puente, the same place we took our language lesson, paid for our tickets, and took our seats.

The theatre was complete with plastic lounge chairs in front of the movie screen with the title of "Chronicle of Rebellion" to whet everyone's appetite until the movie started. It was pretty fascinating to see all the pictures of the native people, historical facts, and finally, understand the story behind the photos of masked men we see around town. The Zapatistas seem to be held in high esteem for upholding the rights of the indigenous people of the land, culture, and history.

Kindra's Journal   8/20/2010

Cold. Partly rainy and partly sunny

It was with great joy that I placed this sticker on the page. Dad finally received the spacers he needed to put tires on, and this spider sticker came in the box.

This afternoon dad and I left in a taxi for the Zocalo to get more pesos. We ended up, however, exchanging wheels for feet because the traffic was so slow. Since it was rainy and we had no umbrella, dad and I walked the five to six blocks to the banks at the plaza at a fast pace. We are quite successful at the whole dollar exchange process now, and were able to get pesos for 900 US dollars.

No more than 5 minutes after we got back, dad had found a truck, so he and I were headed out to the tire store across town to pick up five brand new tires. From dad's wallet proceeded most of the pesos that we had just gotten from the bank for the tires. It was slightly defeating to see 15 piles of pesos stretched across the desk and keyboard of the salesman. We also ordered springs for the Land Cruiser that should be ready tomorrow.

I think they are amused by our attempts at communication. Dad is very good at making hand motions for things. It cracks me up to hear him trying to explain things to people in English. Like today at the bank when the lady wanted his passport instead of a copy, he exclaimed in exasperated English, "I don't have the original document"! Despite the words being in a language she didn't understand, the lady seemed to get the gist of it and used the copy. I don't know why it struck me as so funny. As we stood in this Spanish-speaking country with the bank's constant love for freshly printed copies, the irony of it all greatly compounded our problems. And here, dad hands over this slightly dinghy copy with multiple creases in it, and it was unacceptable to them. It all worked fine in the end.

We drove to the anything but gringo Indian town. Mom bought a coffee cup from a roadside store, and then we went across the street to get supper. The three-sided restaurant run by a church family's mom and daughters had a pleasant atmosphere. The family smiled and watched usl the whole time we were there. They were so kind. Some very strange men came up to us at the end of our meal and, through their long story begging for money, finally caused dad to buy them each a meal, bless his heart.

We stopped at Diego's shop on our way home, and he told us to bring the Land Cruiser in on Monday. He was impressed by the new rims calling them very beautiful and wondering how much they had cost. Needless to say, they have now been painted a flat black color that is very nice and less flashy. The wedding rehearsal was tonight.

Kindra's Journal   8/21/2010

Cold and Rainy

Dropped the Land Cruiser off at Chassis de Oro by 9:00. Dad wanted me to tell them he had faith in them to make sure they knew he was having to trust them. They're very nice.

Our ride home was quite interesting as we talked with our cab driver Jose Luis in Spanish about our religion. We just read the Bible, follow it, and we're not associated with any religious groups. Too many days of taxi driving seemed to have him ready to chat with anyone.

The wedding was changed to be here at Moxviquil, so we all got in on helping with the setup. Dad sweeping, mom mopping, I was tying ribbons on the chairs, and Kacie clipping off dead flower heads. It looked lovely! Excellent idea for the chairs.

Took a walk to our spot up on the Sendero trail, then went to get the Land Cruiser. We stopped at a nice little restaurant next to Chasis de Oro and bought some tacos for lunch. It was such a cute little place. The woman there had her tiny baby girl in a broken car seat on the concrete floor. The little children are so adorable with their tan skin and thick black hair.

One of the things I like most about being here is seeing the native women in their hairy skirts and silky embroidered shirts. Usually, they have a baby tied into their shawls. It's fantastic and different from what I'm used to seeing. There was a young couple I saw walk by while we were eating. The young man looked just like any other man you'd find here, but the girl was dressed very authentically. They made a beautiful sight! Men can only dress so differently I suppose.

Back to Chasis de Oro. The Land Cruiser now has beautiful springs in both front and back. They are so wonderfully strong that every tope we go over just about shakes your back out of order with their stiffness. I'm still very thrilled with the lift they gave the cruiser and that it will be better able to carry a load.

We had to go to AutoZone to get locking torques for the wheels. While we were there around 2:30, all of a sudden, the workers started clapping their hands. They ran to the center of the store with lots of enthusiasm and cheered for Autozone.

The dog food was almost gone, so we stopped at *Chedraui, the* Mexican version of Walmart. Despite its size, it was still third world. While it was constantly pouring rain outside, the noise from the roof was so loud that you almost had to yell to talk to people and dodge the puddles and try not to get wet under the drips.

Dad worked on the Land Cruiser some more when we got home, and after supper, we girls went over to the Coltman's to wash up their dishes from the rehearsal the night before. Had an interesting talk with Renee about Sabbath days.

Trying to wait until Isaiah goes home for the night so I can go use the bathroom in my nightgown without being seen. Okay, I'm back. I couldn't take it anymore. It may have been a success because I quickly and quietly scampered down the hallway.

Had a fun game of Pictionary together. "It's a dog with a cupcake, no a squirrel with an acorn, it's the Zapatistas, Marcos with a ski mask"! Everybody loves the Zapatistas.

Kindra's Journal   8/22/2010

Sunny and in the 80s with scattered showers

Hola! The big misfortune of the morning was finding out that our one burner stove is broken. We were trying to find the broken piece, and in the course of taking it apart, gasoline shot right into dad's eye! Poor thing.

I worked on my letter to our friends back in the states and finished it after five pages. Rhoda is sick with a terrible cold today, poor girl!

Yesterday while we were running errands, I saw a motorcycle with five people on it. A husband and wife, a little boy hanging over the handle, a girl held on to the side by her mom, and another girl between the parents.

Went to Arcotete for a walk. I love the swinging bridge! There was a neat-looking old white troop carrier loaded with happy people. On our way home, we stopped at Ojo de Agua to buy our usual p*ollo asada* and corn tortillas again. Dad also purchased the same grilled corn I had eaten the day I got very sick.

Something makes me feel that same sickness just to think of it! We had fun talking to the man at the *tortilleria* who can speak a little English.

Keegan is here right now giving us a camera and computer lecture. Alicia is here to hear about our trip and visit. When we were hiking at Arcotete, we climbed up a slippery bank that ended up in a vast hilltop of cleared fields and gardens. Dad thought it was probably 100 acres or more! The grass was mowed down perfectly from herds of sheep, and the wooden fences were immaculate. Dark brown soil could be seen between the plants in the gardens. The common corn crop could be seen in the distant rolling hills and an old chimney and house foundation made of rock.

As we turned around and we're heading back, we heard the faint shuffling of hooves and a ringing. A flock of sheep was soon in full view. 25 to 30 of them with their long fuzzy tails. They ran right past us as they nibbled on the grass. Some were big and some small. There were many colors in the herd, such as gray, brown, spotted, white, bluish, tan, and black. A young boy and girl about my age were not very far behind them. They were both dressed in traditional Indian clothing. The girl just stood there with an enormous smile on her face and watched us walk down the hill. I looked back at her a few times and smiled. It would be so interesting to communicate well enough to hear all about their life and how they take care of the sheep.

Kindra's Journal   8/23/2010

Cold and rainy

We took the vehicle to Diego's shop to get the roof repaired and then proceeded down the street as we thought we'd just walk a little way and get a taxi. We walked and walked until we found ourselves all the way to the Andedor!

The road just pulled us in as we walked along. We kept seeing more and more interesting sights. There was a man with a machete hacking away at sugarcane on the side of the road. We passed some hair-cutting salons, multiple restaurants, and a cleaning store with mops and brooms. The streets became more and more crowded with people and vendors as we were literally pressed on. One of the storefronts had a life-sized pig sculpture in the doorway with a harness on it. If it was to draw people's attention to their store, it worked on us.

Inside the store, or shall I say, as we stepped off the street, it smelled strongly of animal medicine. All kinds of feed, even a bag of sorghum seeds, lined the walls. In the middle of the floor were three open bags of whole corn, cracked corn, and sorghum seeds, apparently for those who buy only small portions at a time. We purchased horse wormer for the dogs without much difficulty, and we're again on our way down the street.

A large truck was coming, so we crossed to the other side of the street and found ourselves in a huge Indian market! We wandered into a massive building with a rough rock floor, and there was meat everywhere. The stench was so pungent of fresh raw meat, like butchering a deer but way more potent. Even for me, it was just too much. The smell aside, as we walked through aisle after aisle, it was fascinating.

There were pig heads, chicken faces, whole dried fish of all sizes, cow heads with hooves, freshly killed and cleaned chickens, and pig hooves. All of these items were placed next to seemingly ordinary pieces of meat. Everything just laid out uncovered and unrefrigerated. On our way out of the building, we bought a few things from a sweets vendor. Mexican cookies and other sweets are not incredibly sweet, so they don't seem too bad as far as calories go.

Once outside the building, we were in an open-air market where we bought some greens, a whole large bag of them, for 16 pesos. The people were so happy we were buying their lettuce that they just smiled at us the entire time. Maybe because we were gringos in the market. Or perhaps just because we were foolish enough to purchase lettuce that is almost guaranteed to be grown in salmonella-ridden soil. I don't know which it was, but they were certainly entertained.

In that big plaza-style area that was packed with people and vendors, they were selling flowers, fruit, pottery, fresh produce, common clothing wraps, and various other things.

We found our way to where we thought was the end of the market. We were so interested in the entire scene that when we saw to our left a super narrow street lined with more vendors on either side, we kept going.

The two most interesting sites on that stretch were a stand full of grain sacks filled with all different kinds of beans and corn. Probably 12-15 different varieties total. There were blue, light green, black, pink, brown, and speckled beans along with blue and yellow corn, just to name a few.

The other interesting sight was an Indian lady standing there with four or five live chickens. She had their feet tied together with her arm slipped

through their legs. The chickens were beautifully colored and appeared to be healthy.

After walking a bit farther, we arrived at the Andedor where we met a man from Saginaw, MI, named Patrick. After living in Honduras for a couple of years, his advice was, "don't stay in one place too long." There are so many lovely places to explore"!

We stopped in at a store to look for a Zapatista postcard of Marcos. Let me tell you, with his popularity, it was not hard to find them. The entire store had the theme of "support the local Zapatistas". Little felted dolls of Zapatistas were plentiful, along with fuzzy miniature horses with masks on, shirts that said" EZLN - Ya Basta" (enough already), and pens that said "EZLN" could also be purchased. We were content to buy our few postcards of Marcos on a horse. After buying some inhalers for dad and stopping for a few groceries, we headed home.

Our enjoyable afternoon was dampened as we walked over to Marcial's shop. We were just about to turn onto Marcial's street when we heard that unforgettable slurred and thickly accented voice call out, "Hey, my friend, my friends." Before he got to us, dad said, "I don't want you girls to be near him, so we'll tell him we've got to go. Keep the conversation short". His gang waited on the other end of the block while our "friend" apologized that his English was poor at best since he'd had so many beers.

Dad made sure he knew Biddy was a protector dog and not to be petted. While mom and we girls waited outside of the shop, the gang started walking down towards us. Kacie went to warn dad, and just as we walked away, the gang headed into Diego's shop. We made it back home unharmed. Praise the Lord!

We went over to Eric's house for supper and stayed quite late. Eric educated us on many third-world diseases, cone bugs, and Himalayan sea salt.

Kindra's Journal   8/24/2010

Put the totes back together this morning, washed dishes, and did laundry. I had some writing to do and finished letters and postcards for our friends and family back in the US. We're going to leave our mail with Isaiah to mail out for us on his next trip to the post office here. And guess where we were this afternoon? Yes, the Andedor.

We bought a skirt for Kacie at an artisan store, then walked to the plaza where we got some of the medicine Jamie suggested we buy for our trip. We met an English-speaking man at the pharmacy and some other ladies who also spoke English. On our way to the Andedor, we stopped at El Punto and got pizza. They are good, but you can only eat so many of them.

We're all craving fresh garden produce and bread. Last evening Eric told us that most tortillas you buy at the tortillaria are GMO, so we purchased some homegrown and homemade ones from the lady from whom we like to buy our platanos. We purchased eight massive bananas, a bag of tortillas, and a bunch of grapes for 100 pesos.

Got a taxi to take us to Diego's shop on the way home to check on the Land Cruiser, only to find Santiago sanding away at the roof. We were hoping the project would be finished. The ever-present "*mañana*" (tomorrow) seems to be a perfectly valid way to not meet deadlines here. Walked home and breathed a sigh of relief as we entered the gate.

I finished emails for our friends and family back in the US that I couldn't write letters to. Ate supper with the Coltman's again and got schooled on scalar energy. While Jamie and Isaiah worked on a puzzle, dad and Eric talked about scalar energy. We girls kept Rhoda as comfortable as we could.

We pulled up to the auto store the Coltman's had suggested because they were brothers in Christ. There were a half dozen young men outside who, upon seeing dad, held up an oil filter and waved our vehicle way back into their immaculate shop. They soon had cardboard slid into place, and we're draining the over 2 gallons of oil. It was evident by the almost overflowing pan of oil followed by a barely full one that they were surprised at the amount of oil that flowed out of our vehicle.

While the vehicle was being worked on, dad went seat cushion shopping. As we strode back and forth looking at the great selection, one of the young workers accompanied us with his shop broom. He stood and stared in utter amazement as dad, mom, and Kacie climbed in and out to try out many different seat covers. When dad went to pay, all the men crowded to the office door and just stared at dad. Then as dad climbed into the vehicle and pulled away, they all smiled and waved.

It was strange being out in the dark this evening, but as long as we didn't run into our "friend" who seems to appear out of nowhere and follows us around every time we see him, I was happy. We enjoyed our filled "*pan*" (bread) and cookies from the store for supper.

Mom and dad worked on the tribute to Mexico email while Kacie kept up her agonizing and irritating antics. It's pretty cold here. Until Tomorrow...

Kindra's Journal   8/25/2010

This morning dad took a disappointing trip to Diego's in the Volkswagen bug just to find out it won't be finished until tomorrow.

We walked around the Sendero loop, and my patience was sorely tested. On the way up the mountain, it's my turn to be in front, but Kacie insisted she had the right to pretend the trail was a road. She kept getting right next to me and almost passed me, and loudly honked her pretend horn. At expressing my not wanting her to do that, she insisted she had the right to. At that point, I remembered my verse today in 1st Corinthians 13:4 that "Love is patient, love is kind". I was able to respond charitably. She persistently kept up this behavior all the way up to the top of the mountain, where she insisted was the halfway point. Upon my moving off to the side, she zoomed past and beeped furiously. But praise the Lord, I overcame my tendency to be upset and tell dad.

Dad figured out how to put pictures onto the computer and accidentally got on Skype, haha. Did some Bible study and did some trampoline practice this afternoon. After a quick walk, I finished another mile-long letter to Alaina. We played our game of 5 crowns and had a small supper of yogurt, platanos, the rest of the corn tortillas, the ever-present cookies from the Indian store, some sugar cane, and the two tablespoons of granola dust in the bottom of the bag. Dad continues to lose weight as our diet consists mainly of platanos ,rice, and tortillas these days, but grapes were a very welcome addition. Dad's marveling at all the women with short hair in the Christian mission base here. 1 Corinthians 11:15 says, "But if a woman have long hair, it is a glory to her: for *her* hair is given her for a covering". It seems they don't care much about their glory here.

Kindra's Journal   8/26/2010

We're still here. Poured rain in the afternoon.

We walked a little way up the Sendero trail and enjoyed the sunshine for a moment. Walter and Biddy don't enjoy their cheap food, and I caught Walter just in time to drag him out the door and hide him behind a flower pot before he threw up. Obviously, they don't do well on the cheap food. We got a taxi to Chedraui to stock up on things for our trip. Our hunger added to our decisions, and our total bill was $75 US dollars. There were taxis waiting outside to bring us back to Moxviquil.

We were so hungry after not eating much for supper or breakfast, so we cooked some potatoes, onions, eggs, and chorizo under the watchful eye of Margarita, the maid. It was super delicious and filling.

Dad borrowed some hair clippers from Keegan, and I gave him a haircut. Very short, but that's what he claimed he wanted.

While Mom and Dad went to get the Land Cruiser, I finished packing up the totes and finally found space for all of the toilet paper mom insisted we buy. While waiting for their return, I used some extension cords and jumped rope

100 times. I also decorated our box in the back seat with some of our favorite scripture verses.

Eventually, mom and dad returned home with the new and improved Land cruiser. It was good to have the Land Cruiser back together on the inside.

Kindra's Journal   8/27/2010

Cold, mostly rainy, with a little bit of sporadic sunshine

Hopefully, our last day here. Finally, a welcome change to our routine. We cleaned and packed everything we could into the vehicle. We didn't pack away our sleeping bags, backpacks, or the Berkey filter as we still need them.

I sorted through all of the things that had been cluttered across the cement adobe house we've been living in. Mom and dad spent hours up in the computer room with Isaiah fixing the laptop computer dad bought from Keegan for the expedition.

Dad found some water that poured into the back sides of the Land Cruiser and rusted his chainsaw. Thankfully, most of the wet items were salvageable.

It's 2:30 now, and Kacie is emailing her friends. I got a lovely email from Alaina. I'm trying to read extra in my Bible, so I don't fall behind in the yearly schedule. I wonder what the rest of the day will hold. More later.

Around 5:00, we got a cab to Chedraui, where we purchased a flash drive and dog food, then went to a little restaurant on the Andedor where we all got gigantic bowls of soup. Came home and returned some things to Keegan and went and said goodbye to the Coltman's. Rhoda was busy working on her puzzle and singing along to her tape. It was fascinating to watch her put it together even with her half arm! I was so blessed by the prayer everyone prayed for us and felt encouraged!

Mom and dad are trying to type our farewell email and figure out the computer. Isaiah is planning to stop by before we leave to give us some DVDs and tracts to pass out on our trip.

Trip Summary by Kristi VanderZon
San Cristóbal De Las Casas

Dear Family and Friends,

After waiting for 18 days here in San Cristobal, Mexico, our vehicle is ready. We're heading out this morning for Guatemala. We feel the Lord has taught us much through our stay here. We trust in His timing. From the beginning, we've wanted the Lord to lead us. Our prayer has been, "Lead us to the people you want us to meet, and keep us from the people you don't want us to meet." Perhaps this delay was an answer to prayer.

The Coltman families we spent time with were indeed a blessing to us. They have a mission here translating gospel materials into the Indian languages. They also minister to physical needs by installing water filters and visiting remote villages with medicine and dental care. Many teams from the states come here to help. There was constantly a stream of fresh faces coming and going during our stay here, partly due to a wedding held here last weekend. This contributed to a group effort to get us on the road again.

Eric Coltman brought us back rims from Texas. A man from California brought us the spacers we needed to make the rims fit. Another man here from Florida was a welder and helped David weld and fit a custom brace for the interior roof support. We purchased some heavier load tires here, and the vehicle got new springs put under the front and rear. It spent four days in a body shop, getting a reinforced roof job. The Lord provided for our needs at every turn. Our job was only to wait. "All things work together for good to those that love God, to those who are the called, according to his purpose." Romans 8:28

The Land Cruiser waiting for wheels.

We had two and a half weeks while waiting to get to know the town of San Cristobal and contribute considerably to its local economy. We used taxis to get around and enjoyed practicing our Spanish with the drivers. They were very friendly and faithful to correct our occasional language errors.

We walked the streets and stumbled across an Indian marketplace. It was the first time we saw such a sight. There was a *carneceria* building, full of freshly slaughtered meat in the rawest of forms: Pig, chicken, and cow heads proudly displayed along with the feet. We saw an Indian woman selling live chickens. She was holding about five of them by their feet.

So many vendors with tight, narrow streets winding through them all. We walked on through the city and decided to ask a white man passing by where we were. We tried to ask in Spanish, but he asked, "Would you rather speak in English?" So, we enjoyed a conversation with him and found out he's from Michigan and had lived in Honduras. He had been living in San Cristobal for five years.

We enjoyed our time here along with the friendly people. Communication is always a challenge. For example, David, frustrated at the bank where now the copy of his passport that they insisted on yesterday was today no longer considered valid. They wanted the real thing. That's when

David gave up all attempts at his Spanish and started saying, "I don't have the original copy." He said this many times, and eventually, the woman gave him his pesos. I guess repetition sometimes helps in any language.

Another fun communication blunder was getting the oil changed. About 6 young men, eager to change our oil, ushered us into their shop. Very friendly, but we couldn't communicate, except for the basic fact we were there to get our oil changed. David wrote on a piece of paper the kind of oil he preferred, and eventually, we figured out the filter, and the job got done with lots of smiles and laughing at our attempts.

We were able to attend a morning of Spanish class at the local language school, which did help give us some direction in our attempts to learn the language.

Let me introduce Rhoda. She is the adopted daughter of Eric Coltman. After her mother died, she was abandoned. Later, a woman took her into her home and told her to make a fire while she went to get some food. But Rhoda had a seizure. She fell with her arm in the fire, and as a result, lost her arm. The Coltmans then adopted her and taught her Spanish, as she previously only spoke her native Indian tongue. She is a delightful girl and so full of joy. A beautiful picture of contentment and trust. Last night we watched her putting together a jigsaw puzzle. She was using her stub arm to drag over and fit pieces together. The song "The joy of the Lord is my strength" was playing in Spanish, and she was singing along. Giggling every now and then when the puzzle piece didn't fit. It was a real blessing to watch her. She was thrilled when I asked for her picture.

Thank you all for your emails. Thank you especially for your prayers. We will keep you posted as we travel through Guatemala and see what the Lord has for us there.

Love,

David, Kristi, Kindra, and Kacie

Trip Summary by Kristi VanderZon   Tribute to Mexico

The time has come to leave Mexico behind and experience Guatemala. Before we go, we want to share a tribute to our travels through Mexico.

The night before we entered Mexico, we stayed at Boca Chica Beach in Brownsville, TX. The neighboring fisherman brought in this stingray.

David, Kindra, and Kacie with a StingrayCamping on the beach.

With faith in God, we crossed the border 27 days ago, as numerous warnings had been given to us about the dangers of Mexico. Even the morning we crossed, the border patrol in Brownsville, Texas, gave us little hope of surviving Mexico. However, we pressed on, knowing there were believers on the other side waiting for us, even encouraging us to come.

So, rebuking those fears and doubts in the name of Jesus, we crossed the border, and what a blessing it has been!

From the very first moments of waiting in line for our paperwork and meeting "Pio," a man from Belize, and a dear native woman who gave us some invaluable directions for getting through Matamoros, we felt very welcome here. We had confidence that "The hand of our God is upon all them for good that seek him." Ezra 8:22 and that our Heavenly Father "guided us on every side" II Chron. 32:22.

We loved Mexico and its people. It is a beautiful country. We witnessed spectacular views as we drove through the mountains and lowlands that can hardly be described with words. We want to pass on some of the distinctive memories and impressions from our many miles of road time in Mexico.

Seeing the early morning energy of a town waking up and people busily sweeping off patios and porches, preparing to open up their shops and restaurants for the day.

The thatched roof, open-air little restaurants, with tables and chairs so neatly set up. Many times we stopped for a much-needed meal, and they were so friendly and helpful. Even when we couldn't read the menu, we would ask the waiters, "*Que le gusta*" (what do you like)? And whatever they liked, we would order. One time we got shrimp, another time beef. You never were sure what would be on your plate, but it was always good. When we stopped to eat when Kristi was sick, the waiter went and got some kind of bark to steep for tea that he said would help her stomach. There was a hammock next to the table where she laid during the meal. Pretty great accommodations when you're sick.

The first hotel we stayed at was in Soto La Marina. Matteo, the friendly receptionist, let us do our laundry in their private machine and email on their computer. We gave him a gospel book, which he thanked us for in a very meaningful note on our way out the door the next morning.

The dogs: they are everywhere. Around every corner and lurking in every shadow. "*Perros de la calle*" (dogs of the street), as our Tlaxcalan brethren taught us to say. They also taught us a handy phrase to tell people who were scared of our dogs "*perros amigable*" (friendly dogs). People were constantly intrigued by our dog duo. Walter & Biddy always drew interest and smiles, and occasionally great respect if someone approached the vehicle and tapped on the window to get their attention. Yes, dogs seem to be everywhere in Mexico but are usually timid and run off at the wave of an arm. Well-fed dogs who get to travel are somewhat rare.

Always amusing was the occasional pig crossing the street or wandering through town. A freshly slaughtered one was hanging up at a little outdoor "*comedor*" (restaurant). You get very fresh meat here!

We saw many donkeys in Mexico. They are often tied up on the side of the road, waiting for their owner to get back from town, load them up, and head home on one of those foot trails that disappear up the mountain.

Much road work going on, usually with only wheelbarrows & shovels. The Mexican men truly accomplish incredible feats with only time and a few primitive tools. The stonework on the long walls that line some mountain roads is very impressive.

The ingenuity of the Mexican people in their money-making ventures. One tiny village had set up its own roadblock, using party flags pulled across the road, requiring pesos to pass through. A little boy ran up and informed us, in a long string of Spanish we didn't understand, and held out his money tin. David dropped in some pesos, and he ran, laughing back to his family, yelling, "Gringos!". David played along and yelled "Gringos!" back while smiling his acknowledgment of their observation.

One of the awe-inspiring sights we witnessed was how they haul livestock. Two full-size horses in the back of a pickup truck. And one time, there was a full-size Brahma bull in the back of a Nissan pickup. We counted five cows crunched into the bed of another one.

We loved seeing the farmers plowing their fields with a yoke of oxen and the shepherds watching their sheep and goats on the hillsides. Also, the terraced gardens on the hillsides, and no matter how steep the mountains, you could see neat fields of corn off in the distance. Amazingly, they can farm on the steep hills like that.

That's a few of our memories from Mexico. Hope you enjoyed them!

Love,

David, Kristi, Kindra, and Kacie

CHAPTER 4

GUATEMALA

Kindra's Journal   8/28/2010

I woke up at 5:30, which wasn't much sleep because we stayed up past 12:30 working on emails and dad talking to Isaiah about DVDs. As soon as I woke up, I went straight to packing up sleeping bags and all the other odds and ends while mom worked on the group email for almost two hours. When I went over to make the coffee, Isaiah and the businessman were talking in the kitchen. Isaiah asked about those tomato seeds we forgot to give him. Bummer they were all packed away too deep to retrieve!

Despite our condensing 10 totes into 9, the vehicle still seems to barely contain everything. Isaiah brought out a box full of gospel DVDs, CDs, and tapes to send with us to evangelize on our trip to top it off. After helping Isaiah get a chicken back into its pen, we headed out at around 9:00 a.m.

It was pretty easy traveling to the border town of Guatemala. We arrived at 1:30 at the place of crossing. This town was the smallest town that I've ever seen that was so busy and full of people. I was pretty nervous about entering Guatemala. It was hard to know which one of the many buildings we needed to cancel our visas and vehicle permit.

After a few wrong places, we finally found the right "Señor" who canceled the vehicle and another right "Señor" to cancel our visas. Those two places were 4 km away from the actual border, so we had to drive back through the town to get to the border again, where we, after some bartering, exchanged our pesos for quetzales. They look very similar to pesos.

The Lord always seems to put the right people in our paths. We met some tourists who were waiting for their papers that we got to visit with. We also met a lady who has lived in Mexico for 40 years who told us despite what we heard (that the people in Guatemala are pretty dangerous), the people continue to get nicer the farther south you go! Wow, what joyous words to meet my ears.

The Lord does seem to have given us mercy in the sight of the authorities! Getting the paperwork done for Guatemala was no problem. It didn't even cost anything for our visas. The tire poison was only 18 quetzales, and I think the vehicle was somewhere around 40 quetzales.

The bank was closed for the afternoon siesta but a young man clad in a purple and green uniform with a gun and bullets around his waist welcomed us anyhow. The entire ordeal took about 2 hours, and once we relaxed, it was not all that bad, and the people were pretty nice to us.

We saw some cute sights today along with some unusual ones. On the beloved Mexican side of the border, we passed through a town where four little children were selling grilled corn all by themselves! They were just sitting on a bench playing with some leaves. Dad rolled down the window and waved to them. They all got excited and created quite a din of chatter as they enthusiastically waved back. The Mexican children are absolutely adorable!

Dad mentioned how the street dogs seem to always avoid the vehicles, and you see surprisingly few roadkills. That trend seemed to end today. I've never seen so many dead dogs on the side of the road as I did today. At least 10.

In Guatemala, we noticed many more extremely drunk people than in Mexico. Two men were wholly passed out on the sidewalk at the border, and further down, two young men were helping a very drunk elderly man walk down the side of the road.

The vehicles down here are also piled much higher than in Mexico. True to Eric Coltman's words, not even 5 minutes into Guatemala, we were not far behind a truck with people who were actually hanging off of the side! Another entertaining thing was a dog strapped down on a colorfully decorated bus's roof rack. This is way more third-world down here. Mexico seems so much more put together and orderly.

Biddy continues to take her wrath out on every dog we pass by and is extremely hard to take out for a walk as she ferociously lets loose on any other dog in sight.

As soon as we were out of the border town, we followed a rushing river through the mountain pass. The swinging bridges, waterfalls, hillside houses, and mountains full of green trees all added to the beauty of the countryside. A strange holiday happened to be taking place as we drove through. We saw lots of trucks and buses decorated with balloons and flowers. They were completely packed out with people. Occasionally leading the procession of vehicles were several men running with lit torches. We later learned that this was some kind of tradition!

We were stopped a few times waiting for landslides to be cleared from the roads. We decided to stop and wait until they were removed. We stopped for the night in Huehuetenango, where our courageous efforts of heading down the long driveway to an auto hotel were rewarded. We developed a nice friendship with the workers here, the family who owns the place.

They were thrilled when we decided to stay. An extra bed was hauled into our room, so we had a lovely little two-bedroom with a hot shower and an attached garage with doors. We got to talking with the mother, Marylen, and her children Jocelyn (20) and Juan (9) and soon found ourselves speeding towards some Mayan ruins with Marylen's children along as our guides.

The ruins park was closed for the day. Still, Jocelyn and that persuasive voice-only Central American and Mexican people seem to be able to achieve, she was able to get us all admission. It was great walking around and climbing up the massive stone structures that used to be temples, palaces, tombs, and game stadiums. The blue sky, gray rock buildings, and smooth green grass all contrasting together were gorgeous! Dad took some magnificent pictures, and we all enjoyed stretching our legs in the clean, fresh air.

When we got home, Marylen said she would make us some food, but as it passed the 9:00 p.m. hour, I thought we misunderstood her or she forgot about it. We had all kept busy: mom typing the group email, dad looking at pictures, Kacie taking care of her baby doll Timothy, and I started writing in the journal. At 9:45, our room's audio machine crackled to life, and we heard that our meals were ready.

We were soon sitting in our room enjoying a steaming hot plate of eggs, refried beans, and tortillas with sweet bread and coffee. For some reason, we decided not to get supper, so we were all ravenous! We were impressed to see God is providing us with food like the Ravens that fed Elijah in the Old Testament. Every day my faith and adoration grow more and more for the Lord.

Dad is feeling quite good about himself because he says his Land Cruiser is sleeping inside with him. I'm so tired I'm almost inclined to think that we may have been sneaked some sleepy powder, lol. I'm going to drink some charcoal, take a long hot shower, and probably literally crash into bed!

Speaking of crashes... We almost got in a crash today when a bus stopped in the road, and a semi passed it by, just coming right over into our lane of oncoming traffic. So grateful we are all safe!

Kindra's Journal   8/29/2010

25% sunny and 75% rainy. Cool all-day

Hello, it's 11:30 here, and we're a little ways outside of "Hue-hue." Here we sit, waiting for a massive landslide to get cleared off of the mountain road. There seem to be cars packed tightly together on both sides of the slide for miles. We pulled off onto the side to wait our turn along with hundreds of other vehicles.

Walter already has a growing crowd of natives that are amused by his ball antics. We walked up to the very front of the block where the slide happened. Many vehicles thought they could make it through, but were all stuck waiting for the mud and rocks to be moved.

The patch cut through the thick clay, and mud was almost as tall as the people on the backhoe. The crowd got louder as the local news cameras arrived, and all of the people tried to explain what had happened. Many different kinds of cargo can be seen, such as propane tanks, cabbage, potatoes, and so many busses with people. I wonder how long this will take.

Finally, around 1:00, after 3 hours of waiting, the road was cleared, and everyone rushed to their vehicles to hurry back on their way. We said a hurried goodbye to our newly found English-speaking friend, climbed into the vehicle, and started to move. Our progress came to an unfortunate halt, as once again, traffic on the opposite side started coming. Needless to say, we eventually made it through.

Not long down the road, we encountered another traffic hold-up. A sunken-down bridge. It created a one foot step down on either side. All was going well, but we were, as usual, stuck in the traffic. When going up the steep incline on the far side of the bridge, the car right in front of us stopped, almost causing us to swerve into oncoming traffic. Dad couldn't get the vehicle going again because of the heavy load. We had to back onto the bridge and get a head start to climb up and over the giant step. The onlookers stared at us in disbelief and cheered us on with shouts of " go Americans"!

As we traveled on to Panajachel, we finally found the Atitlan reserve, where we bargained the price down to $1,000 quetzales for a super quaint little jungle house. It had two showers and a toilet downstairs. The sinks were made out of big pieces of bamboo. Upstairs had a huge bed for mom and dad, along with bunk beds for us girls.

Since we hadn't eaten a meal all day (just sweet bread and a few cookies), we ordered some food and had our supper on a neat little deck that a rushing creek flowed right by. We met some people from New York who are also traveling around Central America. Our new friends informed us that we should check our house because they found one scorpion and one small tarantula in the house they're renting right next to ours.

While dad and I unloaded the vehicle, mom and Kacie took the dogs to a little clearing to exercise and discovered a small zipline. Once we figured out how to sit on the rope and successfully stop ourselves without being slammed to a stop, we had a blast. It goes pretty fast! The zip cable is around 1oo feet long.

Mom finished a group email, but we had a problem sending it, so we gave up on it for the day. I enjoyed a hot shower, checked my bed for poisonous creatures, and slept great!

Kindra's Journal   8/30/2010

Sunny in the morning and rainy in the afternoon

It's a beautiful day outside! Got up and played on the zipline, then walked to see the mountains surrounding Lake Atitlan, with three volcanoes on the opposite sides of the lake. There were quite a few landslides from the intense rain on the lakeshore. Having the sun out this morning feels terrific.

On our way back to the reserve, Jerry, the guard, told us we could go up and around the muddy trail. So we climbed up next to the waterfall and crossed a super tiny cable bridge where we could see all the volcanoes at once. The trail was really overgrown, but we made it back to our little house where we enjoyed some coffee and the last of our bread from San Cristobal. We sang some songs and read some bible passages.

We are now heading out to see the monkeys and hike more this evening.

I love it here. Wow, we had such an excellent hike! We bought some bananas and oranges to feed the animals and then headed out. It didn't take long to arrive at the monkey and coatimundis observation deck. We found ourselves throwing bananas to the monkeys and watching them peel then devour them. They informally get into a comfy position and then eat up. The oranges were enjoyed by both the coatimundis and the monkeys, who carefully skinned them and just wanted the juice. At one point, the coatimundis weaseled through the fence and came right over to dad, who was holding its favorite food, an orange.

We walked up next to a rushing creek and came to many bridges that hung over the bubbling streams of water. We came to a magnificent super tall waterfall after crossing 4 or 5 of these swinging cable bridges. One of the bridges went close to the base of the falls, so we got a great view of it! We kept climbing up and soon came to a waterfall, but the trail seemed to end right there. After looking around a moment and studying the map, we realized a bridge had been there. It had since been washed away. We could see the trail on the other side, so despite the precariousness of crossing right where the water surged over the edge of a cliff, we went for it! Everyone made it across with dad's help, and we started to descend down the mountain.

We could see the volcano very well at this point and enjoyed looking at all the flowers, trees, and leaves. We passed the spring that supplies the reserve's water and from there went through some muddy ground that was very slick. This year, they say, has been very rainy. We found ourselves back at the welcome center, took the dogs out to that field, and played on the zipline.

At around 3:00 this afternoon, our sunny weather ended, and it started to rain. Despite the inconvenience of the rain, it's actually beautiful to watch. From the porch of the little house, you can both hear and see the waterfall. I love seeing all the different ways they use bamboo in the construction here. It's in the walls, beds, roof, countertop, tables, and railings. It looks lovely and rustic. We went to look at the monkeys, and we're very entertained by an overly friendly coatimundi who ate from our hand. After looking again at the waterfall from the bridge, we called for a tuk-tuk to take us to Panajachel.

Within 10 minutes, Ricardo was waiting for us. We all squeezed into the tuk-tuk, and were soon speeding down the steep hill into Panajachel. Occasionally we stopped for Ricardo to point out something interesting and explain about some volcano or city. We asked him all kinds of questions about his age, job, and where he lives. Dad's usual questions. He started driving when he was 16 and has been tuk-tuking for 6 years. After an extraordinary tour of Panajachel and Lake Atitlan, he dropped us off on the main street. He said he'd be waiting for us at the end of the road at 8:30, in 1 1/2 hours.

We got out and set off in the dark street and watched our little red three-wheeled tuk-tuk putter away. We walked for a while, then bought a hand-embroidered blanket from a very persuasive vendor. He very convincingly reached his hand into his pockets and pulled out the linings as he explained he had nothing for his kids, and they needed food. He finally made a sale after coming from 100 quetzales down to 18.

We ate at the restaurant Ricardo recommended. It had good music and Italian food. A nice change to our diet! At 8:20, we made our way back to the end of the street just as Ricardo arrived. While we were eating, and of course, dad wanted to sit outside, many vendors tried to sell us things. I enjoyed talking to one of the ladies about being a Christian, but I don't think I had ever been so pestered during a meal! One of these sellers was the shortest lady I had ever seen, and she had the tiniest boy with her toddling around. She came up to us and persistently pecked mom with the chicken potholder, but despite mom's best efforts of "*no gracias,*" I was left to do most of the talking. It almost came to me being a bit rude. I finally told her no thank you, but thank you so much for showing us. She didn't seem to care what I told her, that I don't need your turtle or the chicken potholder because see, I don't wear them. She finally left, giving me a final peck on the shoulder with the stuffed turtle.

So back to the tuk-tuk. Ricardo gave us a nice ride back to our jungle cabin. He let dad drive on the cobblestone road to the reserve. We all had a good time laughing about him being the only gringo tuk-tuk driver here. We got a few good pictures of us with Ricardo and the tuk-tuk, then watched him drive off into the darkness. Checked for scorpions and tarantulas, then went to bed.

Kindra's Journal   8/31/2010

What a great day! After a shower, we went to see the monkeys and coatimundis. They were up to their usual antics. While we waited for the hour of 10 a.m. to come, we tried to pick up our house because we plan to move to the auditorium to camp.

At 10:00, we headed to the reserve center to get harnessed up for ziplining! There were 11 people in our group, including our two guides. After some quick instructions in Spanish and a short practice line, we were off to an intense 15-minute hike up the steep mountain to the first zip line. Kacie pushed me to the front of the line, and after being securely clipped in, I lifted my feet and took off. It was amazing!

As I soared over the green canopy of treetops, I looked to the right and could see Lake Atitlan and two volcanoes. We went on eight zip lines total, all very high up in the air, with some lasting for over 40 seconds! It was fantastic, and we all thought it was time well spent!

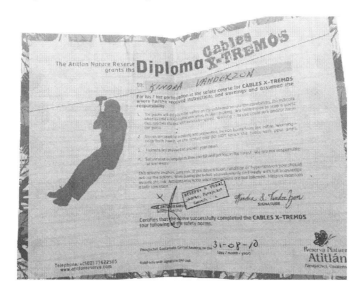

Moving out of our little house was quite the task as we hauled all of our camping things up to the auditorium. We were all glad it would work out to stay another night here. After we hid our things behind the white plastic chairs in the spacious tarp structure, we walked down the little footpath to the office, where we asked Jerry to call Ricardo for us.

Within 10 minutes, our friend Ricardo had arrived. I'll give a brief overview for all those of you who were not here to experience meeting Ricardo. He is super kind, amiable, and has the highest pitched, most fascinating laugh that any of us have heard! This good conduct and happy personality have been rewarded with being the primary tuk-tuk driver for the reserve.

Since it wasn't quite nice enough weather to hike, we headed to town to get a meal and walk around. We meandered through the market streets, stopping at vendors to look at their wares. As soon as you glance at their products, they start calling out *"buy one for two"*, *"we give good price"*, and *"come look"*. Even after you walk away, they're still calling out *"lowest price, I promise"*!

We finally stopped to get something to eat because all we had to eat today was a few cookies, so we were hungry. Almost our whole meal, we were diligently descended upon by women trying to sell blankets. My favorite technique to ward them off is to, without enthusiasm, say *"no gracias"* then ignore their repeated cries.

We walked across the street to where they were selling the woven sweaters that I wanted to buy. After showing interest, I soon had a man desperately searching for the right color and size. After he almost demanded I try on every color and seeing they were all way too big for me, he frantically dug for a smaller size. Unfortunately, the only small size he had was for a child, and too small. At this point, he asked, "what is your name"? So I told him, and he said his name was Victor. Finally, I figured out that he only had two sizes. Despite his begging for me to try on more, we politely said bye and moved on.

Later I finally found one that fit, and I figured it was a safe item to try experimenting with the third world "haggling". After the shop owner brought the price from 120 quetzales to 80, I told her 70 and no more. I laid the sweater down on the table, and she saw it was over. "Okay, for you good price" and now I'm enjoying a nice warm blue Guatemalan sweater! An amazingly successful experiment.

We made it back to the designated spot where we earlier had a battle with the Central American version of an ATM machine. We sat down on the curb to wait for Ricardo. We were amused by the scene of two bus workers shouting out their destination to get more passengers and the policemen chasing them off.

It wasn't long until Ricardo arrived. After we reclaimed our forgotten umbrella from the shoe store, we headed for home. The beautiful view combined with the cool breeze made for a great evening! Raphael came out when we pulled in, and we all had an enjoyable conversation. They said the DVD of the testimony we gave them was great. Praise the Lord!

Ricardo was pointing to Biddy, saying *"macho"* (boy) or *"embra"* (girl)? We were really stumped as to what he was asking. Finally, we figured it out, and dad said quite triumphantly, *"ah mi hija"* (my daughter) upon being so enlightened. We all could hardly stop laughing when he said *"Mujer"* (woman) to clear things up. Closer, but still hilarious! Well, you learn as you go something new every day. We said goodbye to our friends then took a path up a steep bank to see the mountains and volcanoes. It was incredible. The clouds were below the top of the volcano but above the lake! We're enjoying our first night camping out of the states.

Kindra's Journal   9/01/2010

Good morning. It's our last morning at Lake Atitlan, and I feel downright miserable. I suffered from a severe cold all day yesterday. Last night was so terrible, almost comparable to last month's stomach sickness! All night I was lying partially on my mat with the rest of my body on the cold bricks. It seems to have contributed to a headache. Meanwhile, my whole body hurts, but especially when I sneeze, my poor rib cage seems to cry out in pain!

Last night seemed to drag on forever. I didn't sleep a wink until everyone got up at 8:00. They ever so kindly evicted me out of the tent. I sloughed around half in a daze to try and help pack up the Land cruiser so we could head to Ben Palma's house. It's a 2 to 3 hour drive depending on road conditions, so we'll see.

We ordered breakfast from the reserve's restaurant while mom and dad finished packing the cruiser. Yes, it's rare for us to order breakfast. Our seemingly ever-present diet of platanos and cookies, whether from our friends in the states, the Indians, or the grocery stores, has almost vanished. We find ourselves hungry much more than we used to!

Left the reserve a little after 11:00, but stopped not too far down the road because of the landslide, which rerouted us onto a very terrible road. The very one Ricardo had told us to avoid. Every bump we hit sent pain shooting through my body. It was pretty miserable. We had to cross the river where the bridge had been washed away. The Land Cruiser was in its element as we punched through the water. Finally, around 4:00, thanks to excellent directions, we meandered down a dirt road where some men upon a half-framed house waved to us, and we pulled in the gate. We made it!

Lucas and his wife graciously gave us a warm welcome, and we enjoyed a meal with them and the worker Enrique. I still felt very sick, so I went down to the tiny sleeping quarters and, after a sorry effort to check the bed for scorpions, flopped down onto it. As I lay my head down and my eyes adjusted to the dim light, I saw a single dead moth. After picking him off the quilt, I rested for hours in a fitful sleep. I had a fever, and still the aches and pains in my body.

Mom, dad, and Kacie went along with Lucas to the market, which they said was very interesting. By the chattering voices coming from the late-night dinner, I should say they had a great visit with brother Marcos and his wife, Norma. Hopefully, I'll be better tomorrow.

Kindra's Journal   9/02/2010

Rainy and overcast

Woke up feeling slightly better but felt exhausted all day. I got an email for Alaina ready and studied some Bible passages using E-sword. I read all of Joel and nine chapters of Second Chronicles. In the afternoon, dad helped set up a massive tent for the anniversary celebration on Saturday. He said it was so heavy the support poles felt suctioned to the ground. There was a group of American young men and some Guatemalan girls who came to help set up as well.

We met Sharon, a Mennonite from Pennsylvania who is staying in Guatemala for one and a half years at the Mennonite air missions base. I helped move benches that needed to be washed. Ben Palma and his wife Alicia and baby brought supper over to our little house. We enjoyed a delightful visit with them.

Kindra's Journal   9/03/2010

I'm feeling much better today. After some Bible study, we girls set out through the ever-present rain. We helped the native women clean leaves to make tamales for the anniversary celebration of Victor and his wife. We cleaned close to 1,000 of those massive *hojas* (leaves). They were no slouch of a leaf at close to three feet long and one and a half feet wide.

Coffee is consumed in tremendous quantities here, definitely a staple drink. Morning, noon, and night, it seems to be consumed by all. We enjoyed a hot cup of the substance around 4:30 with fresh sweet bread. Kacie and dad have a slight touch of that sickness I had. We played our five crowns game tonight from the Coltman's. Poor dad was desperately dragged down the stairs by a tan calf when he was moving it. The whole scene was pitifully hilarious! Watched the volcanoes blow out fire and smoke tonight.

Kindra's Journal   9/04/2010

High of 69 degrees

Went over to Lucass after being jolted awake at an early morning hour by Lucinda. She needed him to take her cheese to market. After singing together with Lucas's family, we washed dishes. Dad made the treacherous ascent with Lucas to fix the broken water pipes. They have been broken for three days, and the rainwater is almost gone.

Read three chapters of Second Chronicles and also part of The Seduction of Christianity. Dad took a few naps and lots of medicine since he wasn't feeling good. Kacie is also sick. I did a tiny laundry load of my five dirty pieces since I had nothing else to do. Went out and played games with Josue, Stephanie, and Kacie around 4:00. They are the cutest! Let Josue play my guitar. He loved it.

We left for San Lucas with mom and dad, two other church brothers, and Kacie and I packed in the cargo space. Met up with Lucas's family, and we all rode to their friend's house and enjoyed a supper of pupusas together. All the while, Lucas was animating earthquakes and sinkholes for us. It was very entertaining. Met another church brother who has an adorable baby daughter named Alicia. We stopped at a supermarket where we met two young men who were Jehovah's witnesses. Came home and helped Corina peel apples for the morning. Everyone got a good laugh as dad picked up the children's flip-book of Spanish words and said he should take it to church to help him understand the Spanish sermon.

Kindra's Journal   9/05/2010

Woke up and rushed over to Corina's house for a shower. As mom got the water going in the shower next to mine, I could hear her making the same shrieking noises as I had made only minutes before. However, her shrieks were caused from feeling boiling water running over her body instead of the freezing cold water I was feeling. I still can't figure out the difference. Oh well.

We left at 8:00 and followed Mark and Norma out to the very third-world town of Olla Grande. Its cobblestone streets were quite charming. We enjoyed the singing, and I found myself understanding much of the sermon Marco preached about Grace. What is it exactly? We went to a native church member's house for lunch. After my eyes adjusted to the metal room with no windows, we enjoyed visiting with Norma. She showed us around the little courtyard outside the door where three families live. The parents, their two daughters, and their families. So interesting.

On the way home, we drove through a tiny town. Three cowboys were riding horses through town, a little colt loose and trailing behind them. The last one in line smiled for the picture when he realized we were gringos.

Further down the road, we saw a man with a big bag of corn, a cow, and a calf.

Gave mom her birthday book. Went to Guatemala City for a night church and their format of verse memorization was very interesting. Rode to Ben's house with him for supper. It took us about an hour to get there. It was a good visit, and their family is so sweet. Drove home around 9:30 and even the gas stations were roped off and shut. When we commented on the landslides, Ben said he would feel better if we would drive as many lanes away from the hillside as we could. The natural disasters here are no joke.

Kindra's Journal   9/06/2010

Sunny in the AM, then thunderstorms

I woke up and worked on a letter for Grandma, then studied the Bible story that answers Kacie's question: what is an ebenezer? Played soccer with Kacie, then went to San Lucas to get a gift for our host family. Picked up a man on the way out who needed to go to the main road. We found him lying in the road. Dad leaned out the window and said, "*como esta*" (How's it going?). The old man's eyes flickered "*Ah, bueno*" (Oh, good), he said. Saw a man with a black horse loaded with a big heavy load along with a lady whose load was as tall as her body. She had it perfectly balanced on her head! Mom did laundry while Kacie and I helped Corina get supper ready. Played more soccer with cute little Josue and Kacie.

Kindra's Journal   9/07/2010

A little rain and then sunshine

Woke up at 4:30 and had a somewhat stressful time packing up, but we were ready at the appointed time of 5:30. We snaked our way through Guatemala City, trying to stay behind Lucas, who drove as fast as humanly possible on the highway. We made it through at around 9:30, where we met Enrique and his family at a market and headed out on a rough dirt road for 10 minutes.

We parked at a brother's house and started our hike. We hiked with Lucas and Enrique's family back to the church building. A simple structure of cement block and metal. Down the hill from the church was another family with 10 children. On the side of their creek, a horse relaxed by the water, and chickens and dogs abounded. We all crowded into the dark smokey little room. After our eyes adjusted, we were able to see the family. We had a good visit, including a prayer for our trip. Dad caught one of the many ducklings that scattered across the floor. We made our way across the creek and visited a few more houses, all of which only a person who visited in person could describe.

Kacie and I got to pat out our first tortillas, and we all enjoyed our long-awaited breakfast at 11:00. The beans, eggs, tortillas, and coffee tasted great. We made our way back to the trail and stopped at Enrique's parents before heading back to the Land Cruiser. On our way out, when we passed the church, the 18-year-old son ran out to meet us. He had a plate of hot grilled corn *elote* that he wanted us and Lucas to take. These people, some of them with shoes falling apart and others that only have the bare necessities of clothing, we're still giving and thanked us over and over for visiting.

Keeping up with Lucas for the next hour and a half was quite the task, and the Land Cruiser was going as fast as it could. We got rerouted onto a pot holy dirt road because the bridge washed out on the Pan-American highway. Even this, however, could not even keep Lucas's passing habit under control. Not much past Pasco we found ourselves in the crazy bordertown leading to El Salvador. Men rushed up to our open windows, some thrusting official-looking badges through the window, trying to convince us we needed their help. After an intimidating mob of about five or six had gathered, Lucas prayed in Spanish for us. With many sincerely concerned parting warnings from Lucas of *cuidado*, be careful, he left.

It was sad to watch our friend drive away but lo and behold, while dad was struggling to get his copies made, they're standing behind him was Lucas. What a blessed surprise! After driving down the road a way, he decided to come and help the vulnerable gringos. We waited for about an hour to cancel our vehicle permit because the immigration offices closed for a party, yes, the whole nine yards. After waiting a long while with the rowdy group of men and hearing yells from them like, "you need to come out" and "I believe right now or else", someone finally had mercy on us and took our paperwork through a door and returned with it stamped. Praise the Lord.

We headed over to the El Salvadorian side. Despite their friendly service, we didn't get back on the road until almost 3:00. The whole ordeal took 2 hours, but it seemed like way longer. Aside from many cattle in the road, crossing through four tunnels and seeing two oxen carts the rest of the day was relatively uneventful. We made it to the long talked of Surfers Inn, where the owner actually flagged us down. They were thrilled to see us and have made us very comfortable under a roofed patio to camp for $10 a night. We walked to the ocean and found it to have dirty water and a rocky beach. Much different than Oaxaca, still pretty.

Trip Summary by Kristi VanderZon   Guatemala

Hello Family & Friends,

Thank you all for your prayers! It is always rewarding to share our experiences with you at the end of a full day. They are a true testimony to the faithfulness of God and an answer to many prayers.

The most popular vehicle on the road in Mexico seemed to be the Volkswagen bug. Here, Toyota rules supreme. Finally, we blend in. Well, almost. The buses are all colorful and decorated. Also, the amount of people packed in and on top of trucks is incredible.

Regrettably, we didn't get a picture of the truck like the one in this picture, full of pigs. About 10 of them. We followed behind it for a while and were very entertained.

We caught a glimpse of this colorful truck

The first night we reached Huehuetenango and looked for a hotel. Kristi spotted a little sign for lodging with a long driveway down a hill. We looked a little longer then decided to go back and see what kind of hotel it might be. It was a little intimidating, but we drove down the long lane and looked in the courtyard at the hotel. It looked a little run down, and we started to pull away when a woman came running down the lane with her little boy and very enthusiastically asked us if we wanted a room. We agreed to look at one and were quite pleased.

We took the dogs outside the courtyard. The woman, Marylen, and her daughter, Rosie, and son Juan, brought us sliced watermelon to eat. We were having a good time talking with them, and we asked about the ruins that we heard were local. They said they were only ten minutes away, and Rosie and Juan would go with us to show us where. So we all got in the land cruiser, and she guided us through town and out to the Mayan ruins called Zaculeu. We got there around 6:30 pm, and they were closing. But Rosie pleaded with the man and wouldn't give up till he let us in, for a special price, of course. We got a private viewing of the artifact museum and then got to see the ruins. They were terrific, and we had the whole place pretty much to ourselves.

Kristi, Walter, and Biddy in the garage of the auto hotel

Our family on one of the many beautiful ruins

Kristi descending

More ruins...

Kristi, Kindra, and Kacie striking a pose

Our second day's destination was Panajachel, on Lake Atitlan. We didn't get far down the road when the traffic slowed, then stopped. We waited for about 15 minutes for the road to get cleared of a landslide, then continued on our way. About 10 minutes later, traffic again slowed down to a stop. We knew we might be in for a wait when people started getting out of their vehicles.

We got out with the dogs and walked up to see why everyone was stopped. It appeared as if people had been stopped for a while, as some were stretched out sleeping in the grass on the side of the road. Already there were food vendors set up and various peddlers of food and drink walking around. We walked up quite a ways, passing vehicles that had come to a halt well ahead of us. The military was there, stuck with the rest of us.

When we got to the origin of the delay, we saw a massive landslide had covered the road, and a back-hoe was working to clear it. We waited for about 3 hours for the road to open up. At that point, utter chaos ensued as everyone ran to get in their vehicles and started trying to get through all at once.

Clearing the slide

David, the girls, and the dogs, waiting for the road to open

The traffic jam

We saw this man resting alongside the road with his load

This sign appeared more than once, along with a loose boulder signs

Throughout the day, we saw boulders on the side of the road that had come loose from the steep mountainside, some as big as our vehicle. The road was so steep descending into Panajachel, David had to deploy the efforts of both the transmission and brakes.

Our time at Lake Atitlan was relaxing. We were fortunate to get one of the six rooms on the reserve. They are very charming units, with an upstairs, downstairs, a balcony with a view, lush jungle all around, and sounds of rushing water flowing close to our lodging.

One morning listening to the girls playing their instruments on the porch and singing together.

We then went on a most spectacular hike. Here are a few pictures we took...

Hanging out with the coatimundis

Kindra and Kacie on one of the swinging bridges

One of the many beautiful waterfalls here

We saw excellent monkey action in the trees but didn't get any good pictures of them. We crossed many swinging bridges.

As per the usual pattern, it started raining at around 3:00.

Later in the evening, we got restless, so we had the reserve call us a "tuk-tuk" recommended by some new friends we met here at the reserve from NY. Tuk-tuks are the equivalent of a taxi, but more like an enclosed motorbike. Our driver, Ricardo, was extremely friendly and eager to give us a tour of Panajachel. His expertise was evident, as he was able to maneuver through some pretty impressive small spaces. He drove us all over town, showing us the lakefront and some severe flooding damage that just happened recently. There were still small buildings tilted on their sides and abandoned.

Kristi, Kindra, and Kacie with Ricardo our tuk-tuk driver

We enjoyed a good meal at an Italian restaurant (they abound down here in Panajachel). True to his word, Ricardo was there waiting at the appointed meeting place. On the way home, he let David drive the tuk-tuk.

We decided to take advantage of the reserve's Extremo Zip Line Cable Adventure. We were with 8 people, including a family from Long Island, NY, and a couple from Jerusalem. After getting fitted in our harnesses, helmet, and big leather gloves, our Spanish-speaking guide gave us brief instructions (thankfully, our new friend from NY translated for us). After a trial run down a short cable, we hiked 20 minutes up the mountain to where the first of 8 cables spanned a sizable gap.

Kindra was the first to go. You step off the platform and are hurled above the treetops at a pretty fantastic speed. When you see the guide on the other side wave his little red rag, you place a gloved hand on the cable to slow you down. We really enjoyed it. However, Kacie's glove started to come off when she was attempting to break, and she came in too fast for a gentle stop. She still wasn't ready to give up, but on the following cable, she had a moment of panic and couldn't slow down and came in full force for an abrupt landing. She was shaken up but not hurt. David helped catch her. For the rest of the rides, she was riding double with the guide, so she could enjoy the ride without worrying about the braking part. We were thrilled we did it.

We moved to the auditorium to camp for our last night at the reserve. We put the tent on the stage, which had electricity. Convenient for writing this email.

Walter relaxing while Kristi types the group email

We headed towards Guatemala City. The church there has a farm seven miles outside of the city where we can set up camp and stay for a few days. Two families live there on the farm. We were surrounded by crops of healthy-looking tomatoes, corn, green beans, and chiles. We have been enjoying the excellent cooking of Corina & Lucinda and meeting the local brethren.

There are three volcanoes within sight of the farm. One night, we could see the red glow of lava spewing out the top of one. It made a pretty sight on a dark night.

Our day of departure started early, at 5:30 am. We decided to follow Lucas as he was making a trip in the same direction we were going. It was a significant advantage to follow his ford ranger through Guatemala City which contains 6+ million people. Even as we passed through at an early hour, traffic was very heavy, and it was a challenge to keep Lucas in sight. We made good time to Pasaco, where we met a family from the church that had offered to make us breakfast. We drove about 15 minutes out of the small town, parked the vehicles, then walked on a trail back to their home.

We saw the church house, visited four homes, and met many of the brethren and sisters of the church there. A few words about the church here: We enjoyed our time with the brethren in Guatemala. There is a longstanding work here, headed by Mennonite Air Missions, located in Guatemala City. There are 17 different churches located throughout Guatemala from this work, and they are connected by joint leadership. At various times of the year, they meet at the farm where we stayed. We were blessed and encouraged by their steadfastness, concern for the individual families in the church, and their willingness to take the time to spend with us and encourage us as well. It's evident the body of Christ is well and thriving here in Guatemala.

We were able to help make tortillas and were served an excellent breakfast in one of the homes.

Kindra & Kacie making their first tortillas.

We enjoyed meeting the people and seeing their joyful faces, and witnessing their generous spirits.

On our way back, we were met on the trail by the son of the first family we had visited. He was holding a plate of fresh grilled "elote" (corn) for us. We were very touched by the desire of the family to bless us in this way.

Hiking the trail back from visiting our new friends.

Kacie, thrilled to find her favorite candy nerds here in Guatemala

We continued on our way and made good time to the "Fronterra" (frontier or border) of El Salvador for a long but successful crossing.

Love,

David, Kristi, Kindra & Kacie

Chapter 5

El Salvador

Kindra's Journal   9/08/2010

Poured rain all night, but today was nice and sunny.

I woke up and got the coffee going in the tiny shared kitchen. It felt good to be somewhat self-sufficient again! Had some delicious muffins from Alicia Palma that, through the course of our travels yesterday, got flattened and smashed to about a half-inch thick. They still tasted good. Thank you, Alicia! We rented two boogie boards for Dad and me, then headed to the playa. By the way, before I get to the story, all of us are swinging in hammocks. Kacie is sick and sleeping, mom is typing an email, dad is drinking some kind of cold beverage, and I'm writing. A cockroach amigo is lying on his back beneath my hammock. Maybe it's just me, but as he's laying on his back with his legs in the air, 2 inch long antennae swinging softly in the breeze, I picture that he seems to be enjoying the day almost as much as I am!

Anyhow, back to the beach. We watched the men out there for a while as they played and surfed on the large white foaming waves. It looked fun and relatively easy, so dad and I decided to go for it. We strapped our boogie board ropes onto our wrists, carefully picking our way over the large black rocks in the water. We hopped onto our boards. Getting tumbled around in the waves was fun and exciting. We certainly weren't getting the hang of it and needed practice. Before we knew it, we were surprised to find ourselves very promptly drifting out way past our comfort zone and beyond 300 yards from shore.

Fighting the current took all we had, and there was no visible progress. Our task seemed more and more impossible. I was getting quite afraid and could see tiny little mom and Kacie back onshore. The thought of sharks passed through my mind. I knew Mom would be worried, and I kept praying, all the while paddling with all I had! Through many different explanations, Dad got the point across that this was life and death dangerous. I was terrified as we continued to fight the current. Without the slightest rest, the task of reaching shore seemed almost impossible as we continued to steadily drift out.

After we concluded we weren't going to make it in, or I should say my poor swimming ability in a full-length dress couldn't. Dad was doing his best to help me but to no avail. We decided to call the other surfers for help. It wasn't long until two men had paddled out to help us. They assessed the situation quickly and had me trade out the bright orange boogie board I had been using for one of their large surfboards. They said that the boogie board I had was no good and was undoubtedly one of my problems.

For about 15 minutes, the four of us continued to paddle with all of our might towards the shore while angling to the left. The progress was very slow, and suddenly I saw a man take off his shirt, run, and dive under the waves. I kept looking towards a rock destination and paddling with all of my tired might. Suddenly, the man I saw diving into the water came out of the water right in front of my surfboard. He grabbed a hold of it and told us all that we needed to swim to the right, and so we did. Within about 5 minutes of more paddling, my feet were on solid ground.

Oh, sand and rock! I could move around without flailing my limbs in the water. Praise the Lord! We shook hands with the men who helped us out and thanked them very much. Even in their half-dressed state, they seemed like very great people to me at that moment. Dad and I walked back to where mom and Kacie were waiting for us and collapsed down on the seats next to the enormous rock.

Not many minutes later, the third man walked around the corner to talk to us. He couldn't have been much older than me, but he had the solution to our problems! He told us when we started talking about the boards and pointing to me, he said "no more." That was fine by me since you probably couldn't have paid me to get out there at that point anyhow. That man's name was Jesus, what a name! Almost fitting. We hope to bring something out for him tomorrow morning. I sure hope he's there! Praise the Lord, and that sure puts a new perspective on things for me.

The rest of the day was uneventful, and we rested in our hammocks most of the afternoon. We ordered a meal from the neighbors across the cobblestone road. Dad and I each got a *pescado frito* (fried fish). It was the kind of fish with both eyes on the same side, and you can only catch them in Central America, I guess. Despite the way its face looked with its razor-sharp teeth staring at you, it tasted great!

We headed back to the beach around 4:30 to watch dad make some attempts at boogie boarding. His feet were cut up, but he was rewarded as he did make one great surf all the way to shore! The owner brought us some tasty pupusas this evening. Dad is reading Chicken Soup for the Pet Lover's Soul. He must be desperate for a good read.

Kindra's Journal   9/09/2010

Sunny and hot, but pleasant in the shade

Woke up before the rest of the family and reheated the coffee. We went up to the lookout above the store and drank some juice for breakfast. Came back and swept our entire area along with the tent. Cleaned up the tables, and mom washed clothes. We ordered some smoothies from the fish cook's wife. She brought them over in these huge glass cups. They were great, and we enjoyed them with three tiny cookies then headed out to the beach to look for Jesus.

No, we were not looking for the Lord to descend from heaven with a shout, but rather the necklace vendor that played a big part in our return to shore. Unfortunately, he didn't come by so maybe we'll find him tomorrow to give him his book! I hope so.

Came home, and we all took showers. After clearing out the Land Cruiser, we decided to head out for the first time in 3 days to get something to eat. We found a cute little place within 10 minutes that was perched way up on a cliff overlooking the ocean. The breeze was blowing through, and the blue ocean was amazing!

The waiter certainly earned us as customers when he waved us in with his white towel. He brought us out an order of cocktail conchas for us to try while we were waiting. The little plate contained two halves of limes with a few toothpicks and four shell halves with shiny tan things floating in some kind of brown juice. Our waiter told us to put salt and lime on them and then poke them with the toothpick and eat.

This looked interesting, and as our waiter looked on with suspense, along with us girls, dad began to sprinkle salt on the unknown subject. The table erupted in questions as it squirmed around. *Vive* (Is it alive)?. Yes, the thing moved and the waiter said yes, it lives. Wow, what a surprise! The man looked at dad, and we asked "do you eat it live?" "Yes." The waiter got the process moving along by squeezing the lime onto the wiggling organisms and then said it was ready to eat. Dad smiled at us girls and then stabbed the tan shining concha with a toothpick and popped it in his mouth. After a few chews, it was swallowed. "Not bad," he said, and the waiter smiled with satisfaction. Dad pushed the plate towards me.

I picked up a toothpick and pressed it into the squishy thing. As I took it out of its shell, a 3 to 4 in long-tail was hanging down in a very unappetizing manner. I lowered it into my mouth, and not wanting to disturb it into some panic spasm, I chewed it twice then swallowed. Its sliminess made it slide down quite easily, and its taste wasn't that bad. Mom was fortunate enough to have the tail of her concha stick to the shell. Kacie somehow escaped the conchas altogether, and dad ate hers.

He later said I think those conchas are coming back to haunt me, and I don't feel very good!

After that, we drove into La Libertad and searched for an internet connection. However, the search was to no avail. We returned home and took a walk to the beach, and watched the surfers. The waves were really nice tonight. We played a game of five crowns. Earlier, dad was sitting in a chair and letting the waves splash over him when all of a sudden, a neck-high wave hit him and completely knocked him and his chair over. He was on the ground, and his hat and chair were floating away. That was one funny moment, and another was when I learned to never put a spoonful of charcoal in your mouth dry. It almost did me in as the fine powder choked in my lungs.

Kindra's Journal   9/10/2010

Another beautiful day!

We woke up and headed out to the beach. The tide was low, and it was quite enjoyable looking for rocks and watching the waves. We walked all the way down to the next creek by a massive boulder rock and enjoyed letting our feet get wet in the rare big sandy area. I found some pretty rocks: shiny, pink, green, sea glass, shining white, and yellow.

Just when we were giving up on seeing Jesus, we noticed him standing out in front of the Caillou Hotel. We got a few necklaces from him and gave him the Good and evil book and evangelistic CD from the reserve. We got a picture taken with him. We walked back to the Surfer's Inn and had breakfast around 11:00 over at Felipe's *tienda,* then headed out for a La Libertad. After getting some drinks and walking around trying to find the internet cafe, a super nice man showed us where it was. We sent and received some long-awaited emails.

We went to the fish port and took a very interesting walk to purchase our fish for supper. While trying to get to the pier, we were just about grabbed off the street by the restaurant hawkers who anxiously tried to funnel us into their place. You can't appease the masses.

Inside the covered beginning of the pier was every kind of sea creature imaginable. Blue 3 ft long fish with pointed noses, red scaly thick fish, shrimp, tiny silverfish, lobster, flatfish, and stingray meat could all be found at almost any one of the 20 plus vendors.

We walked past the vendors and watched a man cutting up a gigantic stingray. It was quite the scene as knives were flying and a man was running across the table. We continued on past many small boats and push carts with wooden wheels to the end of the dock, where the cranes lifted them out of the water. Some youth were being juveniles out on the end of the pier, while the older and wiser were simply fishing.

Kindra's Journal   9/11/2010

Woke up and packed up camp. Our new friend Heis dropped off some directions for an internet cafe in La Libertad. We left the Surfers Inn around 9:30. Got the Baha lights fixed, then stopped at the internet cafe to no avail as our next host family hadn't sent directions. After a quick change of plans, we headed for the Honduras frontera. Getting going was difficult as we were blocked in by a pickup truck. Dad resorted to English again while trying to sort out who the owner of the truck was. He eventually gained success, and we were on our way.

Progress was short-lived as we encountered a bridge that was washed away. We followed a bus down a side road where the helper jumped off, gave us some necessary directions, and charged us. A little boy ran ahead to where he ran down the bank and carefully waved us through. In the middle of the river, an older man took over the guiding. He took his job very seriously to avoid us wrecking into boulders.

We pulled up to the bank on the other side, where after dad persuaded the men to at least let him drive to the top of the hill, the men began stating their charges for the river crossing. The one little boy we started with now had two men behind who also had helped in the venture. Dad wanted to, without a hassle, get moving. So, he bought them some ice cream and paid them some change. Success, we thought, but a man walked up in the common uniform of just shorts. He tried to buddy up to us and said he was from Maryland. The place where all "friends" seem to be from here. After listening to his story for a minute, we were fortunate to escape despite his demands for food and money. We got out of there just as an angry mob started to move down the street towards our "friend." Praise the Lord we were fortunate to make it through unharmed! The day was continuing on in the same sort of manner if. I wouldn't write about the negatives, but I want you readers to get a complete immersive feel of our trip.

We ended up getting lost due to a combination of poor road signs, maps lacking names, and an uncertain destination. After hours of driving around, sometimes multiple times over the same stretch of highway, stopping to ask the police, and desperately gripping the map, we ended up at a gas station. While dad fueled the Land Cruiser, we girls took a bathroom break and let the dogs out. Just before we left, the man who had been discussing directions with dad handed us a beautiful hand-drawn map of how to get to El Amatillo, the border. It worked! An answer to prayer, praise the Lord.

We traveled on in a restful manner until we reached El Cuco. We ended up getting turned around, confused, and frightened, only to turn around again with confidence. We asked a *policia*, and were kindly directed to a slew of hotels. After looking around a party hotel where although the man assured us "good for family," we didn't quite agree.

We pressed on further down the road until we saw a big gate that said hotel. Dad started pounding on the gate, and we gained entrance to a better hotel. Although above our price range we saw not many other options, so we decided to stay! We took a walk down a staircase to a tiny little beach where we met a man named Ricardo, his wife, and two little kids. He had some interesting things to say about his work of fishing out on the ocean to provide for his little family. He grew up here and is quite content to stay. That's refreshing and good to see!

We went back to the hotel and ordered some food. We waited for a while, watching the storm roll in and darkness fall. All of us were super hungry as we hadn't eaten anything but some kind of say around 12:00, so a supper of refried beans and fried tortillas tasted really good! The night guard keeper, Espia, seemed to take a liking to us and talk to us much about his job in the USA and how he was able to send money back for his family. He does, however, enjoy the simple life and wants to be content making $80 a day. He admitted it's only God that blesses him with a job. We gave him a Good and Evil only by his grace.

Trip Summary by Kristi VanderZon   El Salvador

Hello Dear Family & Friends,

We crossed into El Salvador and began the paperwork there. We had no problems until we left the office and were stopped by an official who said our paperwork had an error, and the license plate number didn't match. Ughh! We thought this might be another start of a long delay, but he radioed an office worker, who ran over with white-out and corrected our mistake.

It took much skill to drive, as David had to look out for severe potholes and cows in the road. We were soon treated to a beautiful coastline drive, with many tunnels through the mountain and spectacular views of the rocky coastline of El Salvador.

Some cows helping themselves to the lane

We decided to stay here at the Surfer's Inn for a few days and soak in the sun & fresh saltwater breezes. It's working out well with the dogs here.

100

It's rainy/off-season, so not many people are around. It's a good, tranquil place to rest in a hammock and let our bodies relax. The owner, Felipe, and family live here and quickly made themselves busy overseeing our comfort. He promptly had four hammocks hanging up and showed us his little "*tienda*" (store), which was fully stocked with cold beverages and snacks. We each have a hammock and are becoming very fond of them!

David and Kristi swinging in the hammocks at the Surfers Inn

We decided to spend one of the mornings at the beach, where David wanted to try out the "boogie" boards that our kind host, Felipe, rounded up for us. Kristi & Kacie stayed onshore to keep track of the dogs and watch David & Kindra try surfing.

Kindra, ready to go....

They started paddling out to the big waves, where many other surfers were already enjoying the surf. However, the current was strong and kept pulling them out farther from shore and away from the other surfers. About 45 minutes later, Kristi, watching from shore, started feeling uneasy and thought they were too far out.

David waved his hands and called for help. Some surfers saw the situation and immediately paddled over to help them. By this time, Kindra was getting exhausted, and the danger lay in drifting further & further out into the ocean. The two men reached them and transferred Kindra to their bigger board, and all gave an effort to get to shore. Still, they couldn't do it. That's when a young man who was selling wares on the beach put down his merchandise and dove into the water, swimming the distance confidently out to them. He felt they should come in from a different angle, and with his help, they finally got to shore. We were all extremely relieved and praised God for the willing men who helped them get to shore.

David and Kindra with Jesus, the man who helped rescue them

David and Kindra resting after their wild time in the ocean

Kacie enjoying the waves from shore

Later, David braved the waves once again, this time alone, and caught a little surf. "It's certainly not as easy as it looks from shore," he later said.

We had some most excellent fish dinners from the neighbor, who is very willing to be our cook. And one night, our host's daughter surprised us with fresh "pupusas." They are a traditional El Salvadorian dish. It's like a thick corn tortilla outside, filled with cheese and vegetables or meat and sealed. They were delicious.

Here are a few pictures of the beach here and our accommodations.

Some natives walking on the beach at sunset

The sand here is black due to a volcano that erupted in the past. It left a 13 mile stretch of black sand.

Walter and Biddy on the black volcanic sand

We're the only ones staying at the Surfers Inn, and I'm sure we're not the typical guests. There is a board in the kitchen with pictures of surfer groups that have come through. We'd like to add our picture and a few statements about our destination and purpose.

We enjoyed the port city of La Libertad, with its fish market on the pier. We saw many varieties of size, shape, and color of creatures fresh from the sea. We bought some kite (not sure of the spelling, but it's a fish with both eyes on the same side) and shrimp. Our neighbor cooked them for us last night. Seafood is the staple here.

We were eating in a restaurant and ordered something with the name "concha" in it. The waiter looked a little reluctant to put it in front of us. We felt prepared to eat anything. There were four clam-looking shells split open on our plate, with pink, fleshy centers floating in a brown juice. The waiter instructed us to sprinkle them with salt, which produced a wiggling action from the fleshy part. We weren't expecting that!

David asked the waiter, "Vive?" (It lives?) And the waiter very proudly responded, "Si, Si, Vive!" (Yes, Yes, it lives). He was worried we would want to return it, but David wasn't about to let an opportunity like that pass. Only Kacie was exempted from tasting this live morsel, being the sickest with a cold of us all. They really did taste alright, just different eating something that is still wiggling on your plate.

On our last night in El Salvador, we decided to look for a hotel in a little town about 10 minutes off the highway. It looked like it was right on the coast, so we figured it would have some hotels. When we pulled into town, it looked a little rough, and we almost gave up, not seeing any hotels.

We stopped and asked a policeman, and he pointed us in the right direction. We started driving down a hilly, curvy dirt road and came upon a hotel that looked closed. It had a heavy, black, iron gate that was shut. David started knocking on the gate, and it opened, and they invited us in. There was just enough room to pull the landcruiser in, and they shut the gate behind us. We had stumbled across a fortress on a hilltop. It was very secure, perched high on a hill, with an incredible view of the coast. 182 stairs lead off the backside to offer access to the water, where there was another gate with razor wire on the top and stone walls on either side.

Inside the walls, it was its own little world. There was a small friendly group of surfers staying there and a little restaurant to feed us all. Although it was a bit pricey for us, we decided to stay and enjoy the surroundings. We had some excellent conversations with Elyon, the night watchman, who was very open about spiritual matters. We were able to share some gospel literature with him.

Here's a picture at the top of the steps. We were grateful for the good night's sleep we got there.

Traveling on,

The VanderZons

Chapter 6

Honduras

Kindra's Journal   9/12/2010

Sunny in the morning, rainy in the afternoon

Woke up at 6:30 and left around 8:00 for the Honduras border said bye to friend Elyon. When mom walked out this morning, he said, pointing to the magazine track we gave him, "I read in here that if you have a problem with your wife, you need to talk to God about how to solve the problem." We enjoyed seeing his simple comprehension. Upon realizing we could not stay for breakfast, the hotel staff quickly chopped up some fruit and packed some granola and yogurt for us. How nice!

It was an easy drive to the border where a worker at the border station persuaded dad to buy the help of one of the highly persistent badge pushers. Here we sit on the Honduran border, waiting for dad and Lewis(the badge pusher) to return with the vehicle permit. It is so hot waiting in the sun for the vehicle upon coming up to the border.

There was a massive line of semis, but thanks to Ricardo waving us through the oncoming traffic, we made it much quicker. As we stepped out of the vehicle with our passports, we just about had our brains rattled apart by a marching band. The 11th of September seems to be some kind of celebration. We saw many women with full dresses dancing, crowds of people, tuk-tuks, and some military men. We were soon packed into a tight line, squished in like the rest to prevent people from cutting. We were grateful everyone was so distracted and in celebrating spirits! We're still sitting here, and it's almost 11:30. We got to the border at 10:00.

I desperately wish I could tell you different, but it's 9:00 p.m., and we're in a border hotel. Yes, it's true. Bless the Lord, because of all days, a white van full of Christian Americans were also stopped because of paperwork! The hours kept dragging on, and we got out of the sweltering vehicle only to be greeted by the obscene calls of some loitering men. I try not to be rude to people, but it just makes you not want to look at anyone when things happen like that. I like people to think that the dogs are not friendly at all!

Ricardo continued to literally run up and down the street, making calls, copies, and arrangements. It was a living nightmare! We paced back and forth in the trashy streets dripping sweat and just trying to maintain our sanity. I was certainly in a spirit of prayer.

The hours ticked by, and the helpers assured us they were doing their best. One insisted we owed him $5 for a cartoonish map that was worse than the one we had! After our moment with the long awaited official had arrived, we talked for about 5 minutes and were sent away no better than before. Around 4:00, they finally told us that mañana they would get our vehicle permit finished.

Panic gripped me as we realized that meant staying tonight at the border, the very thing we try to avoid most. Praise the Lord, we are still okay and enjoyed a small church service in our room! It was such a blessing and a great testimony to hear the singing and praying with people who have just come through the same places we have!

What a surprise to have a church service today on the border. We were all super hungry after not eating since breakfast. We decided to go to the Chinese restaurant that was attached to the hotel. They had the strangest music on, and I was tired. After being served a steaming hot plate of fried rice about the size of a 3-gallon bucket, we headed back to our room with leftover rice for the dogs. We certainly did ourselves in if there was a sleepy powder in the food. Haha, maybe that joke won't be so funny in the future.

I hear men outside the door, and this town is really rough. The room is horrible, and we're all sleeping on one full-size bed tonight. There is a frog in the shower and ants on the walls. May God protect us tonight.

Kindra's Journal   9/13/2010

What a night! Unlike any before, and I hardly slept. All four of us, Kacie's doll Timothy, and Biddy the dog, were crammed onto a full-size bed with a huge dip in the middle. Right now, we're just talking to our American friends and packing up. We're going to tackle the border in the power of the Lord this morning. I hope we are traveling before 12:00. I'm praying. Praise him for protection, more later.

Hello again from Nicaragua! Well, my estimation of 10:00 was not far off as we were sent on our way around 12:30. Yes, 26 and a half hours at the bordertown. Unbelievable. We arrived at 8:00 to the news from Ricardo, "I'm working on it. We should have you out of here in an hour." After four more hours of the paperwork chase, hearing our papers were, at last, ready was wonderful. We were charged lots of money and tried to stay sane in the crazy heat.

The noise was intense, with many people yelling and numerous dogs trying to come past our dogs with them growling and barking. The streets were full of garbage and crowds of people and government workers who seemed to lack any human decency or mercy. Another day of the apathetic workers talking into telephones seemed almost more than any of us could bear.

I prayed now that they would get our work done quickly and graciously. The thought of going back to that awful hotel that all the shirtless truckers had been pouring into this morning for showers seemed almost real. Thinking of sleeping on the ridge of that sorry slouch of a bed and another sleep-deprived night wouldn't have been good for anyone!

When our American friends left with their helper and a celebratory tuk-tuk ride, we girls were left standing on the sidewalk. At the same time, dad went to find Ricardo about the papers. Then, lo and behold, the blissful sight shall not be forgotten! There came Ricardo and "English speaker" as we came to call him, with dad a head taller than the rest with his big straw hat. Upon seeing us standing with smiles of anticipation, Ricardo made a sweeping motion with our papers in his hand and said, "no more of this"! He proudly presented us with our papers. We paid him $20, for which he was thrilled. He and English-speaker accompanied us to the checkpoint and helped us cross.

We were on our way with our American friends not too far behind us. At the first police stop, they provided the perfect distraction. We were trying to hand the police our papers for the dogs when our friend's huge massive white trailer caught their eye. The police pretty well shoved the papers through the window and said, "you're ready, just go." Dad asked in disbelief, "we're good"? And with a half-interested wave from the police, we were off.

We later found out they charged our friends a five dollar fine for some made-up paperwork mistake. We pulled off to wait for our friends, and since we hadn't had much except two tiny bananas, we opened our last package of chips ahoy cookies from Mexico. We all got a good laugh out of dad calling them "crumbs ahoy" as I opened the package, and the form of a cookie was nowhere in sight.

Waiting after every police stop for our friends was a bit of a challenge as going through these countries, you don't feel inclined to just stop. It was a good spiritual exercise to do unto others as you would have them do unto you. We weren't sure our friends and their big white van would get the hint and maybe blow on past. While speeding along, trying not to get passed by them, Dad exclaimed, "this is the kind of brotherhood I always wanted... one that waits for the other". The concept seems to be lacking in the church and the world. In the many ironies of all this, we found it funny, and everyone began to laugh. So without any hassles and with multiple shouts of "gringo" as our vehicle passed, we made it to the Nicaraguan border around 3:00.

With the help of Ricardo's friend Sylvia who was waiting there for us, we were through the border in an hour. Compared to the Honduran border, this one seemed absolutely welcoming. It had two welcome signs. the military smiled and waved. The people were helpful and professional! Yes, praise the Lord. We said bye to our friends who were still tied up in sheets of paperwork and headed out into beautiful Nicaragua on good roads!

The situation was growing tense, however, as the hour of 6 and darkness were fast approaching. Dad finally broke the silence and said it's almost fascinating. No one was saying anything, but we were all way on edge about finding a hotel. After passing tons of the forbidden auto hotels and driving all the way through town, the Lord answered my exact prayer. He provided a nice hotel with a very secure courtyard.

We took cold showers, and I got shocked three times by it. Kacie got some very gratefully received supper, and then we got ready for bed, a huge step above last night, and went to sleep.

Oh, a funny last thought. I had to go to the bathroom super bad when we were driving through Honduras, but we didn't want to stop and lose our friends! After one of the police checkpoints, while our friends were still stuck, dad quickly pulled over. I had to go next to the vehicle on the side of the road while many shouts of "hurry, hurry" proceeded from the Land Cruiser. Not a good situation. I had hoped I wouldn't have to do that on this trip! Oh well.

Trip Summary by Kristi VanderZon   Honduras

Dear Family & Friends,

When we packed up the landcruiser that morning, we intended to travel to a children's orphanage home near San Salvador. On the way out of town, we stopped at an internet café, hoping to get directions there, but were unable to. We then decided to head for the border and scoot through Honduras. This seemed the best choice, although we regretted not being able to follow through with our original plan of visiting the children's home.

It felt good to hit the road again, but shortly we faced our first detour. A bridge was out, and we followed a bus off the main road, wondering how this would alter our day. A man hopped off the bus, very willing to give us instructions on overcoming this obstacle. He said a boy would run ahead of us and guide us through the river, showing us how deep it was, so we could get through. He then wanted some money for telling us this, so we gave him a little and followed along behind the little boy (maybe 6-7yrs. Old).

He did run ahead of us, but now two men also wanted to be our guides, and they were also in the water ahead of us, pointing out hidden boulders and urging us forward. It got fairly deep on the landcruiser, maybe at the bottom of the doors, but we pulled out just fine. Then came our little group wanting their pay. It was a little overwhelming, being in this little village, off the main track, and people very insistent on getting any money they could from us. David didn't have any ones, so he bought ice cream for them so he could break a five, and he spread out the change among them.

113

Our guide helping us through the river

In all, we paid four people during this little detour. Then another man approached the car. He knew a little English and wanted to talk, but it was getting a little uncomfortable as a group of men, standing nearby and watching us, started shouting at him in angry tones. We pulled out with a quick "Adios" and headed back to the road.

Somehow, we ended up getting on the wrong road but didn't figure it out until well over an hour. We ended up having to backtrack a little and finally did find CA2, our road, but it cost us a couple hours.

We arrived at the Honduras side of the border at 10 a.m. We were feeling good. It was early in the day. The mood there was festive, as it must have been some kind of El Salvadorian Holiday. There was a marching band performing there, and a crowd had gathered. (That explains why we saw a marching band in the road earlier, in the seemingly middle of nowhere). When we approached the border area, about 7 men gathered around the vehicle. We're noticing a pattern here at borders…

Our first glimpse of the border

We were going to be firm with our refusal to "hire" any help from them, but this was at a gas station. There was a friendly, English-speaking attendant who suggested that one of these men could provide a good service for us, getting us through "very speedily." One of those phrases that comes back to mind 26 hours later. He said, "they're just trying to make a living". Suddenly, we felt sorry for their lot and hired one named Ricardo, who was confident that for $10, he could speed us along.

He hopped on & clung to the back of the land cruiser and waved us through the long line of waiting vehicles. He was a big help getting us to the initial point of official entry. We got our passports stamped and felt on top of the world, that things were going so well. Ricardo was running around, making copies for us, and doing all the talking, and showing us where to park, etc. It was extremely hot, and the girls and I stayed in the land cruiser with the air conditioning running. The dogs were in the back panting.

David was going with Ricardo to different offices. Every once in a while, he would stop back in at the vehicle to get another paper and tell us "just a little bit more". The next time he stopped in, he was beginning to show signs of discouragement and said, "It will be another hour". We gave up trying to keep cool, turned off the car, and all got out. We found a shady place to sit with the dogs and watched the chaos surrounding us. This little border town was the worst we'd seen yet. It was really run down. The government buildings looked like they had seen no maintenance since they were put there in 1940.

There were a lot of men just hanging around watching our every move. It did not feel good. The office David got to know really well was a real time warp. There was an antique typewriter, and the woman at the desk was arguing loudly on the phone every time he went in. It was over an hour later when Ricardo had to admit, this could take a lot longer, the computer is down. About every hour, he would tell us "one more hour". That phrase became a joke among us when we realized it meant nothing. Around 3:00 p.m., we were getting antsy to leave.

I felt we should go back to El Salvador. The thought of staying in this town overnight seemed incomprehensible. But now, the office had our title, and we were stuck in between El Salvador & Honduras, not able to leave either way. That was when a big white van & trailer pulled up and out piled a bunch of Americans. It turns out they were missionaries headed for Costa Rica. Their leader, Calvin Williams, spoke good Spanish and seemed to have confidence that the paperwork would go through. They were a happy bunch and definitely altered the feel of the place for us. We all waited until it became evident that the computers were not coming back on, and nobody would show up & fix them.

There was a moment of hope when Ricardo said the "official" was ready to see us. We were ushered into a back room, where a very stern-looking man snapped out demands for this or that paper. He then wanted the girls to go outside. David said, "No, they stay with us". So he said they could wait in the other room then, which they were already basically in. It seemed strange, and then, very abruptly, he got up and said, "Maybe one hour". Then he added "50% yes, 50% no" and he was gone. In hindsight, we think it was one of those moments he was waiting for a hefty money bribe. But with no money given, he was gone, and there was no one left to help.

Calvin had been told of the "best hotel in town", with air conditioning & secure parking, so it was agreed we would follow them to the hotel. We rode through the rest of the little town, not seeing any hotel, and were on the main road for a short bit when we came to a police checkpoint. They turn us around & we head back to town. We were all really hoping that "best hotel" was past this checkpoint. We followed, still with the hope this hotel was somewhere. It was, but it was not what we envisioned. It was right back in the hubbub of border town life, with all the same shady characters that had been watching us all day. The same filth and dysfunction. A nightmare was unfolding before our very eyes.

It was tucked in behind a Chinese restaurant. We pulled in through the mud into their "secure parking area" and its short, crumbling stone wall, graffitied with "bienvenidos" (welcome) with a skull & crossbones. A pig and two insanely mean-looking german shepherds strained at their ropes to get at us.

We got out, and some of the group went to see about rooms. They did have two available, for an unreasonable price. Our family got the room with one bed and a bathroom, and their group got the one with two beds and no bathroom. Some of their group slept in their van. The rooms were very minimal. Only a bed with a sheet. No other furniture and no window to let in any light. The door was metal with a small sliding bar to lock it. With everyone there together, we could joke our way through our accommodations for the night, and being a Sunday night, we set up chairs in the courtyard there and commenced to have our own little worship service.

Our makeshift worship service

That's when it started to rain, so we moved all the chairs into our room. We had a very special time singing, reading bible verses, and sharing thoughts on God's faithfulness and perfect timing. With everyone's voices singing "We love you Lord" and prayers of thankfulness for our shelter on this night, our minds were genuinely being transformed to see the beauty of the situation instead of resenting our predicament. We were thankful for meeting these brothers & sisters and considered it a perfect gift from the Lord that we weren't at that hotel, in that border town, alone.

We ate at the restaurant out front, then went to our rooms. By now, it was dark, and there were a lot of men hanging out in the parking lot, acting rowdy, and it was very unnerving. We put Walter in the Land Cruiser and kept Biddy in the room with us. We all commended ourselves to the protection of the Lord and went to sleep. It was strange having no window to see what was going on outside, and the four of us sleeping on the one drooping bed was not very comfortable.

Our room did have an air conditioner, which helped drown out the noises from outside, and we got some sleep that night. We praised God for preserving our lives and vehicles that night. We headed back the next morning, where, eventually, at 12:30 p.m., we were handed our papers and ushered out of town by Ricardo. It was indeed a liberating moment, and the other group was able to leave also, so we could travel together through Honduras.

Kacie & I, and Biddy, staying in the shade and waiting

You can see the Land Cruiser parked in front of this loaded bus.

Our travel through Honduras was pleasant and quick. We were stopped at two police checkpoints, but no problems when they saw the big white van and trailer coming down the road behind us. They quickly

119

gave our papers back and focused on them. Although we didn't want our new friends to have any trouble either, it was comical. We had a great experience at the border of Honduras/Nicaragua. The officials were quick, efficient, and polite. We were happy to see this sign.

Thank you, faithful family & friends, for your prayers. It is truly a comfort when we are out of our comfort zone. Our ordeal at the border truly confirms that "The Lord preserveth the stranger", and he is increasing our faith through these trials!

Love to all,

The VanderZons

CHAPTER 7

NICARAGUA

Kindra's Journal   9/14/2010

Hot and sunny

Woke up around 6:00, and mom worked on an email while I tidied up our cramped hotel room. A few hours later, we were on the road and headed for John and Cynthia Smith's three to four hours away. The big scare of the morning was losing biddy momentarily. With the wide-open gate and stories about dogs being stolen, we had reason to be. Within a few minutes, we heard her clicking on the third story. She got confused and thought it was our floor. Our happiness to find her again was immense. She was shaken up and in a deep depression for several hours.

We received a warm welcome from the Smiths and enjoyed walking around the back alleys to a lake. The water kept rising and forcing people to move their tin shacks further back to dry land! We encountered countless ferocious dogs that, with some quick thinking, we were able to avoid dog fights! All of the people were super friendly despite their tumble-down tin dwellings.

I got to go along with John, who, when he turned the electric transmitter on with a tool from his friend, made the whole neighborhood super happy! It was wonderful to be able to do laundry in the washtub out behind the house this afternoon. Some laundry hadn't seen the light of day since being packed away at the Surfers Inn and sweltering under the campus tarp on top of the roof rack, all the while fermenting.

I had a neat experience of going with Cynthia to buy tortillas. What a blessing because we had a conversation with a man about coming to church here. I'm so tired, just completely done. But like the Energizer Bunny, that's for you, Kacie, I kept going. I washed dishes after supper, then listened to John read two chapters of Angels in the Night. The electricity went out, so we went out to join the party! Just about the whole neighborhood was out there. Most of the men were lined up on our side of the street with the traffic stopped. As John climbed up the pole, the usual ghetto music actually seemed to accompany the whole situation. It was an incredible experience to be part of such a crazy situation. Everyone was happy when the electricity returned.

Kindra's Journal   9/15/2010

Very warm!

I'll try to write while I have a few minutes, even though it's almost 9:00 and I still need to pack my backpack. I also want to email some family and friends! I woke up around 6:00 this morning and puttered around till everyone else was up. After breakfast and devotions, I quickly washed the dishes, and we headed out to the cam mission base.

Touring the storehouse full of medicine, beans and rice wheelchairs, Bibles, and clothing was really interesting. It was a blessing to know that people had donated at all! The neighbor's monkey that was tied to a tree provided much entertainment for us. Making lunch for everyone, washing all the dishes, and making some of the guest beds kept me quite busy.

Cynthia was decorating the cake someone had ordered from her cake business. Just as we were about to leave, Kacie climbed into the Smiths Land cruiser with their little girl Tatiana. The vehicle erupted in a noisy situation as Tatiana threw up all over herself and Kacie! Our big accomplishment of getting all of the children and Cynthia's cake decorating supplies in the vehicle was quickly undone. Kacie passed the little girl covered in vomit off to me and ran to the bathroom. After we washed Tatiana's dress, we all piled back in the vehicle and headed for the city.

As we drove back in the sweltering heat, my mind went back to my new goals from the morning... to be more involved with children.

I got to test this resolve as I was being hit with bags of crackers by the children in the back of the car and having dirty cake dishes thrown past me onto my dress. We got stopped by police on the way home for a minor passing incident. Between Cynthia and us pretending not to know Spanish and Tatiana puking out the window, the police let us go for 5 US dollars and 10 cordobas. Praise the Lord.

I ran around when we got home cleaning up the church in the front half of the Smith house for the night meeting. After picking up the dry laundry, sweeping, and mopping, I took a thorough shower and washed my hair. We had a quick supper then enjoyed the Wednesday night meeting.

Right after the closing prayer's "amen," the electricity snapped off! After almost an hour of waiting for it to cool, the natives couldn't take it anymore and came to the gate and called John. We all paraded out and flipped the switch and enjoyed the cheers that came up from the crowd. Hopefully, this will open a door for ministry.

It's past 11:00 now, and mom and dad just finished their testimony. I have a lot to do to get ready for speeding towards the Darien Gap! I know dad wants to get an early start. Had an interesting conversation about some interesting subjects such as drugs and the communist government. John's jolly mood grew as the clock's hour hand ticked away. He loved the joke about us not waking about tomorrow and thus having to stay and visit longer.

Trip Summary by Kristi VanderZon   Nicaragua

Hello Family & Friends,

We crossed at El Elyono and traveled down CA1 to Esteli, where we found nice accommodations and had some sweet rest.

The next day we were at the home of John & Cynthia Smith in the city of Managua, experiencing a glimpse of life in a *barrio*, the spanish word for inner-city neighborhood. We arrived yesterday, and it wasn't long before we were walking down the back streets and narrow alleyways of Managua.

John and his family were treating us to an insider's tour, on foot, of their neighborhood. We had Walter & Biddy along on their leashes, which caused quite a commotion as many fierce dogs did their best to get them, but thankfully, we made it through without a dog fight. It was a unique opportunity to see life as it really is for many people here. Friendly faces peeked out from doorways and fences. We saw some very poor shacks that people had to move to higher ground to get out of the floodwaters.

Serious drug & gang violence has plagued their neighborhood. Still, John & family moved in here two years ago and became part of the people. They are involved personally with their neighbors, and as a result, have earned the respect and protection of their neighborhood. Yesterday, we got a glimpse of how they genuinely relate to their neighbors.

Due to an overloaded system, the electricity had turned off, so John borrowed a long electric pole to reach the top of the transformer and switch the breaker. The electric company refuses to deal with the repetitive problem, as they feel threatened in the barrio.

Later at night, this happened again, and we went out to watch, but this time the darkness gave the scene a whole new element of excitement. A crowd had gathered as John shimmied up the electric pole, aimed his long pole at the switch high above, and succeeded in turning on electricity for the neighborhood. The crowd cheered, and John was quickly gaining popularity in the neighborhood.

John turned back on the electricity for the neighborhood. We witnessed this 3 times in our short stay there.

Biddy waiting for another dog to pass by at the front gate

We visited the CAM (Christian Aid Ministries) base, located here in Managua, on Wednesday. It was encouraging to see the collective efforts of Christians in the USA. They give money and resources to fill CAM's warehouse with food, medicine, wheelchairs, and baby packages, to be distributed to the very needy in Nicaragua. It is an enormous effort to truck supplies out to impoverished villages and help with disasters, such as a flood that happened recently where a village was cut off from outside supplies and help. CAM gets the supplies by raft to the village and distributes them to each family. There are currently three families living on the base to run the operation.

Kacie with one of the local native babies

We really feel blessed with the privilege of staying with John & his family for a couple days and getting a feel for their inner-city ministry there.

This morning we got up early and departed from John's, but not before we shared a prayer, asking for God's guidance and protection as we continued our journey.

We have appreciated hearing from you all. Your emails really encourage us and keep us from feeling lonely on the road.

Love in Christ,

The VanderZons

CHAPTER 8

COSTA RICA

Kindra's Journal   **9/16/2010**

After three and a half short hours of sleep, we hurriedly packed the vehicle and headed out for Costa Rica at 6:15. Had a fairly difficult time following signs to Peña Blanca. When we turned off to ask the police for directions, they tried to give us a ticket for making a u-turn even though we were off the road. However, after about 15 minutes of talking Spanish, we paid $5, and we're again on the sign hunt. I'm dreading the border, but we should be there slightly before 9:00. I'm sure God will take care of us. More on the whole thing later. I'm really praying.

Well, our border crossing went just great, and we enjoyed meeting several different men and women who are also traveling the Americas. Most were on motorcycles, while another couple was driving a truck camper. It was such an answer to prayer and a blessing to actually enjoy a border crossing for once! John Smith's advice was 100% correct about the tour buses crowding the place. As we trudged through the mud, I was grateful that we had gotten such an early start on the day. I must admit we weren't particularly impressed with the building's looks. Still, I must say many of the people we met there were very friendly!

The rain continued to pour down on us as we drove on at a rather slow pace, sometimes only 20 miles an hour. A police officer waved us over because we girls didn't have seat belts on, but he let us go after a few obscure questions.

We drove through the strangely almost deserted town of Punta Renas. We had no success finding a decent hotel, so we headed back out into the growing darkness to continue our search.

We found a lovely little cabana, and although the room is crawling with ants and other specimens, we are grateful to have two beds to catch up on our rest! Although the electricity was out, we walked down the street in search of something to eat. We found a restaurant selling fried fish for our supper, served by candlelight! I was thrilled when we took the dogs out for a nice walk on the little ocean inlet. I really enjoyed seeing the lit-up fishing boats and the waves crashing up against the shore. Lord willing, tomorrow we should travel the coast and arrive at Mark Kardonas.

Walked out to the beach again around 8:30 to see the pretty sights of the lit-up shops and hear the gigantic waves crashing. Dad was still hungry when we got back, so we got out the bag of bananas from the border. We told him they were for tomorrow, but he still didn't seem convinced. After his comment of "I want to die full," he flopped onto the bed and lay they're propped up on his pillow, enjoying his border banana to the fullest! Somewhere during the process of his banana consumption, he picked up some of the little banana strings and laid them on his shirt. When I told him that he has quite a bit of banana on his shirt, he turned to me, and with a fresh bite of banana still in his mouth, said, "what does that even mean"! Obscenely funny at the moment. Poor mom is suffering from a super snapped neck, and dad is zonked out on his bed with a belly full of bananas.

Kindra's Journal   9/17/2010

Day 52 - Rained this afternoon.

I woke up and emailed our family and friends while the rest of the family walked the dogs. Then, while they worked on the group email, I cleaned the room and tried to pack up whatever I could find into the vehicle. Our travel was slow, and we endured some more rainy driving in Costa Rica today. The vehicle seemed to have a broken part. We pulled over multiple times to check things like transmission oil spark plugs. We added some rubbing alcohol just in case there was water in the tank! Finally, we stopped around 1:00 and figured it out.

The driveshaft was almost falling off so much that it was starting to lose bolts. Between dad's innovative thinking and the assistance of a young man from the gas station, we got some parts, and we're on our way. After laying in the mud below the Land Cruiser for a half-hour, dad finally perfected his word "lodo" (mud). As he was trying to have the young man, who couldn't understand English, get him a part, he said, "uno mas sizo." According to dad, if you just add an "o" on the end of an English word, it will work in Spanish too. We all started laughing!

We enjoyed traveling into the beautiful mountains and arriving at Mark Kardona's home. We met his wife Ellen and daughters, Miriam and Judith. We also met the coffee pickers that live on their property Darin, Daisy, and baby Eliana. The Kardonas have a beautiful place here, with plants growing everywhere. We enjoyed some excellent visiting and fellowship. Their daughter Miriam is so kind and is letting Kacie and I occupy her room.

Today daddy got the opportunity to share with some bandito outlaw club members what Christ did for him and gave them some books. All the tracks and CDs and DVDs everyone has given us our blessing, and I pray the Lord will further bless the recipients. We gave our helper at the gas station a Good and Evil book, and he was very thrilled. He walked away, holding it up and exclaiming that it was a "regatto" (gift) from the gringos. I asked the young man at the gas station if he was a Christian, and he said, "un poquito" (a little). What an honest answer.

Kindra's Journal   9/18/2010

Beautiful and sunny in the morning, foggy and rainy in the afternoon

Woke up slightly before 6:00 and read through five chapters of Zephaniah, then went downstairs. I enjoyed watching the people head out to pick coffee. One of the single moms dropped off her daughters for the day. After helping wash dishes and hang up laundry, our family headed back into San Isidro to get a few things. More dog food, parts for the vehicle, and horse wormer. After zigging around the one-way city streets, we ended up sitting in the hot sun for almost 30 minutes, waiting for the bridge to open back up. It seems like a USA town here, and the apathetic attitude of the people matches the scenery. A very nice man gave dad a used spark club cable for free.

My favorite stop was the farm store to get the dog's things, and I enjoyed looking at the saddles. They were nothing extra and very light! When we got back, dad replaced a few parts in the Land Cruiser, like the seal in the rear driveshaft. We girls played five crowns with Miriam and Judith. Miriam took us on a great walk where we got to meet a sister in the church named Lucy and saw a really neat fj40.

I showed pictures of our trip to Miriam and her mom. Their place here has made me think about Bolivia and our house and the other people there and really made me want to go there! They have the prettiest flowers here, lots of impatiens.

We sat and visited in the living room with Mark, Emma, Judith, and also Edmund who came over for his nightly shower. I ironed Kacie's dress for church tomorrow. Got my shower in, and despite the ice-cold water, that wasn't the worst part as when I was washing my face, the washcloth was so bubbly that I got soap up my nose, quite a problem. Kacie fell asleep tonight while I was reading to her!

Kindra's Journal   9/19/2010

Sunny and perfectly comfortable temperature!

Woke up and left for church. Met quite a few more people and found Mark's message on Luke 6:47 was a real blessing. "I will show you what it's like when someone comes to me, listens to my teaching, and then follows it." Seeing some of the young converts was a blessing. Hearing one of them share their struggles and victories that week and then later pick the song "I surrender all" was an encouragement.

Enjoyed visiting with the brethren and during the fellowship meal and then sang for quite a while with the youth. 11 of us total. From there, our little singing group walked down the dirt road to the house of an old lady who was celebrating her 91st birthday. After a few songs, the girls gave her some simple cards and gifts. We sang for her for about 30 minutes. The singing sounded good under the tin roof. The light coming in from around the boards made our song books easy to see. This old lady wanted to sing a song or three for us in return. We all gave her an exaggerated round of applause!

The group of us walked back to church, and after having some coffee with mom and dad, our family went for a walk on the slippery wet clay roads way past many fields of coffee. It was beautiful, and we saw Darin and Daisy walking on the road also. We put the dogs away, washed the mud off of our boots, and continued on down the road to Marlins. We had a good meal accompanied by fellowship and sharing testimonies. Dad also shared his testimony with the help of Marlin as a translator in church this morning.

We talked about the death road, which got them all worked up. Anita, Edmund, Philemon, Andreas, and I stood around for a long time looking at pictures of it on the internet. Edmund was in an almost continual hysterical state of laughter during all of the death road talk! He provoked me sore tonight, but I must still strive to be kind.

Kindra's Journal   9/20/2010

Beautiful in the morning, sunny in the afternoon

After breakfast, we walked down a road to find Darin among the coffee plants, but our search was of no avail, so we girls went to visit Anna. She has a cute little girl and enjoyed showing us around her little place. Daisy was also there, and we had a good visit. I gave dad a haircut, then Kacie and I went to the store with Miriam. We helped her haul some very heavy grocery bags up the very long steep walk back to the house. Mom and dad did more Panama boat research at Marlin's home.

I worked on a surprise thank you gift for the Kardonas, then helped them hang up laundry and iron curtains. Went down to have lunch and visit with Nathaniel and Carmen at their store and enjoyed hearing his testimony and the progress the church has made in the last four years. He shared some of the brother's struggles with us, and we were encouraged to see them still fighting the good fight of faith!

We walked home in the rain, read our emails, and went to visit a lady named Lucy who lives up the road. Her house is charming and so entirely decorated with flowers that we hardly noticed the floor swaying beneath us. Lucy is a sincere individual, so we had a good visit and Spanish session. She made her parrot talk, and it was fun to watch.

When Isaac got home, we visited with him for a while. He was gone when we got here getting a haircut. Should anyone with thieving intentions walk up to Lucy's door, they could hardly miss the sign saying that someone is praying and the articles in the house belong to God. Interesting.

We enjoyed sharing supper with Gloria and Heidi at Mark's home and sang some songs with their instruments! I had an interesting shower tonight as the mysterious warm water still seems to evade me. The light went off while I was in the shower. It's late, and I need to pack my bag backpack for the morning to head to Panama! Our word for the day is *bastante*, meaning enough/sufficient.

It's around 11:00 p.m., and just about an hour ago, I heard some voices downstairs. I was trying not to be a busybody; however, I still discerned amid the commotion, Edmund's voice. I thought something odd must be happening to bring him out at such a late hour. I threw on my head covering, grateful I decided to sleep in my clothes and headed down to the back porch where Philemon and Edmund were investigating the scene of the crime. The rest of us stayed on the porch watching.

Just a few minutes before, Judith had gone out on the back porch to investigate the footsteps she heard running off into the forest. Upon looking around, she found their laundry all scooted around on the line, and two large boards drug off of the porch. No real harm, just intimidation factors. The men shone their flashlights off into the darkness, up in the trees, then on to the ground to find footprints. It was evident that two people had been there. At this point, if my Spanish serves me correctly, Edmund made a joke about the men wearing mismatched shoes and, despite the seriousness of the situation, started laughing almost uncontrollably.

Slightly before this all happened, while mom and dad were in their room, they had the windows open and the lights on. Biddy had just started going nuts, barking like someone was right outside the window. Our little porch gathering dispersed with people saying in Spanish he is still a friend, and we must pray for him. What a testimony if he was out there. Philemon told dad that these peepers really aren't the ones who will rob or break in. It's just intimidation. Edmund and his friend then made loud whistling noises and bang on a big metal container at several-minute intervals.

All is quiet once again, and we are praying for our protection and their salvation. It's very late, and I can finish packing in the morning. What an experience!

Kindra's Journal   9/21/2010

Woke up around 5:15 and packed up. Said our goodbyes and headed out around 8:30 for the border of Panama. We made it to the border around 12:00, and as usual, leaving the country was the easy part.

Before we even got out of the vehicle on the Panama side, our "helper friend" chased us down. It's incredible how you can walk past them and tell them you don't need help. Yet still, in the end, you end up giving in to their persistence and hiring them. They love being in charge and having your important papers in their hands. I later remarked to Kacie as our "helper" walked around with our documents that I wish I could tie a rope to him!

As always, we got our passport stamped and then started the downward spiral as a worker explained that insurance was necessary. From there, our papers were scattered hither and thither as our "helper" showed us where to unload the vehicle. We girls took our belongings into the room for inspection. Keeping an eye on everything was a task.

While they inspected Kacie's backpack, I opened mine and tried to stuff my wallet with 60 dollars and my ID further down in the pocket. All went smoothly until I didn't have dad's passport in the stack. The lady wanted us to show her our entry stamps. She insisted she needed to see them even though she knew they were there. As I had earlier suspected, the paper receipt from Honduras that was stuck in the passport almost caused a huge problem. Now that I look back on the scene, it was pretty comical.

The lady on the other side of the table reached out for the unnecessary passports and kept trying to get us to give them to her. Even though I told her "no" to the point, she was stretched out across the table, straining her neck, trying to grab them. In order to keep them in my possession, I had to do a lot of stretching. After arriving in Panama and playing the border game for two and a half hours, being stolen from, and just watching the immorality of the whole thing, we were more than ready to leave.

We bought a few coco frios from an old man at the border who, after we drank some juice, cut one open for us and used his machete to make a little scoop to scrape out the white flesh inside the coconut. We drove for about 45 minutes, then stopped in the city of David for the night, and we're able to download some new emails. I loved reading my aunt's very detailed emails, and we enjoyed looking at our Costa Rica pictures. Hopefully, it will be a secure place here tonight.

Kacie provoked me sore today. As I look down at my feet, I have sandal marks across them from wearing my chacos all day everyday from the crack of dawn till dark. Longing for home. Bolivia, here we come!

Trip Summary by Kristi VanderZon   Costa Rica

We made our way to the Costa Rican border and actually enjoyed the border crossing. The paperwork went smoothly, and we met some fellow travelers that were interesting to talk to. There was a couple from California driving down to Argentina in their pick-up/camper combo. They were also already contemplating the challenge of shipping their vehicle in Panama. There were four young men from New Zealand on motorcycles, making their way from California to Argentina. Sadly, they were right ahead of us as we were entering Costa Rica but got turned back at the checkpoint. Probably a paperwork issue.

We then met two brothers, originally from Bolivia, who were now living in Sweden, but were making the trip on some pretty nice BMW Motorcycles. They started in Mexico and said maybe we'll see them in Bolivia, where they plan on ending their journey after they make it to the tip of Argentina.

At the last border we crossed (you might recall the Honduran border nightmare story), we met a man from Britain who was driving around the world. He was in a hurry, but we saw him again here too. It's really an encouragement to swap stories with these fellow travelers and know others are pursuing the same goal.

We drove through some heavy rain today, and it was the first time since we left Tennessee on July 27 (we've been on the road for 51 days) that I've fallen asleep in the vehicle. I woke up to the undesirable words, "We're getting pulled over." When it rains, it pours. It was the 3rd time in 2 days that we've been pulled over by the police. The first two times were for legitimate traffic violations (improper lane change & 'U' turn (which was debatable), and a five-dollar bill was all it took to appease the officers. But this time, he just asked a few questions and let us go. Getting pulled over is becoming more routine and doesn't unnerve us so much anymore.

We found a hotel by the tiny port town of Caldera on the Pacific Coast and were thankful to pull off the road for the day. It was still raining, and we had just opened the door to our room when the electricity went out. Where is John when you need him? We walked to a little open-air restaurant that had some candles going, and they fried us a delicious fish dinner in the dark. We're very thankful for their efforts. The electricity later came on, and I was able to finish this email.

We took the dogs across the street to get some exercise and watched the waves come crashing in. It was a beautiful sight, with the big fishing boats lit up and at anchor for the night and lightning making a stunning display over the water.

Kristi navigating the roads

We then traveled down the coast on Friday. At the first fuel stop of the day, we met some "Banditos," which are members of a motorcycle club. David spent some time talking with them and was able to share some gospel literature and his experience of coming from the motorcycle club scene and being delivered from that life through Jesus Christ. We were excited about that opportunity. As we continued down the road, we noticed an unsettling vibration coming from under the landcruiser. It eventually got so bad that we pulled off at a little gas station.

David spent about an hour laying under the vehicle in the mud tinkering with the drive shaft, which had come loose. He eventually was able to tighten it back up. We enjoyed a beautiful drive through the mountains to the little town of Santiago, which is south of San Isidro de General. We have been enjoying our stay at the home of Mark Kardona, nestled in the hills among coffee groves and banana trees. The view is beautiful as we are surrounded by mountains. There is a little church here, where we enjoyed worshipping on Sunday.

Darin & Daisy with their little baby. They are believers from Panama who are staying with the Kardona's to work in their coffee grove.

We enjoyed the fellowship we shared with the believers here and were encouraged to see a thriving church in the mountains of Costa Rica.

Our last night in Costa Rica included a disturbing occurrence. We were getting ready for bed when one of the young ladies we were staying with opened the back door and heard someone run off into the woods. Earlier, they had noticed some things moved around outside, and we had been suspicious someone had been there. We had thought someone was outside our window, and Biddy had been restless and barking from our room on the main floor. Edmund & Phillip, two young brothers from the church, came over and shone their flashlights around the yard and held watch with us for a while. They said it was probably "peepers" who often come earlier to move things around just for a little intimidation effect, then come back later and try to peep through windows. We still managed to sleep pretty well that night, knowing God sees all these things, and we can trust in him for protection. We woke up with thankful hearts that nothing more happened.

We will need prayer as crossing into Columbia may be the biggest challenge of the trip. We need to make arrangements in Panama City to ship the Land Cruiser by boat and then arrange a flight or cruise for the dogs and us to meet up with the vehicle in Cartagena, Columbia.

With love and thankfulness for all the prayers on our behalf,

The VanderZons

Chapter 9

Panama

Kindra's Journal   9/22/2010

We took a long walk before our complimentary breakfast of a piece of store toast, jam, and coffee this morning. The dogs have super bad worms. The last time we tried to give them horse wormer, it literally backfired. Today we want to try giving them smaller, more frequent doses. A quarter of a syringe three times a day. Today we plan to start our expedition to reach Mark's office and attempt communication. I've been praying for this for so many days, so I set out in faith. Hopefully, more later.

We drove along and got excited when we saw a sign for "SURF CAMP HOSTEL" along with all of the signs advertising expensive-looking resorts. The caretaker wasn't as welcoming as we had hoped, but the place had showers, a toilet, and a nice space to camp. We soon had our tent set up and walked down to the beach. We found a nice spot to swim and there were hardly any rocks and small waves so we could play around in the water. The beach here had even blacker sand than in El Salvador.

It was getting dark so we headed back to the hopping place to take showers and went into town to get supper before it was nighttime. However, despite all our best efforts, it didn't happen so quickly. The shower ended up being a raw pipe out of the side of the building. With all my clothes on, I couldn't quite get all the sand off. Our dressing conditions weren't much better as going behind our tent was the most private thing we could do. Yes, my friends, this was almost my worst nightmare. We drove into San Carlos, or rather the outskirts of it, and bought some cereal, milk, and of course more bananas. We brought them back and ate behind the land cruiser with the light of our two headlamps. Only the Father knows where we'll be tomorrow.

Kindra's Journal 9/23/2010

Woke up around 5 to the sight of Walter, belly up in the middle of the tent. I unlocked the vehicle then started to pack up. I set up a clothesline to give our wet clothes every advantage they could have to dry. A nice man from the hostel called us girls over to show us a beautiful flower that was native to Panama called the Holy Spirit flower. It was white with the perfect likeness of a dove inside, hence the name I suppose. It was a ray of hope and happiness streaming into our gloomy morning. The bulk of the tension was likely produced by the stress of finding a shipping company as soon as we reach Panama City.

Soon after that we were packed up and heading towards La Ciudad de Panama on the monotonous Panamanian highway, with disgustingly immodest advertising. So far I have found nothing impressive or super nice about Panama and just want to get the whole process of getting ourselves and our vehicle to Columbia started. After about 1½ hour of much confusing highway travel with still no map and unclear signage, we found ourselves sitting next to the Panama Canal watching a ship from Japan go through the locks.

We bought some doughnuts which we thoroughly enjoyed since it was something other than the usual breakfast of bananas or nothing at all. Less than 10 minutes into our pleasant and peaceful spot, the watcher of the tourist building blew his shrill whistle at us and motioned for us to leave. I can just imagine his thoughts, "how dare these poor travelers sit over there on our concrete. Didn't they see the $8 admittance fee to tour the building sign?" We went and finished our late breakfast in the land cruiser and headed back out, still without a map. We aimlessly but speedily found ourselves getting onto highways we had no clue about and cruising through the city, ultimately ending up on the same highway we had been on hours ago. Some buildings we passed by in the city were unlike any I had seen before. They were 15 stories high and maybe one stepped above abandoned. Clothes hung out of almost every window. We wondered if the clothes were being hung for curtains or to dry them.

We continued down the same highway ultimately ending up in a super fancy hotel parking lot. It was very expensive and not an option for us to stay. There we sat, in the same area we had been in this morning, not knowing what to do, mapless, and wanting to see if the shipping company emailed us back. After a while of sitting on a concrete slab and reading our almost completely decayed map, mom and dad went to ask a taxi driver about some cheap hotels. They soon returned with smiles on their faces and said that the taxi man is going to show us a cheap and well-kept hostel. God is so good!

We snaked through many streets and soon ended up in front of a big brick building with a hanging sign that said, "Hostel De Clayton." It wasn't much to look at from the inside or outside but the owners soon had us feeling quite at home. One of the ladies went straight to researching shipping companies for us. On the wall were many pictures of people with their expedition vehicles in front of the Hostel. Certainly, I thought, we must be at the right place. We took some pictures of us and our Land Cruiser outside the hostel then parked it to read our emails.

We headed back out in the afternoon. We stopped at a restaurant and bought some reasonably priced hot sandwiches and soda for $3. The owner showed us a really neat picture book about Columbia, the place he was from. It made me excited to get there. These past few days have been a real bummer. The trip has seemed very mundane and uninspiring. We drove to a free overlook where nobody told us to leave and enjoyed watching the ships in the canal. There was one from Monrovia and one from Singapore. It was quite fascinating watching the big boats zoom around by the ships.

Back at the hostel, dad continued his airplane research while mom and I took a shower. A hot shower! The last hot shower was 23 days ago in Panajachel, Guatemala. How time flies. It was good to wash off the remains of sand, sticky salt water, and sweat under the relaxing pressure of some hot water. I just have to read the Bible book of Esther and I will be done with the old testament. My bed on the ground doesn't sound quite as nice after many stories about the lizards in my corner and the big black beetle on the floor! Very hot and sweaty weather!

Kindra's Journal   9/24/2010

Woke up and continued the ship information Marathon. Around 9, we went to the Mira Flores locks again, but this time we surrendered $26 for the entrance fee. We enjoyed watching 3 ships pass through the locks. It was interesting watching the tugboats working with ropes. Occasionally crew members from the ships would wave to everyone on the shore.

We watched a quick movie on how the canal was built and then toured the museum. I think Kacie's favorite part of the museum was the imitation of the ship's navigation room where the view out of the screen "windows" made it look as if you were moving along into the locks. I enjoyed seeing the tanks of fish and bugs displays of tarantulas, butterflies, mantises, grasshoppers, beetles, moths, and scorpions. I'm sure our climate down in Bolivia should be the perfect host for all of those specimens.

We got some hamburgers for lunch and took them back to the hostel where dad was soon on the shipping trail again. We saw a group of coatimundis shuffle out into the field next to the hostel and enjoyed the "Jesus Lizards" running around in the drainage ditch. It's no wonder how they got their name because they can run on the water, standing upright, using only their back legs! It was very entertaining. We went back to the canal this evening and watched the boats till the museum closed. We went and walked on the Panama version of the "sendero" from San Cristobal Mexico. After that, we went to the grocery store to buy some food. Even though the prices seem slightly expensive, it cuts our food bill in over half. Dad accidentally left the lights on in the Land Cruiser, so our battery died. We had to get it jump-started and we were able to give the man who helped us a Good and Evil book. Biddy had quite the encounter with a tomcat. They got so close that the cat actually "left its mark" on Biddy. We gave her a bath to wash all the sprayed potty off.

Quote of the day from Felipe, another guest here at the hostel:

"When you carry around a fancy computer bag you say as well as saying, look at me, I've got the latest technology, please take it."

Kindra's Journal   9/25/2010

Today was the opposite of busy. The day's pace was so slow that I made tasks like hanging out the laundry take as long as I could. I would take the pieces out 1 by 1, shake them, lay them in a flat pile. and then hang them up by categories! Dad continued his research on flights and it turns out they are very expensive! Worked for a while hand sewing my quilt squares, then emptied and repacked my backpack. Went to our little spot to watch ships and got to see a big container ship pass by.

Mom, dad, & Kacie were busy taking and practicing self-portraits of themselves. Around 2, a man named Dyllan showed up to stay at the hostel and soon was sitting at the outside table with us, keeping up a lively conversation. From what he said, I gathered that he is from a broken marriage and heavily addicted to some serious partying. We shared our supper of bread and eggs, which Dyllan accompanied with multiple cans of beer and some terrible rock music.

Another man staying at the hostel was quick to buddy up with him. They were soon cheering with their beer cans and commented on how peaceful it is here. I found this quite amusing as floating out into the night air were the harsh strains of heavy rock music. Bless them for their discretion however because they decided, because of our presence, to save the "heavy metal music" for another time! Having him here is a good opportunity to be a light to him, to show him that the party crowd isn't the only "good life". We saw a capybara at our lookout spot. They're so cute! I'm very thankful when it cools off at night! We heard many bad things about Colon today. We've gone through this before though and God always provides.

"When you're all alone it leaves more room for God." - Alex Tunicci

Kindra's Journal   9/26/2010

Wow, a different day! While taking our walk around the neighborhood, dad was commenting on how the muddy little creek down the hill looked like a prime spot for a crocodile. Sure enough, upon closer inspection, we saw one right on the bank with its head and spiky tail sticking up out of the water. How exciting! This one was about 4 feet long. We continued on our walk, passing some nice duplex houses with well-maintained yards. This neighborhood is certainly on the upper scale of nice. We let the dogs off their leashes in the immaculate,

American-style community park. It was complete with tennis courts, running trails, a softball field, and a playground.

Our morning quickly took on some kind of structure as we ran into the lady who works at the hostel and had a quick chat about some places to see birds and monkeys. We headed back to the hostel, brewed up a pot of coffee, and headed out for the national park in Gamboa. Still hungry, we decided to buy a few donuts before we hit the road. To our surprise, we saw a familiar face behind us in line, someone from the Franklin Farmers Market! The man had just moved down here in July but was a former produce customer of ours.

On our way to the park, we stopped on the side of the road right next to the canal and enjoyed watching a cruise ship and container ship pass through the locks while we ate our donuts and hot coffee. Within 15 minutes of road time, we were in the national park but had no success finding the hiking trail and ended up at a lake. Us girls jumped out to watch a huge, wild, 8ft long crocodile swimming around in the murky water along with many large turtles. Dad asked an English speaker who happened to be passing by where the trails were. This kind man quickly took it upon himself to give us a grand tour of the area. After snaking around through the abandoned, but still in excellent condition, old canal worker housing, he took us to his own house which was of the same style. He gave us a complete, historical tour of the inside architecture, complete with a view of two capybaras he had tamed. They look similar to a huge guinea pig. After his somewhat scatterbrained attempt to explain the attributes of Columbia, he jumped in his jeep and we followed him down to the pipeline road where we had been told it was nice to hike.

Before we were even out of the vehicle we could hear the screaming of howler monkeys. The noise is unlike anything I have ever heard before. It seems to start out with 1 or 2 of the monkeys shrieking (almost like a screaming pig but not so sharp) until the whole tribe is hooting along in unison! On our hike through the thick jungle, we got so close that we were directly under them and the dark monkeys were all around us. We hiked on for quite a while, thinking we would soon come to the end of the trail. However, when the Rangers, who were passing back through in their truck offered us a ride, we found out this trail is 47 kilometers long and goes all the way to Colon! We watched many different varieties of hummingbirds up close at the nature center.

Came home and shared our spaghetti supper with Dyllan. What a sad situation. Everything he has going on in his life seems so terrible. Got to go, it's past 10:30!

Kindra's Journal   9/27/2010

We took a long walk before our complimentary piece of store toast with jam and the ever-present drink of coffee. The dogs have super bad worms and the last time we tried to give them wormer (the horse kind) it literally backfired and they threw it up. Today we want to try giving them smaller, more frequent doses. Perhaps ¼ syringe, 3 times a day.

Today is the day we set out on our expedition to reach Mark's office and attempt communication. I've been praying for many days so all I have left to do is to set out in faith. Hopefully, more later...

Hallelujah! The Lord preserves the stranger once again! It's 3:00 in the afternoon now, and I will try to write down the morning events. We made it to Mark's office building surprisingly easily. Upon stepping off the elevator onto the second floor, we had no trouble finding the Aduana office. After reading story after story of people reaching a point of madness in this very office, it was evident how clearly God answered my prayers of the past week. Apparently, many had resorted to yelling and throwing papers back at Mark. Everything had gone smoothly, and the paperwork went well. As we rode the elevator back down to the main floor, we felt quite successful. We had a map of how to find the vehicle inspection station, a promised personal guide to Colon, and some airport pages ripped from a phone book.

The directions seemed easy enough to follow, but our party came to a grinding halt as we looked around us, trying to see the police station. We strained our eyes to find the building where the map showed it to be but failed to see anything but the scariest looking project housing I've ever seen! Military police were scattered all over the area. Still, they seemed to be all too rare of a sighting among the swarms of unruly students and intimidating men. Figuring we must have taken a wrong turn, we pulled off at an empty bus stop next to the main road to check the map. For all of you who haven't had the experience of driving through a huge third-world city with a tourist map, let me explain.

Many times it seems as if you may as well be sitting on the thing because it seems completely worthless. As far as street signs go, it's rare to see them, and occasionally, the name on the sign isn't even on the map. While mom and dad were in hot pursuit of our location on the map, I looked around to see what was causing all the commotion behind our vehicle. It was us! My worst nightmare was unfolding before my very eyes. This poor old man, a terrifying character, was yelling to his friend across the street and pointing at our vehicle. As the seconds ticked past, he got more animated. He yelled and motioned for his friend to come over, continually pointing at our vehicle. I quickly reached up and shook dad, telling him to quickly go before these men got any closer to our vehicle. Wow, we had a quick escape. Praise the Lord.

As we drove further, we found ourselves lost downtown, which seems to be a frequent occurrence. We just couldn't find any street signs that made sense. We stopped to ask an older man, "where is Balboa Avenue?" This nice old man studied our map to the point where I was beginning to wonder whether he even knew where we were, but then jumped in his car and drove us to the very street we needed to be on. When we would stop at lights, young men from the schools would laugh at us in a very intimidating way and point at us. They would also approach our vehicle, whistling in through the open windows and causing the dogs to get all worked up and growl. From this point on, we rolled up the windows to be a little more inconspicuous. We proceeded to retrace our directions meticulously, over and over again, in an attempt to find the necessary policia station.

Their sense of who's a gringo seems to be almost canine-like, and at times. Everything seemed almost too bad to be real. The honking of horns, rude, impatient people, so much exhaust fumes it gave you a headache, and always being on edge, not knowing what people might do to you was so stressful. Upon dad's urging us girls to try harder to navigate him down the right road, mom explained in her exasperation, saying, "I could burst a blood vessel in my brain if I tried any harder!" So true. We finally ended up back in awful Curundu. A young military man waved us over to tell us what peril we were in, and I believed it.

It turns out we had followed the directions to a tee, and we're right next to the police station. The sign was hard to see. It was a strange feeling having just completed the goal that we spent the whole morning on, only to be thrust straight into another! Now we had to find a place to park and try to safely cross six speedy Lanes of traffic to get to the police station for the vehicle inspection. We pulled up to the garden gate at the main station. We soon had a guard to show us where to go. He was clad in the usual green uniform hat and black boots and bulletproof vests and, of course, a short-barreled shotgun that is so popular to see down here. I really think there's no shortage of guns possessed here either by the authorities or the general citizens!

The guard wasted no time in getting down to business. "Buenos dias, (good morning). Tell me what you need." He gave us permission to park in front and told us where we needed to go. Praise God for the only available space. We were there at a busy time as we saw many men appearing with papers. There was a car with many bullet holes through the driver's windshield. A rough-looking man in handcuffs with a guard passed close by the vehicle. Quite the sights. So we parked, and instead of crossing the street, we crossed over the tall walking bridge. This was scary to me as some of the characters up there looked very shady, and we were quite a ways up! We did make it across and quickly shuffled our way down the corner to the police station. As we walked into the office, we were greeted with stares of and amazement. Everyone backed up as we walked to the desk, only to be told "manana" at 10:00! That's one step closer, and we headed home to rest in the backyard of the hostel. Oh, victory in Jesus! What bliss to breathe in some cleaner air and have our feet on familiar ground.

We relaxed, sent emails, met two girls from Switzerland, watched the Jesus lizards, and went to our canal overlook spot. We sat around our white table this afternoon, but the task of the 10:00 AM vehicle inspection looms before me like a dark cloud. I'm praying hard, and I have not a single reason to believe the God of the universe wouldn't follow through on his word. It's a matter of faith! Many times when we are in a terrifying, dangerous situation trying not to act scared, my mind goes back to all of our friends back in the States praying for us. David, who has been staying at the hostel here, left today, so we gave him a farewell note, Mom and Dad's testimony, and a picture of our family. May God change him. His primary pastime is partying, drinking, smoking, and other things that go along with that. What would you give in exchange for your soul? Listened to the workers laughing away as I was the last one outside.

Kindra's Journal   9/28/2010

Rainy in the AM

Didn't sleep well last night. Mom is cleaning the room as I write this, and the rest of the hostel acquaintances are hanging out in the living room. Fernando is busy helping the girls from Switzerland figure out how to get on the right bus. He gave them a few key phrases, such as "donde" (where) and "por favor" (please). As the girls tried to pronounce them correctly in their strong Swiss accents, I had to laugh to myself. Mom put my thoughts into words by saying, "It's not asking the correct question that's the problem. It's understanding the answer." How true! Well, I'm a little nervous about the whole Curundu thing, but I've spent much time over it in prayer. God does preserve the stranger. I will set out in confidence! More later.

I feel so beat and tired. This was the most running around and busy day I've had in a long time. The only difference between this and the border was all the paperwork was completed without a single problem. A clear answer to my prayers! We aimed to take a more direct route to Curundu but missed our exit. We went far down the highway before we could turn around and try again. Everyone sat in silence. Dad finally broke the silence, and we all agreed that only God could protect us in this bad of a situation. Finally, our navigation worked, and we found the last parking spot. Inside the building, we were surrounded by workers. We all too quickly were escorted back outside to check the VIN number and be told to come back at 2:00 that afternoon. We did have an encouraging little chat inside the building with a man who also used to be a sinner and has, praise the Lord, been saved. With plans to return in 3 hours, we set off to the safe neighborhood of Albrook once again to try and find cages for the dogs. When Dad and I walked into the pet store and saw the price of $260 on the dog crates, his heart almost fainted within him. For a second, he considered just hiring a group of men to take us all through the Darien Gap. With renewed zeal, we walked across the street to the huge hardware store. These stores would even be considered classy in the states.

We were greeted by a super friendly man who enjoyed his opportunity to practice some English with us. Dad was going to look for something to make the cages out of himself but right in the middle of the aisle was a whole stack of dog cages on sale for $60! Praise the Lord just what we needed. As we were standing in line to check out, mom commented on how we used to talk about how in the world we would purchase dog crates in Panama City. Well, here we are! We tried to find a decent shoe store but failed to do so. We're headed back to the hostel to relax for an hour before speeding off again to the other police station. We arrived precisely at 2:00 and had no trouble finding the secretary-general by bouncing from guard to guard and asking. They all seemed to know what we were there for and would say "vehicular inspection" and point in the right direction. We were able to bypass the tremendously long line of people labeled "assistance for victims." We found ourselves waiting in the reception room for dad to file the papers. Sweet success, everything went smoothly. Praise the Lord! We met a few men who were also there to get shipping papers. Unfortunately, they were shipping with Barwell and not with Manfred, so we couldn't share a container.

As we were trying to pull out into the traffic to leave, a bagger with a bloody leg approached us. He was getting really close, to the point Biddy started to growl loudly, and horns started honking at us to go. We barely escaped unscathed as we squeezed between some buses. Dad made it to the u-turn spot, but we were going too fast to actually make the turn. We were shot off onto some random street in Curundu. A big no-no! Dad knew we needed to be on the next street over with his mental calculations, so we zoomed off to the left. Everyone with windows up and mom was saying, "David, I can't believe the choices you're making!" Just as we passed an incredibly scary group of men, the street we wanted came into view.

My heart sank to the floor as I noticed yellow roadblocks positioned across the road. What now? Dad just kept going, and sure enough, at the end of the row of blockers, the Land Cruiser just barely squeezed through. Praise the Lord. Without much further incident, we stopped at the grocery store Ray and then went home to the hostel.

Kacie played with her friends Gabriella and Carlos, which provided entertainment for us as their little ball got stuck up in the tree. Ricardo made quite an exciting demonstration of how to get a coconut off the tree and drink it. I suppose when he saw dad standing there with a hatchet looking at him saying "como" (how)? He certainly took the process from start to finish. Knocking them off the tree, cutting them open, pouring them into the glass, then cracking them in half to scoop out the white flash. He and all the neighbors were quite entertained by this, and everyone enjoyed their cocos. We put together the new dog crates and took a walk around the neighborhood. When we walked down past the "dangerous animals" sign, we spotted a crocodile down in the creek that was at least 5 feet long. We were close enough to see its head and all of its features. Daddy is intensely researching flights. Hopefully, tomorrow we will have a restful day off. The Lord knows the way through the wilderness; all I have to do is follow.

Kindra's Journal   9/29/2010

Extremely hot

Finally, the long-awaited day with nothing to do had arrived. As we sat around our white table eating these unique corn things Ricardo made for breakfast, we realized we had everything to do! We had to find a way to get ourselves to Cartagena, Columbia. There happened to be a taxi waiting right there next to the hostel, so dad and I jumped in. We made the quick decision to make our way across town to Casco Viejo. This historic port city happened to have a hostel that had sailboat services! We were quite disappointed in our taxi driver because he's slowly toured us straight through Curundu and its neighboring cities that were equally as bad. We would have never found it on our own!

We weaved through back one-way passages with many serious gangster men on the sidewalks. We passed by so many people in sad situations. One scrawny old man was stooped over, picking up a pile of trash. A group of young men scooped away at a gravel pile on someone's roof. Another older man was surrounded by police, handcuffed and uncomfortably crouched down to a stair-step. There are so many people in the slummy places that Christ could change into new people! What would happen to gringo's if they moved into one of these dilapidated building complexes? Would they kill you? How long would a person last in those circumstances?

Our driver, obviously confused, kept zig-zagging down one street after another. We were quite impressed with the ancient buildings and ocean views, all of this to the apparent pleasure of our driver. We discovered our driver was under the impression we wanted a tour of the city. We finally figured it out when he asked us if we were ready to go home! When we told him no, we had to go to Luna's coastal hostel, he proceeded to ask about half a dozen people before we arrived with success at our destination. Wow, definitely not our crowd of people, but they were kind and helpful. About an hour later, we were out of there with a sailboat reserve to take us to Cartagena! Perfect timing. Well, getting a taxi back was not as easy as we had thought.

Standing in the blazing sun and watching a handcuffed man surrounded by police on the corner next to us seemed slightly bewildering. But we did find one, and we're able to share our testimony of salvation with the taxi driver. He wished us God's blessing as we left his taxi, and we said, "equalmente" (you as well). We learned this saying in Mexico, and it has been very useful. The rest of the day went by in a blur. Dad and I plan to take the Land Cruiser to Colon in the morning with the mystery guide from Mark's office. We returned the dog crates and got to talk with our English-speaking friend again, who told us that some people were gringos or acted out. He raised his walkie-talkie by the antenna and stuck it down through the air, pretending to strike at someone. Yikes! God has protected us so far, though. Ricardo went straight to work on our dilemma of finding a 4x4 vehicle to take us to Carti. He soon returned, saying at 4:30 Friday morning, he will knock on our door when the vehicle is here. Praying about tomorrow and Colon. God be with you till we meet again.

Kindra's Journal   9/30/2010

Woke up earlier than usual, around 5:40, and packed up the vehicle with everything we won't need for our sailboat trip. Dad and I left around 7:30, picked up some spark plug wires for later, then headed out for Mark's office across the street to find our paperwork and pick up our guide. He was a hard nut to crack. We were thrilled to realize that the other gringo in the office was sharing a container with us. We ended up spending our whole time in Colon with him. We drove the hour drive to Colon and found ourselves sailing through what appeared to be a giant Curundu.

It was easy to find the port as we stayed right behind Klauss's white Toyota van because he had our guide riding with him. Shipping containers were stacked extremely high, and we seemed to be constantly surrounded by them. We did our paperwork to get visitor's passes, but only for dad and Klauss.

Upon Seferino motioning us to get in our vehicles, we drove back to a noisy truck stop where we found our beloved Aduana office. It wasn't as bad as some, but everyone was up to their usual antics. From apathy to immodesty, all their paperwork and stamp slamming it fit all the Aduana requirements. We went back to the port and waited for almost 2 hours while Seferino worked on getting our bill of loading. We hung out, fixed spark plug wires, finished the book of Galatians, toured Klauss's bus, and bought a few little empanadas for 95 cents each from a man who sold lunch to the workers. It was sweltering hot.

The fumes from the many brand new cars and enormous pieces of farm machinery that drove by made my eyes sting terribly almost the whole time. We were relieved when around 2:00, Seferino waved us into the guarded lot. After the downpour of rain, our vehicle was thoroughly sniffed out by a drug dog. The dog wasn't the giant ferocious German Shepherd I had imagined, but rather a little and certainly not over-fed brown dog. Of course, we passed without a glitch and were soon dressed in hard hats and safety vests. As for our helper, after he saluted us and gave us parting instructions of not to go in a yellow cab, we shook hands, and he was off to do who knows what.

After zig-zagging through the maze of containers, we arrived in front of our container. Without much delay, our vehicles were loaded and tied into place. Most of the official workers and some non-official workers have a pistol strapped to their waist. We waited for 5 minutes until Mr. Aduana came out to authorize our containers to be shut. They needed a giant metal pole to tweak the lever and be in place. We toured the Gatun locks to pass the hour between 3:00 and 4:00.

Then we headed over to the train station to wait out the next hour until the train left at 5:00. All of this, mind you, in a yellow taxi. The train ride was absolutely incredible, and we enjoyed the view of big ships and Gatun lake. Flying through the jungle on smooth train tracks was fun. We enjoyed sitting down with Klaus, having completed the task we set out to do. We had a slight scare as a no-name taxi we got into took us on a roundabout way home. We were soon happily united with a distraught mom, Kacie, Cornelia, and Ricardo. It is fun to exchange adventures with each other and get to be together again.

Kindra's Journal   10/01/2010

I was super tired because we girls stayed up till midnight chatting about yesterday's experiences. I slept on the little couch, not the same couch the bums sleep on. It was so short that my feet hung off. So much for Ricardo's knock on the door is he showed up slightly before we were ready at 4:30. We hauled all of our stuff out and sat on the steps of the cement walkway while we waited for our ride to show up. Meanwhile, Ricardo was calling Manuel to see why they were not on time.

They finally pulled up in a nice new white Land Cruiser, a ride worthy of our precious payment of 180 dollars. It was directly followed by an old junky-looking blue vehicle. I quickly pushed the thought out of my mind that this may be the vehicle for us and just assumed it must be a neighbor. Sadly though, as the Toyota Cruiser sped away, I realized yes, this was our ride to Carti. Three people piled out of the vehicle to tie our backpacks precariously onto the flimsy excuse of roof rack. They tried to make a tiny tarp fit over the packs, which ended up being of no avail as it was way too small to ever possibly fit. Jane was not happy with our ride, and neither was dad. Actually, his wrath was quite kindled!

After the stacks of newspapers were tied up and shoved to the side, Walter got crammed in the back, we three girls packed into the seats, and dad was the co-pilot up front. With all of us packed in like sardines, Junior, our driver, took off! We drove through the deep ghetto to drop off the other passenger at a college, then stopped at a grocery store to get the things necessary for the trip. By the time we came back out, dad was in much better spirits and enjoyed telling us that our driver drives the motorcycles with the shotgun rider on the back. He certainly had the look about him that all the police have, except he did smile on occasions when something was truly funny. So we are on our way, going as fast as we could go, passing cowboys and every other vehicle.

Junior beeped at almost every bicyclist, steep curve, person, driver, and vehicle we passed. Maybe with the hope to minimize accidents? Within about one hour, we had left the city and turned onto a dirt road. It had the steepest hills but views that were certainly worth the speedy downs. Obviously, this is what the other passenger who owned the vehicle had in mind when he told dad that this Nissan patrol could go up the steepest hills like nothing! Junior would keep the gas down while speeding downhill to make it up the hill with any semblance of speed. The hills were so steep when you reached the bottom, the front of the vehicle would already be going up. When we came to the top of the hill, Junior would lean way forward out of a seat to peer over the vehicle's hood in an attempt to see the road. That's how steep those hills were! Careening over the top of a hill, we pulled into a little Kuna Indian restaurant where Mom, Kacie, and I speedily made our way to the outhouse.

The main building was a thatched roof with the nicest little wood floor and railings. We sat at one table and our guides at the other. There was no menu. I think they just served one meal for breakfast at $1.50 a plate. Two eggs, two pieces of flatbread, and refried beans. It was perfect because we hadn't eaten much yesterday. Our guides didn't spend any extra time waiting around. We resumed an even faster rate than before up and down even steeper hills through Kuna Yul, an autonomous tribe that takes care of their own land.

At times we would go screeching the tires around corners with Junior Hocking the horn to make sure that anyone else coming around the corners would know we were there. It had been over 2 hours since we left the hostel. The road turned into a bumpy airport runway and ended at a little block and thatch hut. We were almost pushed out of the vehicle. Our stuff was quickly unloaded and hauled off to the boat launch. We had no choice but to follow our backpacks and the groceries that Captain Kyle had asked us to bring. We walked along and found ourselves, and the dogs hurried off the dock onto the launcher that we were told was going to Awab, our sailboat.

The deck was not very big but full of people who were busily unloading supplies for the villages. In less than 5 minutes, we were staring at our new home for the next 6 days. A wooden sailboat, 55 ft long, with beautiful brown strips of wood around the bottom and white on the other parts. On top stood two people with minimal clothing, to say the least, staring right back at us. It wasn't long until we had unloaded several bags of groceries, four huge backpacks, the two dogs, and ourselves. We were introduced to Kyle and Silvia, the hosts and owners of the ship. They were just as surprised to see us as we were to see them.

We settled in, went swimming, got a 50-gallon container of diesel, and then headed out to a Kuna island to fill up on freshwater. The island was absolutely amazing and exactly what I had always dreamed of, with little passageways going between all the huts made of thatch and stick. When children saw us walking around with Walter and Biddy, they came running out. Some naked, some with tiny little undies, and the occasional field outfits on. They ran out after us and tried to work up their courage to touch the dogs. We let a 17-year-old young man named Aril show us around the village, buildings, and the church. He said he was a Christian and that the church there was evangelical. That's good to hear! Dad and I walked out into the water. Now let me tell you, this was not very smart.

We were so impressed with this large pig that they housed up on a platform above the water. A neon sign couldn't have been harder to miss. An outhouse above the water and a pig to top it off! What a parasite party! The people were trying to sell mom one of those molas, an exclusive Kuna type of embroidery with 12 colorful layers of material. They finally wore mom down. Since the Mola had a picture of a turtle on it, Kacie decided to buy it for her turtle collection.

One old man enthusiastically came out to greet us with nothing but the littlest undies on. He introduced himself and shook our hands. We talked with him for a while and then followed Aril back to our boat. We are sleeping on the dark deck tonight because the weather is so nice. We're anchored just off the Kuna Island. The wooden dug-out boats are still going by, and we can hear the people talking. It's a strange feeling out here, way out in the water, and I'm sleeping in my salty dress.

Kindra's Journal   10/02/2010

Woke up this morning to the site of the Kuna men in their long skinny boats silently paddling by. We rearranged our things on the boat to get ready for the three more people coming aboard today. We picked up Alice (27), Blake (30), and (Jake) 29 and headed out to the island with the immigration office. Kyle took everyone's passports into the island while the rest of us swam around the boat. The water is so crystal clear! Unfortunately, the immigration office couldn't resist messing with Kyle, so with the help of $20, we were on our way. We stopped at a little island for a beach break, but guess who we saw on our way in to anchor? Klaus! Dad yelled out to him, "I won't be there till Wednesday." "Me neither," he yelled back. After going through that day in Colon together, it felt so good to see him again. We snorkeled around on the island for a while and saw lots of different kinds of fish. We also got to see the starfish I had hoped to see. Actually, I got to swim past about 20 of them! They are very thick and colored red and yellow. When we got back on the boat, Kyle was a little flustered about all the clothes we were swimming in. After we got them drying, he seemed to settle down about it. We're visiting with the other three passengers in the back area. I'm so tired. The sunset was so beautiful last night! Slightly chilly with a strong breeze.

Kindra's Journal   10/03/2010

Wow, woke up to the sight and sound of dolphins jumping in the water around our boat. After watching people jump off Klauss's boat to snorkel with the dolphins, dad decided to do the same. He was soon swimming off towards the fins and tails that frequently glided above the water. Breakfast this morning proved to be lacking as everyone was super hungry afterward. Especially since supper last night consisted of some chopped tomatoes and a tiny square of quiche. The food is good. There's just not a whole lot of it.

Swimming as much as we have, seems to make you quite hungry. Back to breakfast. Our family went through the line last, and all that was left were four thin slices of bread, a boiled egg for each, and a few slices of banana. That's all right. We're determined not to complain and stay on the captain's good side. We're now on a 4-Hour stretch to a different island where we will anchor for the day and swim.

Since my clock has ceased to function with any form of reliability, and the ship doesn't have a visible clock, we're just going along for the ride. Mom had to cut Kacie's braid short because it was harboring an unconquerable tangle. I am sure her shorter hair will be more manageable to take care of now and less of a hassle for Mom. Of course, Silvia had to wonder if we also had some strange idea about having long hair. This presented an interesting opportunity as we shared some thoughts on Christian femininity with her and first Corinthians 11. Still alive but scared about going out to sea in the morning. We encountered a storm this afternoon. Kyle and Silvia are always more worked up than they need to be, but when the sunny, pleasant weather changed to a dark and windy storm, the situation caused stress levels to rise.

To make matters worse, just as it started to pour rain, the rope that held the sail snapped! Waves made it hard to balance, and as we hauled all of the couch cushions into the cabin, I got pretty worried! Finally, everything was strapped down outside, and everyone except the dogs went inside. I look through the window and rain out at the poor pups who were getting wet despite the overhead umbrella. The windows around the cabin caught my eye as Kyle tried to jam a stick in one of the windows to hold it shut. The cowhide in the middle of the floor had a wet spot growing bigger in size with each strip from the ceiling.

When we asked where the life jackets were, it seemed to upset Silvia. She told us that it was her responsibility to keep us safe and that she will provide the necessary items if the time comes. We did pry out of her where the life jackets were located, so that's good. I sure hope we don't encounter a worse storm because I was very scared about the one we already went through. We anchored between four very close islands and were able to snorkel on a reef. We saw all kinds of interesting fish, coral, squid, jellyfish, barracudas, and pretty little blue and yellow fish schools. It was great and just what dad had wanted! Also lots of other fish and many other sailboats four to five here. Also we know where Klauss's boat is :-) I'm going to read some scriptures to calm myself.

Kindra's Journal   10/04//2010

As soon as we woke up, Kyle was there telling dad he had a cup of coffee waiting for him. It was time to take the dogs in the dinghy to the island for their last potty break before we set out for the open sea. I quickly took down the laundry and began arranging things below deck for a long trip of rough tippy sailing. The bilge pump broke, so Kyle was busy in the engine room trying to replace it with a new one. Unfortunately, the new pump brand used 12 volts instead of 36 volts like the former one, and Kyle had to take quite a bit of time to rewire it. Finally, we motored up and headed out. I had no idea what we were in for!

As soon as we passed the reef that divides the Caribbean from the Atlantic, we were in two to three-foot swells. The boat immediately started tipping at disturbing angles as it rolled around in the waves. I was scared! Mom commented, "wow, we finally found something that scares Kindra!" That is sadly true. While still trying to grasp the idea of spending two whole days on these terrifying waves, dolphins suddenly started jumping out of the water right next to our boat. It was incredible and just like the pictures! I could see them under the water, then they would start jumping out five or six at a time! Kyle insisted we take some Dramamine pills for seasickness, so we did, and wow, we got so tired. Maybe that's what people use for sleeping powder? You can't really do anything but sit.

For example, venturing down into the bathroom is quite the expedition. I always end up banging into things and losing my balance. Trying to hold still enough to unlatch the bathroom door is always a task in and out of itself. So far, so good. Since we have no clock, I'll say it's sometime in the afternoon. We have already eaten two good, but not exactly huge, meals. Still, we all have the familiar hungry feeling again. Lord willing, more later.

It got stormy around 3:00 and was raining on and off. Kyle and Silvia lowered sails just before dark. Our family has the outdoor cushion relay down to a science now, and we shuffle them back and forth quite often. As darkness fell, the rain descended. We were all stuck inside the cabin. Everyone was hot and sweaty. With no fresh air or horizon to keep our eyes on, our feeling of seasickness increased. Allice, one of the other passengers, started up a few riddles and mind games to keep ourselves occupied. The pitch-black windows and being tossed to and thrown in the waves felt very odd.

Dad and I curled up on a pile of the outdoor cushions in the corner to keep from throwing up while everyone else got a bowl of soup. Getting from the kitchen, up the stairs to the pilothouse, and with a bowl of soup was a challenge for everyone. Unfortunately for us, Jake failed the test! Upon arriving at the top of the stairs, Jake slid through a puddle of water, heading straight to the pile of us sick ones who were cramped under the table.

Not wanting to spill the hot soup all over us still held on to his bowl. Not being able to stop himself crashed into the window above the table. His bowl of soup went flying, landing on the table. At that point, dad and I woke up and, not knowing what happened, thought that the boat was coming apart and that Jake had thrown up! This caused a chain reaction as I grabbed an empty plastic grocery bag and headed for the door. Dad did the same. The next moments weren't glamorous as the boat tilted violently to one side and the other, and the rain got us wet. I waited a few minutes and then basically slithered down the stairs.

I curled up next to mom, trying not to be rolled across the floor with each tremendous swell that caused the boat to tilt at extreme angles. The boat tilted so far that things started to fly off shelves and out of cupboards, causing quite an unnerving clatter to arise. Silvia grabbed a little blue ribbon and stuck her head out the door to see which direction the ribbon would fly to figure out the wind direction. By this time, the seas were really rough, and all I could see when the boat tipped was white foaming water close to the windows amidst the pitch blackness. Silvia, who is quick to hit the panic button, was, however, right this time when she said, "Kyle, the wind is blowing like bloody hell out there. This is really bad!"

At this point, dad said we girls should get our life jackets on. No problem, I thought. A mom snuck down into our Captain's bedroom to find the life jackets, I prayed she would find them. She found one, which I put on, and we found Kacie the small one she had from the day before. Mom sent me down to look once more, and as I went down the stairs into the Captain's room, my thoughts of what might be the case quickly became a reality.

I opened the bag that was supposed to be full of life jackets, but it was full of national flags. I then went to the closet where the rest were supposed to be kept. I poked my head inside, trying to see amidst all the ropes. Praise God I found one, though old and thin it was. I was happy to bring it to mom. When I emerged up into the cabin, a look of disappointment washed over dad's face. Fighting the impulse to throw up again, I quickly crumpled up with my bulky life jacket on the floor. I could hear dad asking Kyle, "Is there a life jacket for every person on this boat?" He responded, "No." Well, at least he was honest. From there, dad went on to ask how to activate the EPIRB and the supposed life raft. We laid there, waiting for hours to slowly tick by.

One moment with our feet above our heads and the next moment heads above feet. Around 11:00, Kyle went down into the engine room again. My guess proved to be correct as he emerged for the fourth time with the bilge pump. As the boat continued to catapult back and forth, Kyle continued to work on it and finally figured out the problem and fixed it. The funny thing was that much later, mom heard a continual thumping. She woke up to see what it was and decided to ask Kyle, who was sitting on the ground, obviously producing the noise. "Oh, it's just stupidity," he said. The floor cover to the engine room was upside down, and it happened to slide into place while he wasn't looking. For the whole situation, it struck us as kind of funny.

We were quickly sobered up again as around 12:00, Kyle announced that the GPS and his compass were not matching up in degrees! There wasn't much we could do other than pray. Just like the rainbow God caused to shine earlier today, when Kyle and Silvia came into the cabin saying, "it's much calmer out there now," I know God answered my prayers. We're heading at speeds of up to 30 knots. I've never seen people listen to those iPad things so much in my life. I mean, Allice, Jake, and Blake seem to be plugged into those things almost 24/7. Another noteworthy time when I woke up in the middle of the night was when Kyle announced, "you want to know something scary? We're 2 miles deep right now."

Kindra's Journal   10/05/2010

Dad went out at 2:00 this morning when it calmed down a bit and slept outside with poor Biddy and Walter, who were stuck outside all night. We encountered two more rainstorms that really shook the boat, but nothing too serious. The boat has finally ceased to make me nervous with all of its tipping. The mainsail got ripped last night. They said we're lucky the sails weren't completely shredded with the way the weather was. I found myself slightly irritated when I saw Kyle pick up my huge backpack dripping with water from the supposed tarped box. That will be a job to dry! 6 to 8 foot swells today on our way to Cartagena. We saw lots of dolphins jumping around our boat. They really do speed along right under the clear blue water, so we could see them really well. I saw a mom and a baby together! I am so tired of Silvia's cooking. It's all green peppers.

Trip Summary by Kristi VanderZon   Panama

Dear Family and Friends,

We drove to the Panama border, arriving around noon, and it took 2 ½ hours to get through. We pulled over on the early side in the city of David in a nice little motel called the Panamericano. Then we headed towards Panama City. The week's big challenge will be to get the paperwork to ship the land cruiser to Colombia. Then find a way to get us there, probably by airplane.

When we arrived in Panama City, we were happy to find the Hostel de Clayton. After sitting in front of an expensive Holiday Inn, we asked a taxi driver if he knew where a cheap but good hotel was. He nodded enthusiastically, and we followed him to that place. An excellent base for finding our shipping vessel and flight to Colombia. We might be here for a few days. We have our own room but share a common living area, kitchen, and bathroom. Not a problem as we stay outside with the dogs most of the time. Hostel de Clayton is less than a mile from the Panama Canal, near the Mira Flores Locks, also minutes away from Panama City and shipping agencies.

One odd occurrence... We were in a parking lot at the canal when a taxi pulled up, pushed open his back door, and whistled and patted the seat for Biddy to hop in. Biddy approached the car, and David called her back. Was he going to take off with our dog? Strange. You really do have to watch everything closely here. We're glad Biddy didn't go for a ride in that taxi!

We were getting road-weary, but the walls were covered with encouraging pictures of other travelers who stopped here on their journey. Some with vehicles, some on motorcycles, some on bikes, and all on their way to Colombia. It lifted our spirits a little to know this can be done, and others have gone before.

We stopped at a little pizza restaurant to get supper, and the owner wanted to hear all about our trip. It turns out he is from Colombia, and he had a picture book he was proud to show us of his country. It was wonderful and helped inspire our thoughts about the next leg of our journey.

Overall it has been a good experience. I never thought I would write that when we were sailing down an unknown road, overlooking the ghettos of Panama City. It had its challenges, but the Lord has been faithful to guide and protect us as usual. Thanks for praying. It's truly a comfort.

161

Camping at the Surf Camp the night before last at Rio del Mar

Kindra, watching some ships come through the canal. We saw one from Japan and one from Singapore.

We toured the canal at the Miraflores Locks. We really enjoyed watching all the ships come through.

In front of the Hostal with our Hostess, Jane

Paperwork is officially underway to get the vehicle shipped to Colombia! We're one step closer, and after being stationary for five days. From the first day in Panama City, I feared Curundu. Curundu is the ghetto we witnessed from the highway, Thursday. High-rise project housing and vacant buildings lend to an ominous air about the neighborhood. The tourist guide book at the hostel says to avoid it altogether.

We pulled up to a station and talked to a soldier guarding the parking lot. He agreed to let us park nearby. One vehicle parked there had about 8-12 bullet holes through the front window. We parked and walked over a bridge to the other side of the street and entered the police station, where the officer inside the door was plainly shocked to see us four file through the door. We had a conversation with a police official, with whom we shared our testimony in brief form. He then said his life was changed by faith in Jesus Christ. We all said "Gracias a Dios". What an unexpected blessing right there in a run-down ghetto in Panama City, in an obscure police station. We were able to join with the policeman in expressing thanks to God for changing our lives.

I don't know if any of you were praying for us today. We surely needed it and are thankful for all of you who remember us in prayer. We rejoiced to hold in our hands the official document of the Republica de Panamá Policía Nacional. It was obtained not without great effort and determination. The paper grants permission for our vehicle to leave Panama via ship for Colombia. Praise the Lord!

We were pulling out in front of the police station onto the busy street when it got very chaotic. A beggar, whose leg was all bloody, was approaching my window. I felt compassion and asked David if we could give him some money. Just then, Biddy, who was hanging out my window, started barking at him. Cars started beeping from behind, going around us. We finally jolted out, half pushed, into the lane with two buses barreling down on us, blasting their horns. David stepped on the gas and got us on the road, but we missed the turnaround lane we wanted.

Before I knew what was happening, David bolted across the other lane down a street of unknown destination. All I knew is we were heading deeper into Curundu. Would this nightmare never end? But David didn't stop there. He quickly turned on to a side street that looked like a dead-end, complete with men hanging out on the sidewalk and no businesses around. Yellow partitions were closing off the road when we got to the end, with just enough space for the land cruiser to fit through. We squeezed through, getting onto another road, which David calmly announced was the right one.

I was trying to catch my breath while sputtering out my disapproval of his unexpected navigation. We did indeed come back onto the main road and made it safely home without further incident. Reflecting back on the whole scene, it was pretty exciting. David really did a most excellent job of making quick decisions and getting us out of there. And for all of you out there praying, praise God for his protection in Curundu today!

Curundu

Here are a few pictures that David snapped of our surroundings at the first police station amid my pleas of "Don't let anyone see you." He truly has his patience stretched at times traveling with three females.

You really would have to be there to get the full effect!

Walter

Biddy

Although the dogs take considerably more effort to travel with, they are a comfort. They provide substantial vehicle protection when left inside it.

Lots of rest and recharging

Ricardo let us enjoy some fresh cocos, and showed us the harvesting process start to finish.

Kacie and her friend Gabriella

We took advantage of our time here by taking a jungle hike. We heard and saw many howler monkeys that screech and call to each other with a staggering volume.

Kristi, Kindra, Kacie, and Walter ready to hike

David and the girls on the trail

Well, we are nearing the time to part from our faithful vehicle for a few days. We will be like the other backpackers we see traveling. We'll only have our backpacks and two dogs. Thursday, we drive to Colon to drive it into a container and see it loaded on a ship. It ships out Saturday. Now to figure out how to get ourselves there.

The drug-sniffing dog inspecting our vehicle

Kindra sporting a hard hat and smile after successfully loading the Land
Cruiser into the shipping container

Finally, we left the hostel and were picked up at 5:00 am by an ancient
expedition vehicle in pretty rough shape. We were disappointed as
we had paid a premium price for a newer vehicle to take us. All our
backpacks and the dogs to a little drop-off station at a place called Carti.

171

As it turns out, this older vehicle showed up, strapped our backpacks on top, and strapped them down with a frail rope. A young woman was riding along who needed to be dropped off at a university. Consequently, we found ourselves riding around the city, packed in this little vehicle, and surrounded by stacks of newspapers that were also headed to the San Blas Islands. After the extra passenger was dropped off, we had to stop at a grocery store to pick up our captain's list. There are no grocery stores out in San Blas.

David and Junior

We quickly warmed up to our driver, "Junior," an off-duty police officer. It was about a 2 ½ hour ride that became more exciting than the extreme cable ride we took back in Guatemala. About halfway there, we stopped at a native restaurant. A thatch roof hut and some tables. It was great food – some delicious fry bread, eggs & coffee. After continuing on the road, the ride really started to get wild. It was getting very hilly & mountainous, with beautiful scenery all around and very curvy. Junior had a way of accelerating at the bottom of every hill and hitting the curve and uphill with increasing speed and intensity. There were screeching tires around some of the curves. He was going so fast. We were laughing and enjoying the excitement, which seemed to encourage his enthusiasm. We all agreed it was truly as close to a roller coaster ride you could get without actually being on one.

David, Kindra, and Kacie enjoying their Kuna breakfast

We crested a hill, and far down below, we were amazed to see the San Blas Islands, all spread out amid the sparkling, blue Caribbean Sea. We came to a Kuna checkpoint, a primitive little hut on the side of the road. Two men were stationed to collect the road tax of $6 per person. There was a sign announcing we were in Kuna Territory. The road came to an end, and there was a little building and a dock. Our arrival sparked much activity. Young men quickly brought out little carts and started loading our groceries & supplies onto them. We hurried along to keep up, each loaded down with our backpacks and trying to keep track of the dogs. We came to a dock, and all our things were loaded onto a little boat, and we all managed to clamber down into it, along with the dogs, and it immediately took off for our boat.

We approached the Awab, our sailing vessel, and our captain stuck his head out of the cabin window & shouted greetings. His girlfriend was also on board as our official cook. From the looks of the situation, this was going to be a grand adventure. We pulled up next to the boat, and with great effort, I managed to pass the dogs up on deck to David, who was the first one on. We passed up all our things, then the little boat sped away, and there we were, looking at each other. He said we were very different from the normal backpacker guests and was glad to have us on board, as this should be interesting.

Our first glimpse of the Awab

Top view of the Awab

We had a wonderful day and had good conversations with Kyle & Silvia throughout the day. Silvia cooks all the meals and bakes bread every night. They took us to a Kuna village, one, they said, was not on the usual tourist circuit, but they had to fill up with "sweet" (fresh) water. We pulled up to a little island packed with little thatched-roof huts. We unboarded with the dogs and disappeared into a whole other world.

We disappeared into a labyrinth of narrow dirt trail passages between huts. Little children ran from every direction to see us. Upon seeing the dogs, they would scream and run away. Finally, we stopped and told the crowd following us, "Perros amable" (Dogs are friendly). I got next to Biddy and showed them how to pet her, and David pointed to one of the little boys and motioned for him to pet Biddy. He ran up, touched her, and ran away. From then on, about 10 children were holding onto Biddy's & Walter's leashes our whole time in the village. They mimicked perfectly everything David said in English. There was a chorus of "Biddy, come, come" and "Biddy & Walter." It's amazing the element the dogs bring to this trip. They cross all language and culture barriers and bring joy to many people.

Most of the little boys were just wearing underwear or nothing at all. The little girls were usually dressed in little skirts & shirts. The man usually had pants & shirts. One man emerged from a hut in his underwear to enthusiastically welcome us & meet us. The women are the most fascinating. They wear colorful dresses, and on their legs, they wear a beaded wrap. Their hair is generally short, and some wear some color on their faces. We saw many reddish-pink circles on their cheeks, and one had a black design down her forehead and unto her nose.

The women would stand in their doorways and hold up the colorful "molas" their people are famous for. It's an art of fabric cutting and stitching that produces a spectacular design on a black background, made out of about 12 layers of fabric. Kacie is collecting turtles on this trip, so she bought a tortoise mola.

We had a self-appointed guide. A youth about 17 years old named Aril, who spoke a little English, which he was very proud to try out. He walked us all over the village and took us to his home, where his grandmother brought out a collection of bracelets she had beaded. We bought a couple of those and then followed Aril out of the assembly of huts to a beachfront of sorts. A pig was in a cage on stilts above the water, and children were swimming and bathing. It is a tiny island filled with huts, a church, and a school. Their outhouses are built on stilts above the water.

All construction is out of natural materials. The ocean provides their income and tourism. That's where the road tax, etc., comes in handy.

They take out long canoes carved out of a single tree and paddles to travel the sea and rivers like a roadway. They free dive (diving with only holding your breath) to the bottom, bringing up big concha shells and other sea creatures like lobsters & crabs. They also fish. They came by our boat many times to sell their ocean bounty. They also take their canoes inland, via a river, and farm the land there. Rice and yucca are their main crops, and tropical fruit is abundant.

We would have loved to take pictures, but our captain had explained, the Kunas do not like their pictures to be taken. It wasn't a regular tourist island, so we didn't even try to pay them for photo rights. We just became absorbed in the moment, and the pictures are forever etched in our minds. We thoroughly enjoyed our time in the village. We docked just a little ways away for the night and slept on the deck. In the middle of the night, Biddy gave a little bark, and David sat up to witness 8 canoes. They quietly glided through the night, right by our boat and out into the sea. We don't know where they were going, but it was a beautiful thing to spontaneously witness. I was sorry I slept through it. It was a day we won't forget, and I think we're really going to enjoy our time at sea.

Kindra got a picture of a Kuna in one of their long wooden boats out a boat window.

A typical cluster of islands where the Kuna people live.

Kindra & Biddy enjoying the sail.

Our 3rd day onboard the Awab, strangely, felt like we were on the show "Survivor," and we joked about how perfect it would be if a camera was recording this all. Nine people on board from various walks of life plus limited shared space on a 55' sailboat for 5 challenging days equaled inevitable drama. It's hard to believe we have found ourselves here.

That day started out crystal clear, and we woke up to the sound and sight of Dolphins swimming all around. It was beautiful, and "tropical paradise" was the word that kept coming to mind. It didn't last for long… After a meager breakfast, Captain Kyle announced we would be sailing for 4 hours to another set of islands to play on.

David, Kindra, and Kacie enjoying a swim in the beautiful caribbean water

David, Kindra, and Biddy lounging in the back of the boat

The food on board is good, but there never seems to be enough. An undercurrent of dissatisfaction seems to create a low murmur among the guests as the feeling of hunger is not what we're used to. We all feel we paid a hefty price for this cruise and were expecting more food. The Captain, Kyle, and girlfriend Silvia, are a little stressed out on the particulars of, for example, over usage of our limited "sweet water" and don't get the best response after correcting our fellow shipmates on some of the finer details.

The real stress came when, 1 ½ hours into our sail, the weather turned, and it became very windy & rainy. The sails were up. A line snapped, causing a flourish of activity and lots of panicked shouting and running around by Kyle & Silvia. We have noticed they do not calmly respond to potential trouble when it comes to the boat. In fact, often, they disagree and argue over the right thing to do.

It made a bad situation seem worse than it was, and we asked if we could see where the lifejackets were stored. This seemed logical information to know. I had asked about lifejackets the first day but never saw one produced. They had assured us they had all the necessary safety equipment on board, including life jackets and lifeboats. Now, it became a problem that we had asked to see a life jacket, and Silvia surprised us by saying, "Look, I am the captain of this ship, not Kyle. He owns the boat, but I am the official captain. I hold the License, and I am responsible for everyone's safety. I will hand out the lifejackets only when you need them." Wow. We were hardly prepared for this. That means the "Captain Kyle" from the website is a lie.

This, obviously, was greatly disturbing, but we had to suppress all that was going on in our minds. We assured the girls that God was in control of this boat no matter who the captain was. We also assured them that many people were praying for us, and we need not fear. Silvia later said, if we really wanted a lifejacket, she would get us one, but we would have to be responsible for it. Tomorrow we hit the open sea, and we definitely want proof that these lifejackets exist. It's a volatile situation when you are on a boat with people. You don't want to create tension, or bad feelings, as you have to live with them for a time. We kept it low-key and did not address all we wanted to. We have two days to go where we sail across the great wide open to Cartagena. There are no more stops, no more getting off the boat to swim, and no taking the dogs to shore. It will be stressful, but we're praying and hoping for calm weather and calm spirits here on board. We are being observed closely, as we are unusual to them, and we want to represent a Christ-like spirit through it all.

Praise the Lord! Thank you all for praying. We have made it to Cartagena. Let me tell you about our voyage....

We left in the morning under overcast skies. We asked to see the lifejackets and were hurriedly ushered in by Silvia to her bathroom. She rudely produced one and vaguely explained where all the others were. Our confidence was sinking in our Captain team. We're not even sure who the captain is. Are there really life jackets and a lifeboat on board, as we had been assured there were?

Nevertheless, we purposed to enjoy the sail, and it was exciting to leave land behind and feel the boat's sway. Dolphins were having a race with us, and we got to see them up close as they swam ahead of the bow of the boat. Kyle handed out motion sickness pills. It was nice to lay in the back and relax. Soon it started to rain, and we had to move all of our cushions into the cabin. We had been sleeping out on deck in the back of the boat, so every time it rained, we had to move all the cushions in. This was about the only physical activity we had for two days.

The waves turned to swells, and the swells got bigger. We were all (7 passengers + Kyle & Silvia) packed into the cabin with the windows shut. It was so hot, and hour after hour passed until it was dark. It was becoming a storm now, and things were beginning to fall off of shelves, and it became a little unsettling.

We had packed our cushions under a table that was attached to the wall of the cabin. David, Kindra, and Kacie were resting under this table.

Silvia cooked supper and urged us to come get our bowls, but no one was hungry. Nevertheless, with her urging, a few of us filed down the steps to the kitchen to pick up our bowls. David, Kindra, & Kacie, were feeling sick so they stayed lying down. One of the men from Ireland was the last to get his bowl. As he came up the stairs, he slipped on a wet spot on the floor just about the time the boat tilted. He went careening toward the window that was above the table David & the girls were under. With a loud smack, his head hit the window full force and broke it. He came down on the table, which broke and came down heavy on David's back, leaving a few 2 inch long gashes.

The man's soup was all over the table and wall, the sight of which was the last straw for David and Kindra, who thought the man had gotten sick. They rushed up the stairs, threw open the door, and got sick. This was enough for the captain. Kyle said everyone should go to bed. It was the first night we had to sleep inside, and we had minimal space to spread our cushions. We managed to pack in and close our eyes, but no one was thinking of sleeping.

The storm was picking up, and the boat was getting tossed pretty good. Things kept falling out of their places, and Kyle & Silvia were unusually silent and calm. We decided to get the life jackets, so we would have them near in case of emergency. I went into the bathroom where she had shown us but could only find one. I looked in all the places she said they would be, and there were none. I went and got Kindra, and she looked too. She found one ancient one. David asked Kyle, "Are there enough life jackets?" Kyle replied, "No, but enough for you and your family." He had to search for quite a time to produce the last one, but finally, he emerged with a tattered one for David. Kacie had one she had been using the whole time.

The other three passengers didn't appear the least bit worried and were lying on their bunks listening to their iPods. We felt really let down. They had lied about there being plenty of lifejackets on board. Were they lying about the life raft too? It was a disturbing time to have these questions, as we're being tossed about in the ocean. David then questioned them about the IPERB they had said was on board, and they did produce it and went over how to use it. It's a device that, in an emergency, sends out a satellite signal and distress call. It is supposed to be able to pinpoint your location and dispatch help. They also went over instructions on inflating the lifeboat and told us where it is stored, although we never did see it. After that, there was nothing more to do but lay down, pray, and try to get some sleep.

I don't think any of us slept until about 2am when the waters finally calmed down, and the hard rain turned to a drizzle. It lasted from 4pm-

2am. Very unusual, Kyle said. Another concern during our sail was water collecting in the bilge. The pump that was supposed to take care of it was not working correctly. Kyle had to bring it up many times and work on it. Kindra had a tough time staying calm. She has been nervous about the voyage, especially since her episode in El Salvador with David when they drifted away and had to be rescued. It was hard to reassure her when our confidence was shaken in our Captains. There was much reassurance when we prayed and knew many others were praying too.

During the storm, around midnight, Kyle commented how many birds were trying to get in. He went over to the window, pulled it down, and rescued one that had been trying to fly in. He sat it in front of him, by the pilot's wheel. Later, I woke up to see it perched on Kacie's finger. She was sleeping deep and didn't even realize it. Then it hopped on Kindra's head, and she, too, just slept right through it. In the morning, it was set free. We don't know how those birds were so far from land and had found our boat in the storm. When I saw Kyle bringing in the little bird to the safety of the cabin in the middle of that storm, It made me think of the verses from Matthew 10:29-31: "Are not two sparrows sold for a penny? Yet not one of them will fall to the ground outside your Father's care. And even the very hairs of your head are all numbered. So don't be afraid; you are worth more than many sparrows." It gave me great peace to know just like the bird was rescued amid the storm, so we were safe in our Father's hands, safe in the storm.

During all this, the dogs had to remain tied up in the stern of the boat, where we usually sleep. There was a floor space, and they were both on their leashes and secured to the boat. This was a rule that Kyle was stern about. The dogs could not come into the cabin. It was stressful to know they were out there. Walter constantly barked throughout the night, but Biddy never made a noise. I think she was terrified, as she was hiding under the bed, which all fell apart and came down on her. They did survive, though, and were thrilled when we could come out by them again. One of the stresses was not being able to take them on shore to relieve themselves. Amazingly, they made it the entire 36 hours without an accident. Mental stress, yes, but they were champs!

In the morning, we saw the sail had ripped, and the "umbrella" shade structure above where we slept had fallen down. Overall, the boat fared well, and we were making good time.

We had an uneventful conclusion to our sail and arrived at the port last evening around 7:00pm. We had to stay on the boat and wait until our passports were checked in by customs in the morning before we could leave. So this morning, Silvia took in our passports. Even though we were supposed to get breakfast and lunch on the boat today, she apparently decided she was through cooking, so no breakfast. She wanted us off of the boat before lunch. We had all been famished, and we have learned that Kyle always says "yes" to requests, and Silvia always says "no." While Silvia was gone with the passports, I asked Kyle if I could cut up a pineapple for us all to eat. Of course, he said "yes," so we did have something to eat.

It was raining again, and the other three people left for shore, and it was just our family left. David, Kindra, Walter & Biddy went with Kyle to a nearby supermarket with an internet café. This is where our customs agent operated out. He needed to see the dogs and get their papers. Kacie and I stayed on the boat with our backpacks. About an hour later, Kyle cruised up on the dinghy to pick up Kacie and me with all our gear.

The packs were so heavy, especially Davids. The backpacks had been stored under a tarp on the boat's deck during the trip, and everybody was disappointed this morning when we uncovered them, and they were soaking wet. We put on the packs at the dock to prepare to walk the few blocks to the supermarket. Kyle put on Davids and carried the bag of dog food, I put on mine and carried Kindra's backpack, and Kacie had on hers and carried the dog food bowls. It was so difficult to make that walk! After two days of almost no activity and the constant swaying of the boat, I was feeling weak and trailing quite a ways behind Kyle. Kacie was a little ways ahead, urging me to keep up.

When we rounded a corner and saw Kindra standing outside the store with the two dogs, I was relieved. We waited there for a while, where I emailed you all yesterday. They were told to bring the dogs back at 3pm to the boat, where the animal inspector will come. Thus begins our adventures in Colombia. We appreciate your continued prayers, and to everyone who responds by email, a big "Thank You." It's always encouraging to hear from you!

A cruise ship on the horizon

The harbor at Cartagena

A few notes on Kyle & Silvia…..We really warmed up to Kyle. He had a harshness about him and could be offensive at times, but he had a calm, easy-going manner. He often would stop to talk to us during our time on his boat.

Silvia tended to make "mountains out of molehills" and liked to have things her way, and I think it was difficult for her to share their boat with people for five days at a time. She was an interesting character. Silvia was only 20 but seemed more like 30. She is Italian and grew up in Rome. She's a model, and after this trip, they were going to sail to Miami, where she was going to work for a while.

After witnessing their reactions to problem-solving, we realized that things are okay when they are arguing and yelling. The night of the storm, they were very quiet and worked all night together in perfect synchrony. There were times they had to get on deck and adjust the sails, and with the waves and the boat rocking like it was, we were worried they might fall off-board. They did their very best and guided the boat through the storm.

We don't hold anything against them and genuinely wish them the best in the future. Still, we would warn anyone attempting this trip to do more research and get references if possible before picking their sailboat. When you get out in the ocean like that, you realize the gravity of the situation. There's no land or other boats for as far as the eye can see. But we are glad we did it. The experience was great, and we did make it safely here.

Thank you all for your interest and prayers!

Love,

Kristi for us all

I could only squeeze a fraction of the pictures I wanted to share in this book, so here's the link to our website where you can check out extra pictures and videos!
https://welcometothejourney.us/

If you would like to hear more adventures from before or after our Bolivia trip, feel free to drop us a line and let us know here. Mom has over 10 years of daily journal entries that recorded our life in the Amish and homesteading. I'm sure before she shares them she'd love to hear some encouragement from her readers!
https://welcometothejourney.us/?page_id=7

If you have any questions feel free to post them here and I will do my best to personally answer them!

https://welcometothejourney.us/?page_id=16

Chapter 10

Columbia

Kindra's Journal   10/06/2010

Oh, wretched bathroom! I was so sick last night. I almost threw up all over the dinghy. I barely made it to the other side of the boat before the horrendous feeling overtook me once again. I knelt there, my fingers clamped to the side of the boat, engulfed in misery. I laid down again in the bright lights from the city, and the high-rise buildings all seemed to spin around me. The rocking of the waves made me just hate being on the boat. Later we repeated the motion of moving the cushion almost in our sleep. Then while mom, dad, and Kacie crammed into the stuffy hull of the boat to sleep, I spent the next half hour plus in the tiny bathroom having my insides horribly mashed. I barely made it to the control cabin before literally crashing onto the couch. I was cold but sweating, just miserable.

Kyle let us get a small snack before departing the Awab. It was a good thing because as soon as we finished eating, Silvia got home and mandated we get the backpacks out from under the tarp, gather our things, and head off the boat. Wow, Jake put his foul language to work as he took out his wet documents from his pack. We were all really displeased that Kyle let our packs get soaked through! Getting rid of us was 100% harder than losing the other passengers. Kyle and Silvia took dad and me along with Walter and Biddy to the grocery store/internet cafe, where we whittled away many hours.

Everyone went inside, and I was left to wait with the two dogs. The street was busy with donkeys and carts, fruit vendors (or shall I say yellers), taxis, and bicycles. The sights and sounds soon grew old as the hours lagged on. My sickness was resurfacing, and I doubtfully gazed at the bushes and just tried to keep my stomach under control. Occasionally a street dog would pass by, sending biddy into uncontrollable fits of rage. As I tried to brace myself against her tugging on the leash, many people found the situation quite entertaining. I gathered by the many people with raincoats or ripped garbage bags that this unrelenting rain was far from unusual. Finally, Kyle came out and said I needed to go with him to get our backpacks, Mom, and Kacie.

I took a few steps as if to go with him when the simple idea struck me, and even though it seemed quite childish, the phrase "never go with anybody I didn't tell you to go with seemed to ring in my ears." "Kyle," I yelled after his retreating figure. "Does dad know I'm going with you?" "It's what you need to do," he persisted. "Did dad tell you I could go?" "Just come along," he said. "I'm not leaving without dad telling me to do so," I retorted. "Whatever," Kyle said, his answers thick with irritation. He disappeared down the street. So I stood there waiting to see one of my family and ignored this older man who kept saying things to me in Spanish.

Finally, I picked out two and then three people out of the crowd who were not even close to blending. Mom, Kacie, and Kyle all loaded down with our backpacks. When mom saw me, her face just lit up with a mix of joy and relief. Mom is just the best! About an hour later, we made an appointment with Manfred for the dogs at 3:00 on the pier. We loaded ourselves down with dog dishes, dog food, Kacie's 5 lb doll, the two dogs, and our four soaking wet packs. They weighed in at close to 45 lbs because they were saturated in water. So with some vague directions to try and find a hostel, we set out. We figured we had found the right place when about every other establishment was a lodging place of some kind.

We saw many street scenes throughout the day, but the most interesting was a man stripping the paint off a bed frame with a bladed machete. After asking around and around for a place to let us stay with our dogs, we finally found one. Our clock was an hour off, so we were way late on our appointment for the dog's visas, and Manfred had already left. However, we met some nice boat taxi drivers who talked to us. That was a bright spot in our day. We got to give a homeless man an orange on the way home. That was pretty neat! Enjoy the Browning things from the grocery store. When we got home, we had hardly eaten all day. Guess who we saw across the street? Blake and Jake! Lucky for dad, his cries of "down with the Irish" weren't heard. Kacie thought it would be funny should they end up in the two empty bunks in our own room. Imagine the disappointment.

Took the dogs out for a walk after dark. I was grateful to have a fully armed military soldier on either side of us with the many shady characters in the streets. We talked to them, and they seemed quite friendly. The nightlife around here is at least twice as happening as the day. Unfortunately for us, we are right on top of a bar that is playing the strangest music. It's past 10:00, and they're still strong into it. A poor homeless lady is sleeping on the stairs across the street. When a bus road passed us earlier, they all started yelling gringos and taking pictures! Taking a shower was pure bliss. May God keep our spiritual growth unquenchable. Praise Him for the little things. Good night. Someone stole $20 US dollars from my wallet that I had hidden to no avail! What a disappointment.

Kindra's Journal   10/07/2010

What a day! We left our room at 8:15 and proceeded to wait outside the Carulla grocery and internet store for 7 hours. Almost all for nothing due to Manfred's snails' pace progression for what avail I do not know! The sights were nearly the same as yesterday, aside from the few fj40s that cruised by and a donkey pulling a cart full of hardware and tools. The continuous obnoxious songs of the fruit vendors and the apathetic stares of the city people walking by made the wait seemingly drag on forever. It was frustrating that the appointment we made with Manfred at 9:00 didn't even start until 10:30. Payback, I guessed, for our accidental hour-long delay yesterday. Or maybe because Manfred was just too busy.

Dad dealt well with the whole ordeal. I even witnessed dad sincerely smiling very amusingly at Manfred as he droned on in his depressingly slow tone of voice. He wasn't getting the paperwork done but perhaps telling one of his off-the-wall stories. I finally got to set foot inside around 1:00. I didn't hang around to listen but quickly seized the opportunity to email friends and family. I headed back outside to take another shift with the dogs. Dad and Kacie went to find something for lunch and came back with two fruit granola and yogurt press containers to share. It was buffet-style, and poor dad misread the sign that said 5,000 Colombianos per pound and thought the price was per container. Oh well, "why not round up instead of down?" said dad. That's just life.

Finally, around 3:30, Manfred shuffled out to the taxi with dad and left for the customs office. Let me describe Manfred: past middle age, yellow hair, medium height, but what he lacks in height, he makes up for it in roundness. He wears a giant waist fanny pack around his middle under a shirt adding to the whole effect. His eyes and hair make it look as if he has not slept for a week. He talks with every breath sounding like his last, and his almost constant consumption of cigarettes doesn't help, poor man. As soon as dad and Manfred left, we girls set off with the dogs for our hostel at a very brisk walk.

By the time we arrived, we had worked up quite a sweat as it was hot and humid outside. We got our clean clothes from the manager, and after I sorted them, I went to take a shower. When I went to put on my clean clothes, imagine my disappointment to find my favorite tan blouse shrunk and bleached a distasteful peach color! All of a sudden, the Latino's fascination and obsession with laundry irritated me. You should never bleach a tan shirt! I couldn't stand the peach top with a brown skirt combination, so I decided to put my second favorite outfit on. As I slipped the linen shirt over my head, I realized it, too, had shrunk. The hours spent sitting at my beloved treadle machine working on the shirts quickly came back to mind as I contemplated where I may be able to buy some more matching cloth!

Well, I couldn't do anything about my most used and loved clothes being messed up, so I set my mind to pray for dad along with mom and Kacie because he still wasn't home at 6:00. He got home shortly after and had quite the runaround adventure that could be summed up in one phrase, "typical third world." Dad's heart sank as they told him there was no record of our container arriving in Cartagena and was possibly on a ship heading for America. The real scare came when they told dad it wouldn't arrive back in Cartagena until November 14th. After some searching, they realized our vehicle was indeed there, what a relief!

Met up with Klaus and his group at the pizza shop across the street. He told us all about his experience with his crew and ship. They had had such a great time at sea that they are all still together! Saw Blake and Jake again. The military men have disappeared from our corner, but God will protect us. Sometimes I feel really scared that we won't make it to Bolivia. alive, but then I feel bad because God has brought us through so many trials. Why would I doubt him now? Here I sit in the most partying town imaginable, music blasting from the bar below and floating up over the little balcony overhanging the busy street.

I can reflect on how God has really cared for us and brought us through both the happy and the terrifying times of our trip. I know he is with us. Sounds like tomorrow is going to be busy, so I better catch some sleep while I can. Most of my day was spent at the grocery store waiting with the dogs, feeling still on the verge of seasickness and accompanied by a terrible headache. I almost fell over while trying to walk this morning due to the continued boat moving illusions. Manfred's best quote of the day was, "Awab is a nice boat, but Kyle is not a captain."

Kindra's Journal   10/08/2010

Rainy

Last night was crazy outside, but we managed to get some sleep. The hour at 5:30 rolled around way too quick. Dad got up and prepared to catch a taxi to get the vehicle to a 7:00 a.m. inspection. I laid there in amazement that the world produces such hard and heavy pillows as these. The task of us girls trying to find insurance seemed to loom before me. But time marches on, and we found ourselves marching with purpose towards the building that Dad told us to find. I knew it was not the right building as I stood there looking at the flashing casino sign and the vendors and vehicles littered around. We decided this must not be the place after all.

We ended up asking a half dozen people who kept pointing us to the following bank. We worked hard escaping dog fights and dodging vendors and rain puddles along our route. We finally ended up across from the supposed correct building, only to be chased off by a man asking for money with his mangy street dog. This caused severe problems with Biddy trying to attack it. The whole situation was really frustrating. Feeling defeated, we walked back to our hostel through the park, where we got to see an iguana about 3 ft long. That was pretty neat! We bought a few pieces of sweet bread for breakfast but then felt quite ashamed of our 0% success rate. We set out to try again. To make a long story short, a very helpful man showed us the way through a dirty dark alley.

Kacie and I waited for mom, who rode up a crowded elevator, only to be told we didn't have the proper document! At least we tried, and we brought some information back to the hostel. Dad arrived with a similarly depressing story of wrong papers and typical third-world governmental operations. We went down the street to get lunch, something uncommon. We usually only buy one meal a day. Perhaps we'll skip supper? I loathe all this waiting around, and the noise of the city is just terrible. Dad caught a ride with Klaus to the port with Michael, a man from Klaus's boat, and we girls were left to wait till he returned at 7:00. We were so worried about him that we knelt to pray for an hour until his return.

A man on the street was waving to us and later came up to our room for money. We hid our valuables, then crammed in the vehicle and wound down some side street so skinny that it took multiple maneuvers to turn a corner. We found a guarded parking lot thanks to our friend David Lopez. As we were standing in the parking lot waiting to pay, there was Klauss. We were all overjoyed to see him again! We went next door to his hotel room and visited while he and dad returned the other traveler's shoes they had traded at the port so dad could get the vehicle. Apparently, regular shoes are not up to spec here.

He took us to a little restaurant down the street where we got supper. It was $2 for a bowl of soup and a scoop of rice. Some of the soups had chicken feet and fish heads in them, but they were good! When we went to the vehicle to get our dogs, the guard came up to us with eyes huge with excitement. He tried to show us his best example of peering into our windows and having Biddy go crazy. When we took our growling snapping dogs out of there, he sat down in his chair, clearly amazed by our dogs. We yelled "adios" then took the dogs to the little grass spot.

Contrary to my beliefs that Friday night would be way crazier than the rest, I found there to be less noise and fewer people. Don't get me wrong, though. It's still crazy! Well, tomorrow we leave, Lord willing, so I'm going to cool off with a shower and head to sleep. God answers our prayers in amazing ways. He brought dad home and protected us on the street. Praise him! We did some map research and wrote down highway names. Good night.

Kindra's Journal   10/09/2010

Woke up, packed, and we're on our way to the airport to get the dog's papers by 8:45. We were so happy to be leaving that mom even waved to a few people as we left. Blake and Jake we're so drunk this morning! They were at the hostel next to us, and we're barely able to keep their eyes open. They kept leaning way over the railing but were happy to have some fellow backpacking women to get drunk with. Poor things. When they are old, they will not be satisfied unless they find the one true reason worth living for! This morning as we were packing up, we gave out three tracks. I realized this afternoon that I may have been more motivated to empty our track supplies a little rather than rescue souls. I was so ashamed of myself. Praying for the right attitude. Also, there are only 54 blank pages in this journal, and I am a little worried our trip won't all fit. That is if we even make it in 54 days!

We followed a taxi to the airport, where we waited for 20 minutes to talk to the man who was supposed to approve the dog papers. He was very rude and unprofessionally told us he would not help us and that we weren't even at the correct place. We later learned he was right. So we left and decided to head back to our hostel. With a feeling of defeat, we rented our room for another night. Mom called Manfred to figure out what to do. I again checked our email for a letter from Jeremiah Garcia but didn't find one. About 10 minutes later, Manfred had it all worked out. He gave us a man's name to tell the airport worker, and we found ourselves heading back to the airport. Dad marched triumphantly with expectation up to the office door.

As we entered, the man almost immediately reached for our papers and started to get the process in motion. As he told us how great his work was and how good everything was, his hand began to slowly reach for the necessary papers. It was all we could do to keep from laughing. A slight glitch came when he read on the paperwork that Biddy was a pit bull. He pulled out the law book stating pit bulls cannot enter the country. We assured him she was a terrier which is true, and with a look of skepticism, continued to fill out the paperwork. He asked us some questions about them having operations, and we looked confused. He picked up the picture of our dogs to pretend to inspect them as if they were the dogs themselves. We all started laughing.

From that point on, he seemed slightly more good-natured as he proceeded to stamp our documents with barely visible stamps and multiple of the same for each piece. He followed that by writing up a receipt. Actually, six of them. He seemed quite caught up in the whole ordeal as he slammed his stamp down repeatedly for a total of 12 furious bangs. Papers began to fly into various piles, "yours, mine, yours, mine," until they were all separated to his satisfaction. Finally, we paid him, and he enthusiastically stapled The fragile money to his receipt. We thanked him, and we're on our way. By the time we got home, it was past 12:00, and we hadn't eaten all day aside from a piece of chocolate.

Dad seemed intent on finding a cheaper place to eat, so we walked around for a while. I still don't quite know what he was looking for as we ended up almost next door. I got two quesadillas and a half for $2.50 USD. From there, we set off for a long walk. We walked up on the old city walls that went down into the water, and we saw an iguana leap all the way down! Then we bought some dog wormer at a pet store, a hat for mom, and a cocoa frio for dad and Kacie.

We walked to the center of town and saw replicas of old Spanish sailing ships, then under some massive arches where we went on a map hunt. We ran into a kind English-speaking man named Kyle, who led us to a bookstore where we were able to buy one. We saw two horses pulling carriages and were impressed that the one didn't have a bridle on. Barely escaped several dog fights. Saw a few monkeys and cute bull terriers. Came home, rested, and then went out around 7:00 to do the same frustrating food-finding run around as before, only to end up next door again. It's such a poor diet with no not many veggies and definitely not cheap either. Bolivia seems so far away. Will we get there by December?

Kindra's Journal   10/10/2010

Last night was terrible! The music blared on, and I finally got up around 2:00 a.m. I went to the bathroom and took a cold shower, then watched the immorality and drinking outside for a few minutes. It was hot, so hot! The music continued until 4:00 a.m. We woke up and discussed plans for about an hour. Where to go, at what pace, how can we live cheaper, and what to do today.

We finally decided to walk around in the old city for a while. We sat in the little plaza with the waterfalls for a while. Dad seemed quite frustrated with the price of things when he asked a man how much a coco frio cost. The man just started to get him a coco instead of answering. Dad thought this quite rude but paid a dollar anyways. We try to be as wise as we can with money. As expensive as the restaurants around our red-light district seem, we saw places in the old city for 10 times the price.

All that aside, the streets are beautiful, with lots of pink and purple flowers hanging off balconies down into the narrow streets. I really like the colors they paint the buildings. Orange with white, two contrasting greens, or white with brown. Sometimes when you're lucky enough to pass by one of the ornate doors that are open and look inside, you can see a beautiful courtyard. The courtyards usually contain a fountain, flowers, and beautiful woodwork around the house. We walked on top of and around the thick old wall and found its height and rough Gray color beautiful against the contrast of blue sky and green grass. The ocean in the background, the Colombian flag flapping next to the lookout tower, and cannons on the wall made it a perfect picture opportunity. Where's the camera when you need it?

We walked back by the ocean. It was fun having the huge wave smash into the rock break wall, creating a soft but forceful crash, then splashing up onto the sidewalk with all of their white foaming fury. I now know that the only way I enjoy waves is when my feet are on solid ground!

Eventually, we ended up back at the hostel, and while the rest snapped, I washed some of my clothes. I hope they dry quickly. Klauss came for a visit and told us about a community hangout spot in front of an over 500-year-old church, so we headed out to see it for ourselves. We ended up staying for the evening, visiting with Klauss, Michael, and strangers alike. Enjoyed some pizza for 2 million Columbianos (or 50 cents USD) a slice and had a lovely time just observing the whole situation. People of all ages hung around with friends and family. The little children were running around the middle of the plaza. Around 5:30, the church bell began to ring, and you could hear the priest droning on. We walked in to observe the scene. The architecture was amazing, but the people seemed to have little to no interest in the priest. A man outside the enormous doors practiced juggling, which was fun to watch. Around 7:30, we headed home. Hopefully, this was our last day here.

Kindra's Journal   10/11/2010

Woke up all to you soon since it was actually quiet last night. As soon as dad returned with the insurance papers around 10:00, we packed up and left for Jeremiah Garcias. True to his word, he was waiting on the edge of the city to welcome us. He hopped in the Land Cruiser to guide us the rest of the way. Barranquilla wasn't near as bad as I thought it would be. Although, I'm sure we were spared its less comely parts. We later walked the dogs through a nice neighborhood for South American standards.

We received a warm welcome from Jeremiah's wife, mother, sister, brother, and family. Enjoyed a relaxing afternoon of fellowship. Since they didn't have a place to park the Land Cruiser, we set out to find a place for it. It turns out plan c worked, and we have a safe place for our vehicle, I hope. Thanks to Jeremiah's English, we could discuss more spiritual things together. Still, I was grateful for the opportunity to visit with the rest of the ladies in Spanish, thus hoping to expand my vocabulary. We walked the dogs around the neighborhood and met a young man on the side of the road. He was reading his Bible, and his name was Milton. Milton told us about his conversion 7 months ago and sang us a song about God cleaning our hearts and making them strong. Very interesting. We spent the rest of our evening visiting and getting what we could out of the Bible study. From what I gathered, it was about repentance. We sang a few songs then headed our tired selves to bed, but not before taking a shower. It feels great to be on the road again, and I feel a renewed excitement about our trip. Giving out tracks today was an immense blessing when I did it with the proper perspective. Praise the Lord. I should make this journal more interesting than I am. So here: our beds have blue checkered sheets, haha!

Kindra's Journal   10/12/2010

Had a lovely day relaxing here with our friends. Went to the store this morning with Carrie, then spent the rest of the morning making dress and blouse patterns for Cynthia. Trying to explain how to make a dress to a novice sewer in Spanish was very difficult, and I kept the word book busy! Enjoyed helping out with the cooking. Under the scrutinizing eye of Karen, I may have sweated two times as much despite the hot kitchen. Their way of peeling potatoes was good but took a bit of getting used to. Another girl who is a believer stopped by. We had a great visit and then a little meeting where dad shared on letting Christ shine through us to be a light to the world. We also got to sing hymns!

This evening while sitting outside in the gated courtyard by the road, dad saw a donkey in the street and ran out to take his picture. Big mistake! He soon had a mob of five boys and men after him for money. Not being deterred, Jeremiah walked up next to where dad was, and they both, without a word, took off at a brisk pace down the road to the vehicle park parking lot. While they were gone, Cynthia finally persuaded the men to leave. Praise the Lord. Spent the rest of the night visiting and enjoyed deep doctrinal conversations with Jeremiah. A good day and the question still stands "why is the church like it is, and why are we all alone?"

Kindra's Journal   10/13/2010

Woke up and hurriedly packed our things into the land cruiser. After breakfast, we were on our way. We were delighted to have Jeremiah accompany us to show us the right road to take. We got pulled over by some transito officer pulled us over. It was apparent when we kept producing every necessary paper with ease that they became frustrated. Hoping to find something wrong with us, they started to tell us we needed more documents and possibly a front license plate.

Dad and Jeremiah insisted we had all of the necessary things, so after 20 minutes, they gave us back our papers and let us go. We said Thank you and gave them three tracks to divide among themselves. As we were about to pull away, they started to yell "Uno mas," one more. That was the kind of problem we like, and we were glad to hand them another. After about 45 minutes of driving, we dropped Jeremiah off and said goodbye. So many goodbyes on this trip that are difficult! While Jeremiah returned home on a bus, we continued towards Medellin. Since the passports were left in mom's backpack, we stopped to get them. We had so many opportunities to hand out tracks today that we surpassed our record.

Travel was fairly normal, and it was much nicer to be out of the city. We passed a few interesting scenes: A group of military men making sandbags to hold back water from a major flood that has driven hundreds of people from their farms and homes. Four or five goats strapped down live onto the roof rack of a jeep. Tons of donkeys and motorcycles with people just piled on, sometimes with up to four adults or a young couple with all their children. Around 11:00, we were coming up to a checkpoint with the all too familiar scene of military men with machine guns. One stepped out into the road and had us pulled off the road with the simple but mighty wave of the hand. We soon found ourselves outside of the vehicle, being watched by one man while another searched our vehicle. It is good not to have to worry about having something wrong in our possession. We had a good laugh with the army men when one of their fellow militants walked up to help search our vehicle and ran away as our dogs went crazy on him. They treated us very well and let us go, thanks to two more tracks.

We had a few hours of concern after we stopped at a gas station and realized we only had 52 dollars worth of Columbian currency and still needed more gas, a hotel room, and a little food. If you had seen the towns we were going through, it would need to be almost a miracle to find a bank, let alone an atm. As an answer to prayer, we ended up stopping at a little gas station that took visa cards. The very friendly man there told us where an ATM was. There was a nice hotel for the night behind that gas station. God answers all of our pleas of desperation!

While getting money in town, we were trying to decide to stay or continue when a nice English-speaking man came up to us. After asking a few questions about our trip, he told us there were no more hotels before the next town and not to even stop in the next town because it was so dangerous! Wow, had we continued, we'd be stuck in the mountains right about now! Praise the Lord for all his tender mercies. The gas station hotel was only $20. We ate supper at the adjoining restaurant and took the dogs for a walk. Enjoyed our first pony maltas, thanks to Fernando's recommendation back in Panama City. God is good!

Kindra's Journal   10/14/2010

Woke up early at 6:00, and we're on our way within an hour heading towards Medellin. It wasn't long till we were in the mountains, and we stopped around 9:00 in a speck of a town and a little restaurant for breakfast. As we sat at our table, a cat lounged in the chair next to us, and its kittens played around my feet. Military men in full attire ran hither and yon up the hill to their lookout and back down. Two military men came over to the store for their break time and to make a phone call. They appeared to be barely 17 years of age and very young. Seeing them buy some ice cream in a vain attempt to keep cool and walk back to the checkpoint with their machine gun slung across the shoulder was quite an amusing sight.

As always, wandering through the mountains was fabulous, but with the road gone in some places and hardly 200 ft of visibility through dense fog in others, it kept us constantly on the lookout. The views down either side of the ridge being either vast green mountains or thick clouds were, as "Captain Kyle" would say, "absolutely stunning." In many places, the roads were terrible. Full of potholes, huge rocks, and bumps. We came to a spot where three little boys were repairing the road with dirt and shovels in an attempt to evoke a peso over two out of travelers. Seeing the little boys leap triumphantly in the air was far worth a few pesos! Medellin was much nicer than expected. With the Lord's blessing upon us and mom's sense of direction, we managed to stay on the main highway through town without a problem.

As we neared the edge of town, we spotted a pet store and made a stop to buy more dog food and stop at an atm. All in all, Medellin was definitely one of the nicer cities we have passed through! I was so blessed to have God directly answer my prayers as all of the military and police who pulled us over were kind and merciful to us. Most of the time, they are just curious. It started to rain around 4:00, and as we drove on to the town of Santa Barbara, we hoped to find a hotel there.

As we pulled into the town around 5:00 with darkness fast approaching, we all sat in strained silence, looking down a side street with hopes of seeing a decent-looking hotel sign. No success was granted, and we all felt truly let down. All we saw were falling down brick buildings and a youth riding his bareback horse down the street swinging his shirt wildly around in the air above his head. Well, in the whole town, not a single stayable hotel could be found. We drove on into the fading light on the mountain roads.

The curves were so sharp at times that all the traffic in our lane would have to stop so a semi-truck could drive into our lane to make it around the curve. Not a flat stretch for a long time, then suddenly, there was a sign for cabanas. We swerved off the road and up the steep driveway.

We were thrilled to see the little establishment in good working order. Although we were not their usual clientele, they were happy to get us a cabin. So here we are in the very place I prayed for all day, happy and content. Having no door to the bathroom or handles on the sink was no big deal as we slept off a day of intense road time. Mom, Kacie, dad, and Biddy occupied the bed with Walter and me on the floor. Grateful to be in cooler weather again. God is so good! Tonight after dark, a horse trotted by out on the road. It made us all really miss our community back in Lobelville.

Kindra's Journal   10/15/2010

Last night was terrible, and I hardly slept at all. Background noises of Ryan brakes on the highway next to us, a perpetually screaming pig, mosquitoes constantly buzzing in my ears, and the unsoftened noise of dad sick in the bathroom without a door all blended together and kept me awake. Around

3:00 am, I finally grabbed some clothes off the floor to cover my face. That kept the mosquitoes from biting, which made a big difference. We were on the road by 7:00 am and soon found ourselves in a tight situation.

The semi in front of us and the semi coming up the other lane were stuck on a sharp curve with a dangerous drop-off. The one driver had to back up the hill while we waited. More terrible roads today, but we were rewarded by driving through some amazingly immaculate old mountain villages. My favorite town was Rio Sucio, where the narrow road wound around through the cute little buildings. As we climbed out of the little town, we could see all of the city with its little brick buildings down in the valley. The people weren't gangster-style like other towns, but rather friendly and kind.

In another spot on the road, we stopped and looked over to the cleared valleys, surrounded by steep mountain ridges. Many families had small houses and places to graze their cattle on all the green pasture. Later as we passed a town called Ansurma, we realized that we were on the wrong road and had been for a few hours. Maps are irritating down here! Thankfully mom made a quick plan and, still driving in the right direction, had us out on the main road in about 2 hours. It was slightly unnerving being out in the middle of nowhere on those red roads we see on the maps and try so very hard to avoid! Since dad was still feeling utterly sick to his stomach, we started to look for a hotel around 2:00.

We passed auto hotel after auto hotel, all the while driving towards the massive city of Cali. After passing through industrial towns and coming to Cali, we soon realized that we had no choice other than to drive through, thus smashing our plans for a short driving day. I gave dad a back massage to help his insanely sore neck and back feel better. With only a slight detour and some skillful driving, we found ourselves on the right road. Staying on that road was a whole different story. The road kept splitting, and almost all of the few highway signs we could find were covered up by overgrown trees and bushes. Praise the Lord that he guided us out of there and our search for a much-needed hotel continued till nearly 5:00.

We stopped at some little cabanas, where, in all their run-down junkiness, they couldn't even find a key to show us a room. When we asked how much it would be to camp in their mosquito-ridden plot, they quoted a grim to 20,000 pesos $70 usd. That made the decision easy, and we were soon on the road again, speeding along with dad holding his mirror on with one hand and driving with the other. When I asked the lady at the toll booth if there were any safe hotels nearby, she said she couldn't understand me even in my simple Spanish. No sympathy whatsoever. After resorting to charades with simple words "hotel," "for the night," "habitation," "dorm," it was clear that she just didn't want to help.

But, God answers prayers and within sight of that very toll booth was an open area with a gas station, hotel, mechanic, and restaurant. It was perfect. God had prepared a place as always. Without even knowing our intentions, the receptionist lady met us out in the parking lot, asking if we would like a room for the night. What a blessing and answer to prayer to have this little spot provided for us. In that big city of Cali, there were so many horses and carts trotting around. I really hope I can get another horse someday. We are thrilled with our little brick hotel room with two beds because it only costs 25 million pesos (14 USD). Dad is in the "woe is me" spirit of things tonight. We are all ready to be home.

Kindra's Journal   10/16/2010

Had an uneventful day of traveling on dirt roads. Traveled through the mountains in the am then found ourselves descending way down into a deserted desert valley where we drove for about 2 hours. The heat was the most impressive I've ever felt. The dry cracking ground, cactuses, and sparse shrubs only added to the effect along with hardly any houses to give the place an extra lonely feeling. As we drove back up into the mountains, we encountered the strangest area. It was the most barren land with some falling down houses. People frequently stood along the side of the road with their arms outstretched, trying to wave us down for a ride. Of course, we were full up and couldn't squeeze in any extra passengers, so we couldn't pick them up.

For the next 20 minutes, they were constantly along the road sitting under scrappy plastic roofs, waiting for a ride. Questions crossed our minds like where they would go, what they would do when they got there, or if they had a home to come back to. One young girl about 10 stood next to the road wrapped up in a thin white sheet for her only clothing. Old ladies stood there with their backs hunched over from years of hard labor. Everyone wanted to leave that place. One old man hobbled along the road crooked on his crutches that were too short. What is our responsibility? How can we really make a difference to them? What can we do?

We traveled back up to the mountain town of Pasto, where at 9,000 ft of elevation, it's so cold people have on scarves and stocking caps! Walter and Biddy got quite the workout sliding across the platform around every steep mountain curve. Around 3:00, and after much ado trying to convince some paramedics to let us camp in their lot, we decided to turn around and drive back over the military guarded bridge and go to the gas station hotel. It turned out to be really nice, and dad was thrilled to pay $11.50 USD for it. It has no hot shower toilet seat or bathroom door, but we're all happy to be off the road! The beds even have some blankets. It's freezing up here.

We got a very warm welcome from the station owners. We gave our last two Good and Evil books to the two young men who live close by. The hill across from the gas station had one of those curious little mountain trails that wind up and up that we often pass by and wonder about. We ceased the opportunity and found the track up the steep rocky zig-zagging mountain path. Very rewarding. On our way up, we passed a very friendly old man watering his garden. When we reached the top, the view of the mountains around us was spectacular!

The many small fields with different crops made a neat patchwork effect, and the blue sky was full of the most perfect white clouds.

We met a lady on the trail who talked with us for a while about our trip. She ended our conversation in Spanish by saying, "for the Christian, God is with them always." Praise the Lord for the blessings he always sends our way. Got pulled over three times today. First, in the morning, by a very smiley young military man who didn't even really look at our documents. The second was a pair of very interesting native cops who did check our papers without many extra words. The third stopped us right before a toll stop and were the typical very nice Colombian military. Still, no internet to send emails to family and friends. I'm sure Cindy is about to send out a search party for us by now. It was a very good day. Tomorrow we will enter Ecuador.

Trip Summary by Kristi VanderZon   Colombia

Hello Family and Friends,

Upon arriving in Columbia and leaving the sailboat behind us, we were given instructions where we might find a hostel. We set off on foot, with all our gear, for a 15 -20 minute walk into the old city of Cartagena. Cartagena has a modern part and an old part. An ancient stone wall surrounds the old part of the city, from back in the early days of defending it from invaders. We made our way down narrow streets, and after four stops at different hostels, we finally found one that would take us with our dogs. We have a room on the second floor, with a balcony facing out to the street. It is the noisiest, most chaotic city we have been in yet!

Today when we were walking around, a helicopter kept flying over. Ambulances and police go by frequently. Horn honking and loudness are all around. There is a strong military and police presence in the city, so it feels pretty safe, even with all the chaos. There are many backpackers here, but no one like us.

When we walked back from the dock today, a city bus went by with lots of people hanging out the window. A few people had their cameras out taking pictures of us as they yelled "gringos". I guess they find us fascinating, with our dresses and head coverings. We're really different from the backpackers they're used to seeing. As it got later, the street scene below keeps getting wilder. There's loud music coming from a bar/ nightclub below us. Lots of traffic and people. Some of the places we find ourselves are so ironic.

David on our balcony overlooking the street.

Our hostel at night. It's on the second story, with the balcony.

We woke up early, after a wild night of noise and activity on the street below. It must have gone on until 3 am. It is evidently party central where we are at. But, praise God, we are in a comfortable room, and all is well. It rained heavily last night and stormed. This morning some of the streets were flooded. The internet was down, so I had to wait until the afternoon to get all of our mail sent out to you.

We're learning that mistakes are costly. Yesterday, we had an appointment to meet the animal inspector back on the boat at 3 pm. Our computer clock was ahead an hour, so we got to the boat dock one hour late, and the inspector was already gone. We were told to meet our customs agent at 9 am this morning, and we would get it all worked out. Our customs agent is a big man named Manfred who is extremely slow. He talks slowly, moves slowly, and watching him remove staples from our papers today was excruciatingly slow. He speaks English but is from Germany. He tells more stories than helpful information. Most of the time, we have no answers or idea of what is happening with our paperwork. It would have been much easier if we would have shown up on time yesterday, but we're trying to forgive ourselves. At 3 pm, we had to split up (I hate doing that).

When we got back, our hostess had our laundry washed and ready for us. We were grateful for this service, although it ended up costing about 5 times as much as doing it ourselves. But, all our clothes were wet from the boat, or dirty, and with being gone all day, I'll have to say it was worth it.

Now, for a little recap of David's afternoon with Manfred. They took a taxi to the Port of Colombia office, where there was a problem locating our vehicle. After looking at our papers and staring at the computer screen, the official told David that the shipping container never arrived in Cartagena. A moment of disbelief hung in the air as he went on to say that they have no idea where it is. A long silence followed, and even Manfred had nothing to say. Several phone calls later, and at one point, with one phone in each ear, the official was pleased to announce, "Mr. VanderZon, your vehicle is here in the port." What welcome words! You never know what is going to happen next here. Manfred and David continued on their way, making about four different stops. With a list from Manfred of what needs to be done tomorrow, David arrived back at our hostel. He received a very enthusiastic greeting from us girls, as it was a little past 6 pm and getting dark. We had been praying everything was all right and that he would get home safe. God is good!

David & I ventured out to get a pizza across the street. We ran into a group who had arrived in Cartagena this morning. After sailing from Panama. We were exchanging stories, and one man said to me, "What are you driving?" I said, "An '84 Land Cruiser FJ60". "What Color?" I said "Blue." "Does it have a big box on the top?" I said, "Yeah, and covered with a yellow tarp." He said, "I'll show you a picture of it." He got out his phone and, sure enough, had a picture of our Land Cruiser on it, at the port. I was so thankful to see the proof that our vehicle was indeed here at the port and not on its way back to the US! Also with this group was Klaus, the man from Germany with whom we shared the container. He had spent time at the Port of Colon in Panama with David & Kindra.

We're tired out tonight. But it seems the city is just coming to life. It's amazing how loud it is out there. In the middle of it all, sometimes you see a donkey & cart, and tonight a horse and buggy came down the road. It made us just a little homesick for the beauty and quietness of our community in Tennessee that we left behind. Well, as a good brother prayed for us the day we left, "May the Lord guide you like a cloud by day, and a pillar of fire by night." We are confident that he has and will continue to!

David brought the vehicle back to our hostel. It was great to have it back, on land, in South America. We parked it in a guarded parking lot last night, just around the corner from where we are staying. Right now, we are packing it up and getting ready to leave. We have one stop to make on the way out of town, at the airport, to get the dog's official papers. Then we may go to Barranquilla or Bogota, depending on what we decide at the last minute. Please pray for clear direction for us as we make this decision.

Here's a picture looking down on the load. It feels good to be all packed up again!

We are packing up & preparing to leave Cartagena and travel to Barranquilla to stay with a brother who's expecting us. It's about a 2 ½ hour drive, so it should be an easy day. Barranquilla is a coastal city northeast of Cartagena. David is going to meet a couple of friends to get insurance on the vehicle, so we'll be all legal to drive the roads here. After that, we should be all set to leave.

Klaus, in the red shirt, is the man who shared our container. He is from Germany and is driving a white Toyota van. Michael, the other man, was on Klaus's boat, sailing from Panama to Colon. We met Michael while waiting at the supermarket for our papers. He's driving a motorcycle from Oregon to Argentina, where he's originally from.

Staying here a couple extra days proved to be a good thing. We walked all over the old city and relaxed. Last night, we walked through some side streets and ended up at a plaza outside an old catholic church, where the locals gather to socialize at night.

We got there early enough to see it fill up and come alive. Children were playing, and a man was juggling. There were lots of families and people. Vendors were selling multiple choices of food & drink, and we enjoyed sampling a variety of tastes. The people were amicable, and we were approached by many wanting to know about the dogs. Many children wanted to pet them. The local "plaza" dogs were not thrilled to have these new intruders on their turf. Still, the people seemed to enjoy chasing them off, as well as seeing the occasional rise it got out of Biddy.

A Typical street in Old Town

Girls & I in the "old town."

Our last night here was quiet and peaceful, as the bar below us was closed on account of it being Sunday. We feel well-rested and ready to move on.

We had a wonderful time of fellowship here in Barranquilla with Jeremiah Garcia and his wife, Cynthia. We stayed at Jeremiah's mother's house. We enjoyed getting to know her and his sister, brother & family, who also live here. We were fed extremely well. Senora Jannine, Jeremiah's mother, enjoys cooking and sets the table with no less than a feast at every meal.

Enjoying one of Jannine's Colombian meals

We had good fellowship and spent time reading scripture and sharing songs we know. This is a small group of believers living out the New Testament doctrines in Barranquilla. We were encouraged by their love for one another, the joy they share, and the gracious hospitality they showed us. We are so glad we decided to stop in and visit. All praise goes to God for making a way to meet these brothers & sisters in the Lord.

We departed Barranquilla this morning, after one more delicious meal by Senora Jannine. Jeremiah rode with us in the Land Cruiser to see us out of town. We were almost out when the traffic police pulled us over. We had every document they requested, but they still weren't satisfied. They were trying very hard to come up with some violation to intimidate us with. Jeremiah calmly told them repeatedly that we had everything we needed. David was confident if we were patient, they would give up and let us go. And that is what happened. They suddenly tired of the nonproductive stop and handed back our papers and said we could go.

209

New country, new continent, same games. They were good sports, and shook our hands, and wished us a good trip. We handed them all a "La Antorcha" gospel booklet, which they gladly received. Jeremiah rode with us a little further, then we said goodbye, and he took a bus back to the city. We truly appreciated our time with Jeremiah and his family.

A donkey with a fruit cart

A cleaner and his push cart

As we drove on and the landscape changed from city to country, our excitement grew to be back on the road again. It's been 23 days since we arrived in Panama City and started the paperwork to ship the vehicle and ourselves to Colombia. The realization that we have actually made it to Colombia and are driving in South America made us feel triumphant.

Our old favorites began to appear in the scenery again. The donkeys, the cowboys on horses, cows in the road, and the little villages. We had missed it. We saw flooded streets and homes, and our sympathies went to the people displaced. We were surprised to see four goats strapped to the top of a jeep. Never a dull moment. We had our first military stop where we all had to get out of the car while the soldier inspected it. The inspection was cut short when Biddy got startled and suddenly started barking crazily. He shut the door in a hurry, and that ended that inspection. They were in good humor, though, and laughed about it.

We all agree Colombia has had the hottest weather yet. We were thankful to find a nice hotel for the night in Caucasia, about 270 kilometers north of Medellin. Our room has an air conditioner, and we are finally cooling off.

The next day found us south of Medellin, outside the little town of Santa Barbara. We found some charming cabanas for the night, perched upon a hill, with a great view of the surrounding mountains.

David & I enjoying the view

Our Cabana

Being back in the mountains again makes for exciting driving. Very curvy roads with steep grades. It takes a lot of concentration for David to drive. A lot of passing goes on, in unbelievable spots, like curves and hills.

A sign that was frequently seen

Two semis passing on a blind curve

A tight curve to maneuver

The military has a strong presence here. This morning at a little mountain restaurant where we ate breakfast, Kacie spotted a soldier sitting on the ridge of a hill. I would have never noticed him. He was so well camouflaged. We noticed some of them look very young, maybe 16 years old? It was almost comical to see them walking around with an ice cream cone or lollipop in one hand and a gun in the other.

Kindra took some photos of the military.

We had another full day of driving. It was an exhausting day, especially for David, as he was up a lot the night before with a bad case of intestinal chaos. We're not sure the cause but felt sorry for him as he was tired and not feeling good all day. At one point, the road got very mountainous, with extreme curves, and there was hardly any other traffic on it. For the first time on this trip, I switched places with David and drove for a little while, so he could have a break.

I was enjoying the challenge of all the curves, and we were going very slow. There were hardly any other vehicles. When we switched back, I started studying the map and realized we were on the wrong road. The main route somehow had turned off without us catching it, and we were on a secondary road high in the mountains. It wasn't too big of a problem, though, thanks to a very detailed route book we had found in Cartagena. We ended up enjoying the alternative route, although it did cause a little stress and uncertainty at times. The scenery was stunning, and we saw some picturesque little villages.

Saving some energy and enjoying a free ride

A cool looking cowboy, ironically at a gas station with his horse

Later in the day, we drove through Cali. The route looked really simple on the map, but the critical signs were covered up by trees when we got into town, and the road kept splitting. So many options, so little time to decide. David did good, keeping the vehicle moving, and we were amazed when we ended up on the right road out of town. Praise the Lord! After that, we were ready to find a hotel. It was just starting to get dark when the perfect one appeared right by a gas station and a little restaurant. The only thing it's missing is the internet, so I can send this out to you. Kindra and David spent some time studying the route for tomorrow. We've got our sights set on Ecuador.

I thought we had been traveling through mountains, but I realized today they were only big hills, at least compared to what we drove through later. Until now, we were traveling from town to town, on a pretty nice highway. Today, the towns started getting sparse, and we found ourselves driving through a desert region of Colombia. There was a long stretch of a couple hours without any towns or houses. The scenery was a nice change. We were seeing giant cactuses and vast expanses of land.

Some cacti from the desert stretch

Then the road started climbing up. We went through a stretch of "forgotten" people. The few houses we saw were crumbled and broken down. It looked like no one was living in them. But all along the side of the road were people with their hands out, wanting a ride. They all looked pathetically poor and hardened by dire circumstances. One girl was wrapped only in a sheet. A man hobbled along on crutches. It was bizarre. We wondered where they came from? How far had they walked to get here? And where did they all want to go? We figured they wanted to be anywhere but there.

Some of the "forgotten" peoples

As we climbed higher into the mountains, it became beautiful again. Grander than anything we've seen yet. We went through a couple of tunnels through the mountain and over some pretty high bridges. It got colder too. We noticed people had on ponchos and hats. We found a nice little room for $11, the cheapest hotel room yet and only an hour away from the Ecuador border.

One of the many tunnels we drove through

Biddy enjoying some breeze

Walter snoozing away on our pillows

Across the road, a trail disappeared up the hillside, so we decided to take the dogs up it for a walk. It was a very steep trail, and as we walked along, we saw a man out watering his crops. A little further on, we met a lovely woman coming down the trail and talked with her for a while. We walked on and came across a couple of charming homes. The view was beautiful, and we were amazed at what we came across on those little trails that we always wonder about. They went on and on. We walked back to our hotel and ate at the little restaurant there. The owner was thrilled to serve us a delicious Colombian meal of fish, rice, beans, salad, potato, soup, and fried banana. It was a good conclusion for what should be our last night in Colombia.

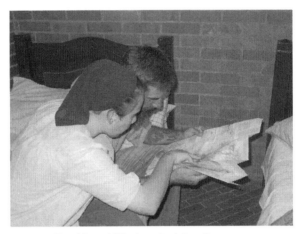

David and Kindra studying the map

A few reflections of our time in Colombia:

The military/police are very friendly. When pulled over at a checkpoint, they always shake David's hand and ask how we're doing. They rarely check our paperwork and seem to just be interested in where we're coming from and where we're going. Did we bring those dogs all the way from the US, or did we get them in Colombia? We get pulled over about 3-4 times a day.

The gas prices here are the highest yet on the trip, at $4.65 a gallon.

We can't get a good cup of coffee here, ironic for being in Juan Valdez's backyard. If you can find a cup, it's very tiny, but we haven't had coffee for 3 days now.

Motorcycles are everywhere down here. They definitely outnumber other vehicles on the road.

Internet Cafes—Where did they go? We can't seem to find one to plug into.

Love,

Kristi for the vanderZons

CHAPTER 11

ECUADOR

Kindra's Journal   10/17/2010

Took our time getting going this morning and took a walk up some mountain trail, the same one as yesterday. We got an excellent opportunity to see a young man riding his horse past us and up the steep mountain trail that we had been walking on. Said goodbye to señor Jorge and our new friends, then headed for the Ecuadorian border.

On our way back out across the heavily guarded military bridge, dad yelled "Buenos dias" to one of the young, heavily armed men. They all seemed really excited about that. Many of them can't be much older than me. After stopping in a little town close to the border, we finally downloaded some long-awaited emails. We proceeded on to the border town of Ipiales, where a policia was kind enough to show us the right road on his motorcycle. That cleared up all confusion as to how exactly to get to the border. It was the easiest border crossing yet, at only 1 hour and 45 minutes.

We didn't have to pay a thing to get out or in, and there was not a single glitch in the paperwork. The most entertaining person at the border was the Aduana man. He was super old and apathetic to our situation. After a pathetically slow walk out to the Land Cruiser for inspection, he warmed up to us. He painstakingly put in the correct info into his computer with seemingly increasingly slowness. At one point, we even found him watching the television in the corner of the room. But despite all that, he was very nice and sent us on our way with supposedly the right piece of paper. A fantastic border crossing, and we were not even bombarded with the usual helpers.

Ecuador is beautiful, and everyone seems friendly. Many gardens on the expansive hillside make quite a spectacle, and the temperature is wonderful. It must be mid to upper 60's and definitely sweater weather. We are glad to see more indigenous cultures once again. The natives are distinctly dressed in ponchos of wool with little black hats perched on their heads. The women usually have on a skirt with a wrap-around belt over the top. Around 4:00, we saw a sign for Cayambe Coca resort and got all excited about reliving our Atitlan, Guatemala camping experience. Our hopes were soon dashed into pieces as we turned off the main road. The direction that the big sign had pointed to only came to a tee in the road without a sign. How strange. After about half an hour of people sending us from one end of town to the other, we gave up all efforts and headed back down the main road.

Praise the Lord, he protected us and provided us with a lovely Cabana for the night, owned by a nice man named Tomas. He lived in Miami for 2 years, and we enjoyed talking to him in English. We took the dogs for a nice walk through the fields close by. I beat Kacie in a race back to the house, which of course, she was in denial of. Haha! We enjoyed a lovely meal in the adjoining restaurant. It was a nice change from the same somewhat mundane, typical Colombian food of beans, rice, meat, salad, soup, and potato.

It's hard to believe we are less than an hour from the Ecuador border tonight. We have only one country left between us and Bolivia. Fortunately for us, this place has a hot shower that we are all taking advantage of. First one in 2 weeks! We all really enjoyed reading the emails from everyone tonight. Got to go. I, too, want to get a shower while there is water in the tank. God is so good to us every single day.

Kindra's Journal   10/18/2010

Saw a man driving just the frame of a rusty old truck down the road today. Took the dogs for a walk. After we packed up the vehicle, we talked with a man named Bolivar Morales, who also spent the night there. Went into town and stopped at one of the many cafes that sold the bizcochos cookies that this town is famous for. They were delicious. They are about 5 inches long and thin. You eat them with fresh cheese and hot chocolate.

We bought some organic coffee from the lady next door, and she told us about two British men who had a big organic farm about 15 minutes down the road. After asking the gas station man for la Finca Organica, we took off down a side road and had no problem finding it. Wow! A nice young man gave us a tour of the place. We only understood very little. It was great to see the companion planting, good bugs, compost, lovely old buildings, fields of tall alfalfa white concrete buildings, lots of guinea pigs, rabbits, cows, and pigs with their old piglets. It got us really excited to get a farm going again! The whole place was beautiful.

From there, we got on the road to Quito, the capital, and had a great time stopping at the equator and taking all kinds of pictures. We managed to make it through Quito finally after an hour of driving around trying to figure out where in the world we are! Very frustrating. We stopped at a mall and bought a map. Traveled on through slummy city after polluted and abandoned town with their perverse advertising and continual string of auto hotels. Dad got real bummed out on the whole trip when we got lost. He is disgusted that a country can have such inadequate navigation systems. Between the lack of maps and ridiculously poor signage, it can be discouraging. He felt obliged to find a free place to camp and had us on the lookout for any abandoned lot. So after stopping at an $80 hotel, we settled on a gas station.

We had our apprehensions about it not having 24-hour security but decided to go for it. We had earlier asked the toll station who referred us down the road a kilometer to the police use station who sent us back to the toll. Anyhow it was about six and time to get off the road, so being as inconspicuous as possible, we hurriedly put up our tent. It was starting to rain, and we had the rainfly on and tight and record time! Dad jokingly suggested we sabotage the fellow trucker's vehicle by taking off a spark plug wire and replacing it in the morning. He was worried they might try to kidnap us and haul us off in the back of his truck.

Oh well, God knows we are here and can protect us no matter what. I will be praying much throughout tonight. It will probably be a long one. Saw the snow-capped volcano and Cotopaxi national park.

Kindra's Journal   10/19/2010

Wow, we are still alive, but last night was so cold. Thanks to our sleeping bags, we slept surprisingly well despite the many trucks pulling in and out with their deafening backing sirens. Occasionally you would see semis pass by the tent from the truckers thinking around with their semis and their trucks with bald tires and in poor condition anyhow. We got picked up in a hurry, and we're on the road by 6:15. It was super cold, and we could see our breath as we pulled our tent stakes out, refilled water bottles, and fixed the mirror that is always on the edge of falling off. For those of us without socks, our toes were so cold. It isn't surprising since we were at almost 13,000 ft of altitude. We stopped in a little town and had breakfast on our way out of the mountains. It was $7 total for us to have juice, eggs, and a piece of bread. What a deal! After about 2 hours of traveling on a new and half-finished mountain road with lots of detours and unpaved sections of rough road, we were again down in the lowlands. It felt good to take off our sweaters and warm clothes.

We had to go through several large cities today. Often, as we're approaching cities, someone mentions how the city looks really nice. I now know that not a single one has turned out that way. But, as we approached the city, the nice buildings turn out to be abandoned with busted-out windows. But that's okay. Much of today was spent trying to follow the terribly flawed signs to our destination. Sometimes you actually have to go past the supposedly correct road and find a turn-around to come at it from the opposite direction to read the signs. The whole sign and map thing is frustrating and completely ridiculous.

The rest of the day was a slum of travel as we drove on and on through the heavy highway exhaust and passing through deserted city after trashy town. Lots of terribly poor houses and unhappy people. They were not happy to even sell you some yogurt. Around 3:00, we neared the border town and did not find any places that were even close to suitable for spending the night! We knew we were getting super close to the border as police checkpoints increased along with a $15 fuel limit complete with military personel right at the pump to enforce the rule.

We stopped at Aduana to cancel the vehicle. Dad had stomach problems again, so he was intent on finding a bathroom. The bathrooms were locked, and convincing a military man to find the man who had the key to open the bathrooms took so long. It made dad quite nervous. Finally, a man hobbled up with the key, and our problem was solved. We drove on into Huaquillas, the major city on the border town. We drove until finally, as we slowly bumped over a tope, a hotel came into view. The sign was painted and advertised hot water, comfort, internet, and a garage. We got all excited as we read the word garage, and we're soon pulled through the gate into the courtyard. It cost $32, and we all got a bed. We washed the thick coating of mud off the Land Cruiser, which was fun, and we're surprised to see our European fellow travelers on the motorcycles roll in. Travelers think alike, I guess.

Walked the dogs to an empty lot. Days have been long, and it's good family time, especially when dad is in his funny moods. The continual straining of my eyes to see the microscopic towns on the map, watching with all ferver for the passing signs, and working together with mom to make that split-second decision is wearing on me. But the most miraculous part of the day, to me, after praying all day that the Lord will prepare a place for us, is always ending up at a place that's a blessing. Whether a gas station or private cabana. We always find a place, but I'll enjoy a home so much. Even though the hot shower and AC didn't work, it was still nice to be inside real walls for the night. Repaired the holes in my shirt and skirt and made up riddles to keep Kacie entertained.

Trip Summary by Kristi VanderZon   Ecuador

Dear Family & Friends,

We crossed the border into Ecuador. It was the most straightforward border crossing yet, and totally free.

Coming into Ecuador.

We had a good day traveling. Right away, we realized this is the best country to be driving a gas hog through. Gas was only $1.46 a gallon, the cheapest we've seen yet. The scenery was beautiful, and the roads were in good shape.

We stopped for the day at some rustic little cabanas about 20 minutes away from the equator. It's cold here, and we dug out our wool coats tonight. We had a triumphant moment when we arrived at the equator, called *Mitad del Mundo* (Middle of the World). Just for fun, we pulled in and took pictures to remember the significant moment we crossed from the Northern Hemisphere into the Southern.

At the equator monument

Kindra & Kacie in different hemispheres

We stopped at a coffee shop and found some excellent organic Ecuadorian coffee, nice and robust. We chatted with the owner for a while and shared our appreciation for all things organic. She suggested we might like to visit a local organic farm she purchases from. We thought this sounded like an exciting prospect. We followed her directions and found the farm. A worker was happy to walk us around and show us all the vegetables growing. However, what we found more interesting was the "*Cuy*" barn. *Cuy* is the Spanish word for guinea pigs, and they're a popular cuisine in the local restaurants here.

Freshly fed *cuy*

This was a self-sustaining organic farm, and they have a profitable method of operation. Here, the worker is feeding the guineas alfalfa hay. In turn, he uses their manure to add to the garden compost pile and uses the cuy for food. In addition, the farm had milking cows and a pig that had just had two piglets. We enjoyed our tour of the farm. It inspired us to get back to tilling up the ground ourselves and having our own farm again in Bolivia.

Later in the day, we saw a bicyclist obviously packed for a long journey. We slowed down so I could ask him where he was from. "Argentina," he replied. But he started his trip in Alaska. Wow! We told him we were headed to Bolivia, and he yelled back, "You're almost there!" We laughed at first, but it was a big encouragement to hear those words from someone. "Almost there"... I guess it's perspective as we still have a long way to go, but we feel like it's getting closer.

Bicycling from Alaska to Argentina

We couldn't find a hotel, and it was getting dark, so we decided to camp at a gas station. It worked out really well. It was fairly quiet all night, and it was free!

Camping last night

Later that afternoon, we faced the challenge of driving through Quito. Our map situation has been lacking. We had one general map of South America, no GPS or compass. We decided just to try picking the right-looking roads. While we did avoid the "Centro" of Quito, we got spit out on the wrong side. It gobbled up a couple hours, getting straightened out and back on the right road. During this time, we saw a mall and went shopping for a map. We found an excellent road guide after searching through 3 different stores, which has been immensely helpful.

This morning, we started early and drove on towards our goal of the Peruvian border. The road started out beautiful, weaving through the mountains, and we enjoyed some spectacular scenery. Then we came across a detour, and when we got back on the main road, it was pretty rough going. Evidently, it's still under construction in many parts, and sometimes it was down to one lane. It got pretty rough, and some stretches were unpaved. Many times we had to question, "Was this still the main road?"

We made it to the town of Huaquillas, just minutes from the border of Peru. We found a nice hotel to stay at and officially passed the 6,000-mile marker of our trip today. In celebration, we gave the Land Cruiser its first bath of the journey. It had acquired a fair share of mud and grime.

We are excited to enter Peru, Country #10. Thank you for all your prayers!

Love,

Kristi, for the VanderZons

Chapter 12

Peru

Stayed up till almost midnight by myself researching Google Earth on how to travel through Lima. It seems like everyone else got up so early this morning. Nevertheless, I managed to pull myself out from under the warm blankets, get dressed and throw things in the correct backpack, so mom could finish emailing. We wanted to get to the border when it opened, and as we packed up the roof rack, we realized the motorcycle friends must have had the same idea as they, too, were packing up. The horror story we read turned out to not be even close to true in our case as we pulled up to a neat row of shipping containers that served as Aduana. Praise God. The traffic officer directed us to the immigration office, where we set off with confidence.

We were promptly sent back to the Aduana office from yesterday to get our passport stamped out of Ecuador. This is frustrating as we had tried to do this, and the officials told us they couldn't do it there. So we found ourselves a few miles back into Ecuador to convince the immigration office to stamp them. This took so unnecessarily long that even the security guys were going around asking, "what's up?" Whether we really had to go to a different office was highly debatable. Still, the man drove with us into town and pointed us in the right direction, and we had to wait and line. I suppose we haven't quite figured out the whole third-world way to wait in line since people usually end up cutting in front of us. The lady behind me obviously had it figured out as she had her chin almost resting on my shoulder and the whole time frequently hit my back with her passport. She left no room for cuts!

About 45 minutes passed before we finally got our passports back and successfully stamped. We had no problems with the vehicle, and after they had thoroughly coated our tires with pesticides, we were off. No big checkpoint or anything. It didn't take long to get to Tumbes, what I would describe as a manageable large town because the road went straight through it.

Since there were no pestering friends at the border, neither were their money changers, and we were left to find a bank. Thankfully some old men directed us to the plaza. With some incredible driving on dad's end, we ended up in the main square surrounded by banks. The people were very unfriendly. For example, we asked a moto-taxi where the Centro de Turismo was, and he thought for a minute and said he knew and to get in his taxi. Dad asked, "can't you just tell me?" No could do. It ends up if he would have pointed behind him less than 50 feet down the road was the place we were looking for. How frustrating! We eventually did find the site only to see they did not have any real road maps. The rudeness of people can really wear on you!

We traveled on and on, finally stopping at a little stand next to the ocean. We bought a few cakes and some wafers. I know it's unbalanced and unhealthy food, but you can't just walk up to a vendor and find carrot sticks, cucumbers, and tomatoes. When we walked down to the beach with the dogs, we saw lots of crabs and a huge dead seal. What a find.

From there, we got stopped twice. Once on the main road by a traffic officer, who, when he saw how we were dressed, was convinced we needed to go to the religious conference in Chiclayo, a town almost two days away. At the second stop, we were routed onto this detour that scooted us right through a checkpoint. Our vehicle was soon swarmed by people, young and old, as they peered in the windows. They patiently waited for their many questions to be answered. What kinds of dogs, where are you from, what religion, why, and where are you going. They were kind and let us go without a hassle. These *policia* don't seem to share quite the ridiculous paperwork addiction, as do their neighboring Central American cousins. We stopped around 3:30 at Sullana. After inquiring at a hostel and being rudely sent away, we chose its only hotel neighbor for the evening.

We spent a lot of time out with the dogs then ordered a few sandwiches. After not eating anything but cookies and bananas (yes, back to our road diet), we were severely hungry. When the waiter brought us less than tea saucer-sized wonder bread sandwiches, we tried not to laugh. Talked a lot about Bolivia.

Keeping Kacie busy on name riddles is a full-time job. God is good. We enjoyed seeing two policemen playing around with a few little children in town. Police seem to be some of the most decent people so far. Saw huge herds of Nubian-looking goats today. Very cute!

Kindra's Journal   10/21/2010

I packed up while mom and dad took the dogs out. We were on the road by 6:15 and soon made it to the big town of Piura, where, after turning off the road and following the signs to Chiclayo, we found ourselves utterly lost. We were starting to wander the streets as we saw no more signs for the city. After a chat with several people and feeling reasonably confident that all of their answers seemed similar, we set off. We're glad to find ourselves once again on the right track and headed for the desert.

We failed to find any place to buy food and continued through the desert with our stomachs on empty. The desert was exactly what I thought it would be. Vast, sandy, and flat. After two hours of driving on flat, straight roads, we emerged into a tony town and stopped for breakfast. By now, it was almost 10:30. As we drove through the town, a little boy pretended to point an imaginary gun at us. We all agreed it was disturbing. It was a bummer of a day and a long day too. Seeing so many abandoned, poor, and stinky towns in the barren desert added up to a very depressing scene.

We got lost again in the outskirts of Chiclayo, but once again, through asking lots of questions, we were funneled down a one-way street. It was a crowded, distressing street, but sure enough, we were spat out on the other end of town. Not bad for a city encounter. We saw some super poor people out in the desert where the city dumps all its trash to burn and blow about. The dwellings are not much to look at and closely resemble the garbage itself. The tiny huts were made out of plastic scraps and looked like the harsh desert winds could just blow them over. Men and women alike were all squatting, digging through piles of garbage with hands or hoes. What a sad state of affairs.

We were pulled over five or six times today. The most amusing time was when mom rolled down her window to give the officer our insurance. He just started laughing, and with a look of surprise, kept saying how beautiful mom was. Where in the world did he come from?!? The desert became more sandy, and we're all impressed by the sandy ridges made by the wind. Around 5:30, we were just coming out of the town of Chimbote, the first successful city navigation of the day. Just as we said, we were resigned to not finding a hotel and staying in a vehicle, we drove past a hostel that was not covered in hearts and lips. We decided to give it a try. And for 20 Soles ($7.50 USD), we were happy. The room smelled of smoke, only had one bed, no toilet seat, no shower cover, or handle on the door. Still, it was a treasure.

Took the dogs out to play. Enjoyed a family hand of Five Crowns and ate a few cookies with some yogurt. I spread Kacie and my mats out on the floor. Everyone else is in bed, but before I hit the sack, I'm going to enjoy a hot shower with the absurdly big shower head. I'm super tired from my lack of sleep last night as guns kept going off and people were running to and from the shop behind our room anyways, praying for God's protection and a good night. It's noisy outside. The shower was deceiving, no hot water! The room is so small that with a full bed, two camping mattresses, and Walter laying the ground, there is hardly any room to walk.

Kindra's Journal   10/22/2010

What a day! After a good but noisy night, we headed out for Malachi Reed's house. Traveling was fast and through the usual oceanside desert. Immensely beautiful, with the sand making perfectly smooth ridges on the mountains. We decided to venture off on a long flat road leading to the ocean. We could see enormous waves sending spray way up into the air when they would crash into the enormous rocks and cliffs. Of course, the Land Cruiser always looks spectacular, but on a desert bluff, we just had to take a picture of it! We then walked down the path to the inlet between the bluffs that were towering up above us! The dogs went really wild playing on the rocky beach.

Further down the beach where there was a washed-out cavelett we found some fisherman's boats. The mere thought of trying to even get out of the inlet and attempt to fish in those tiny boats seemed nothing short of impossible. As I watched the enormous waves crashing against the cliffs, it made me shudder just to think about getting out into the ocean. While I was waiting for the others who were also following me down to that side of the beach, I ventured out on an intriguing little rock ledge.

I found where the boat owners stored their ores in a neat little crevice in the rock. All of a sudden, I happened to look out and see a huge wave coming in. It turned my little area of exploration with no water into a terrifying knee-deep, white, swirling pool. I clambered up onto the rock to keep my footing. I somehow managed to look back and see mom, Kacie, and dad all running backward to the dry shore. Apparently, dad didn't see the rock behind him and tripped, which sent him headfirst to the ground. He fell in the icy cold water and got his back all wet.

I was beside myself for a few seconds while the space between the rest of the family and me was full of angry-looking surges of water. As the water receded enough so I could see rocks to cross on. I looked out to see another enormous wave racing towards me, and without wasting time, cautiously ran to the shore. I barely escaped getting drenched. The sea and I are really striking out. Just a bad combination, I suppose.

We walked back up to the Land Cruiser just as a father and son were coming down to work on their boat. We had some fun driving around the dunes in the Land Cruiser and taking all kinds of pictures. Too many, I'm sure. We drove until dad had all of us girls almost beside ourselves and adamantly protesting against his excursion. He was driving the Land Cruiser on a hill going down to the ocean cliff. With the angle we were on, the view out the window was frightening. Despite all this, dad was in his height of glory, testing the Land Cruiser's capabilities.

Around 2:00 we found a payphone and called Rebecca Reed, who gave us directions. About a half-hour later, and asking around for the "gringos", we arrived at the gate. We knocked, more like pounded, on the massive metal gate and honked the horn. After a while, Malachi's younger brother John opened the gate for us. It was nice to be among believers again and actually be in someone's home. Us girls did our laundry, and after I came back from the line with a basket for the next load, I found mom, dad, Malachi, Rebecca, and Kacie all drinking matè. Mom wanted me to try a sip, so I did. Then she told me everybody drinks off of that same metal straining straw, what a shocker. Had a good time this evening. Mom and Dad shared their testimony. We're camped out in the half-finished house in our tent. Kacie isn't feeling well, so I'm out here with her while they visit.

Kindra's Journal   10/23/2010

Woke up at 5:45 and did my hair. No one else was up yet in Malachi's house. Mom read us some interesting emails, then we helped make breakfast. Over breakfast, we formulated a plan of driving into town with Malachi and John. Malachi is headed to Lima for a Light and Lamp student conference. As soon as he had everything ready, we piled into the back of the moto. It's a motorcycle converted into a people taxi. Three wheels total with the passengers in a separate compartment than the driver. We visited with the brothers and sisters while Malachi waited for the rest of his travel group. As soon as his group was all assembled, they took off down the street with their luggage.

We made plans with the two young single sisters to meet us for a hike at 1:30, then piled back into the moto and headed out for the market. Well, it wasn't long until our ride came to a halt two blocks down the road. We peeked out the little window to see John reach into his pocket and pull out a map. His words could be heard even over the loud rumble of the motor, "I'm just starting to figure things out around town." He made a u-turn and cruised down another street. We again stopped to read the map. Just then, one of the church brothers drove by and was able to show us where the market was.

We were soon walking down the crowded market ways. I tried to keep Evelyn's little six-year-old hand in mine as we strolled along. We failed to find any skirts and soon found ourselves perusing the vegetable section so John could buy the things Rebecca needed. It was a massive market with not as distinct an Indian culture as San Cristóbal de las Casas, so it was different. We successfully found a package of six squeaky balls in the toy section for the dogs, two pineapples as a surprise for our hosts, and a small wooden spoon for our soon-to-be home. We walked through and enjoyed the sites of a chair weaver and charcoal maker. It took us a while to see everything, and about an hour later, John suggested we stop and get an Inca Cola before we left. We stopped at one of the corner crossroads at the market. John bought a large unrefrigerated bottle of the bubbly banana soda. We all drank what we could till the last drop was drained.

Once back, we girls did laundry again while dad worked on changing the oil. At lunch, dad announced that the oil filter was stuck, and he couldn't get it off. Finally, dad and John came up with a magnificent idea of strapping a ratchet strap around it and tying it to a tree so they could tighten it, and it worked! Our group of hikers assembled and set off for the distant hills. It was a serious hike all the way to the top. The view of the green valley below was amazing, and we stood on the mountain of billowing dust. The landscape was barren all except for the few scraggly flowers that survived here or there. Occasionally someone would want a picture, and then soon, one person would be juggling four people's cameras to get a group picture! Running down was the super fun part, and the dust clouds people would kick up from the fluffy loose soil was quite impressive.

By the time we got back, everyone was hot, dusty, and in the mood for a matè tea break. Everyone sat in a circle, and we all passed around the metal cup packed with tea leaves with the straining straw in it. Someone was designated water pourer, and the cup passing began. Everyone drank down to Mark, the youngest participant. Partakers continue to pass the cup until you say "gracias," thus ending your turn. I was the first to quit after the second round, while more committed tea fans drank on. Rebecca and John drank till the pitcher was empty. Took down the laundry and answered many questions from the children: "have you been to the Moon?", "do you know who you're going to marry?", and "why do you sinners put that strong ink on their skin?" They were truly miffed about the "strong ink," which is what they called mom and dad's tattoos.

Kindra's Journal   10/24/2010

Kacie is being quite absurd about taking up too much space with her mat no matter what I say! I got up in time to see the rest of the Malachi Reed clan and John leave for Lima. I got the instructions on filling the water tank and locking the place up. It was nice to have a little family time to talk about Michigan and then get ready for church. But the morning turned into chaos as dad tried to install another filter on the Berkey while I finished dishes. The filter was almost a goner until mom came to the rescue with an extra gasket. Soon I had the hair trimmers in my hand and was attempting to give dad a haircut, but the limited voltage made it difficult. We soon figured out someone would need to hold it only part way in the outlet. In order to let Mom and Kacie finish our last load of laundry in time, dad crouched in the corner to hold the plug halfway out while I tried to finish a remotely decent haircut. We got the job done and were soon following Simon Slater's family to church in the city of Huaral.

The meeting was interesting about the different kinds of joy and sorrow and what kind should be seen in Christian's lives. It was a small meeting with three families in total. Afterward, we enjoyed talking to Brenda and her husband, Harvey mast. They used to attend Pleasant View church in Michigan and knew some of our friends quite well. We went to Simon and Christine's for lunch. After doing dishes, Kacie, I, and their oldest daughter Sonia (13 yrs. old) hiked back to some neat ruins where we found old pottery pieces and lots of bones. It was fascinating walking around back there. Came home, and mom worked on a group email while dad and I cleaned up the cruiser. Had supper ready for when Malachi's family, John, and a Bible student man named Dickarrived. We had a pleasant evening of visiting. Did the dishes then our family took the dogs for a walk. I love the climate here, but our legs are insanely sore after that long hike yesterday.

Kindra's Journal   10/25/2010

It's perfectly cool here and makes for ideal sleeping! Packed up, then enjoyed a breakfast at the mines before heading out. It felt good to be out on the road again, and we were surprised how easy it was to find our way through Lima, the capital city with over 13,000 people. When we got to Lima, it was super foggy with about 50 ft visibility until we came into the city valley. The road turned to a six-lane highway at times. Even with a detour and some crazy driving, dad managed to drink coffee through it all. We had heard It takes nerves of steel to drive through Lima, but we found it wasn't too bad.

It's just past 2:00, and we're sitting at a busy highway intersection waiting for Owen Yahtzee to come. We couldn't find a phone to call him, but two nice ladies at a gas station took mom and dad over to a little brick building where they paid a few soles and finally got a hold of him. I wonder what the rest of the day will hold. More later.

After 40 minutes, Oliver arrived, and we found ourselves in the inner city. Oliver took us to Petronella, a church sister's house. She, unfortunately, was away for a few days. Her brick house was very unlike any house I had ever seen. As we stepped off the sandy city sidewalk into her home, I found myself stepping onto the same sand as the street. It was a strange feeling to be inside walls and windows with simple furnishings, and yet it was all on sand. The two beds and table in the main room we're crooked but sturdy enough to use. Concrete flooring could be found in the kitchen, but the bedroom was also sand. While they discussed the vehicle, Oliver took us out back and said we would enjoy watching the guinea pigs in their abode at the farm. The misfortunate rabbits who were abiding in a tiny travel cage built for one small rabbit. The poor things tipped their cage right off its sad wobbly stand as Biddy made an over-enthusiastic approach, causing them to leap back in fright. We visited there for a few hours and drank coffee while mom and dad shared their testimony.

Headed out to Sylvia's farm and set up camp for the night as our vehicle will be safer here than in the city. Sylvia rushed up to us from her alfalfa patch along with a half dozen dogs who run the place. She chatted along in her high-pitched Spanish, telling us to please stay for several days since she is lonely. She ran off to tear her dry laundry off the line, all the while continually chatting about how welcome we were. We set up our tent, which she found delightful. It was soon dark out as we crowded inside the kitchen, if you could even call it that. We crowded into where Owen was preparing a dinner of noodles, tomatoes, and tuna served alongside their beloved *chocolo:* boiled giant field corn. He preluded the meal by saying, "I'm not sure how clean everything is, but I will tell you I've never gotten sick yet."

In the dim lighting, one could see guinea pigs underfoot, in every corner, and under every table. They gathered around the piles of alfalfa and table scraps wherever Sylvia had seen fit to throw them. Should you fail to see them in the dim lighting, they made their presents quite known by their sheer whistles and chirping noises. Three four-story cabinets constructed from cane lined the walls of one room. I dare say the hundreds of floor guinea pigs had the better end of the deal. You can imagine how much manure all of those guinea pigs make. Maybe dim lighting is best in that situation, haha.

As we ate supper, I realized I had to eat a little bit of each thing on my plate. As soon as I finished one portion of either chocolo, sauce, or noodles, Sylvia would publicly demand that someone put more of whatever it was that I had finished in my bowl. Trust me, as soon as I had it figured out, I made sure to leave a few of the large white kernels on the cob and a scoop of tomatoes next to my noodles to avoid any unusual attention.

After listening to dad and Owen discussing the usual doctrinal subjects, coldness and tiredness overcame me. I wandered out to our tent, where mom and Kacie were already fast asleep. When we asked where the outhouse was,

Oliver paused and somewhat hesitantly went into how we'd have to haul water from the pond to use the toilet way out in the outhouse. His directions seemed to end there, and we decided just to go elsewhere to which he seemed to think was best. It's absolutely raw living back here.

Kindra's Journal   10/26/2010

Woke up to the sound of barking dogs, guinea pigs, Sylvia's hardy morning chatter, and a dog marking the tent right on the other side of my head. Very disturbing! Mom and dad drove the Land Cruiser out to the main road so that our dogs could run around. I had to dig a hole so Kacie could use the bathroom. She was unfortunately not feeling well. I picked up the sleeping bags, mats, and pillows while the rest packed up the vehicles and sent me to help him prepare breakfast.

Oliver put me to work cutting up a large papaya. First, he had to scrounge a dirty bowl, knife, and broken piece of tile for a cutting board. I washed them in the buckets outside. After trying to sanitarily cut up the papaya, I had what could be considered a relative success. While we waited for dear brother Oliver to cook the porridge on Sylvia's little one burner, I took note of the dusky surroundings in the brick building. Guinea pigs ran to and fro, but remained centered around the scrap pile containing breakfast preparations of papaya seeds and pieces of burnt pancake that Owen kept tossing over to them. The kitchen included the dishes, cooking utensils, some various odds and ends, and some split boards covering the tiny corner table.

A dead guinea pig lay along the wall, kitty-corner from the stove.

Mom was surprisingly disturbed by the whole situation of this tumbled-down shack with pigeons, cats, chickens, and hundreds of guinea pigs dwelling with the people. Mom and Kacie sat in the screen surrounding the dining room until breakfast was ready. Just as the gnats and mosquitoes smelled the pancakes and barley drink, Sylvia flung open the door, thus perfecting their entrance despite the screen. Everything they served was quite excellent!

A newly converted couple, Robert and his wife, came over before we left to visit. Dad shared a few verses with them from James. They were so excited. I mean, it was like they were hungry for the truth! So good to see. At 10:00, we took pictures with everybody and gave Robert and his sweet wife a ride out to the road. Those two were such a blessing and sent us with lots of sweet bread for our trip. It was really special and a blessing to us from their hearts. Kacie and I rode out to the main highway on the back of the Land Cruiser since it was full of people. On our way out, some men riding on the back of a huge green truck passed us and got all excited and happy when they saw us two girls catching a ride the same as they were.

Travel was easy today, and we drove through the remaining stretch of desert to the mountains. We listened to some preaching CDs. Finally, we reached Nasca, where we finally found the correct way off the main road and into the mountains. The paved road is very narrow, steep, and has tons of sharp curves. I made for some extra alert driving. We passed two bicyclists from Japan! As we got up to the top of the foothills, we drove through some kind of nature reserve. We saw a bunch of these mini alpaca-type creatures that were super fuzzy and cute. Also saw a real alpaca further down the road as we searched for a suitable camp spot for the night.

Dad had no idea how far away the next town was, and consequently, we're on "E" road right now. Supposedly the town of pisco is around the next curve here, so hopefully, they'll have gas. I'm praying that they will. We had success finding a pull-out for the night out here in the middle of nowhere. It is situated by some cow pastures and falling-down houses in a deep ditch. It just happened to conveniently be here, and behind the ditch, we are hidden from the road. How handy. After running around to set up camp, we barely beat the darkness but had enough time to pause to see the mountain sunset. It's super cold in the tent. After eating some bread and bananas, everyone else went to bed. It's only 7:30. Praying for safety, good night.

Kindra's Journal   10/27/2010

Woke up around 5:00 and enjoyed the strong sunshine as we picked up our camp spot. The cows on the other side of the rock wall watched us with undisguised curiosity. In the morning light, the yellow prairie grass looked beautiful. Within about 5 minutes, we arrived in the quaint little town of Pisco and loaded up on fuel. It was good to see the fuel gauge rising from its resting place on E.

The town seemed to just be waking up. We were able to find a little store where a warmly dressed lady welcomed us and told us the name of each thing we looked at, from bananas to dad's new favorite lucuma yogurt. It was one of those really friendly towns where the people make you feel welcome, a rarity these days. We drove on through the mountains, our headaches reaching a climax as the elevation reached 14,500 ft. Wow, that is the highest elevation I've ever been at!

We passed through lots of alpacas with ribbons in their ears. The expression they have on their faces is absolutely hilarious when their front teeth stick out. We also passed by lots of huge, crystal-clear mountain lakes that were super smooth on the surface and a beautiful blue color. It was like we had the road to ourselves because we rarely saw any trucks. Seeing the snow capped mountains in the distance was neat, and when we got close enough, we enjoyed getting to walk around in the snow for a while. You could really feel a difference breathing in the thin air. It was strange.

Passing through the tiny villages, though few and far between, was always interesting. We saw a young couple and their little baby, a lady spinning yarn, men packing up alpaca wool, and people who seemed totally happy and content with life. Seeing the people in their native colorful clothing is awesome, just like the picture books. Twice we passed little girls walking on the side of the road, maybe six or younger, going who knows where. I wish we could just take them home with us! When we finally reached the town of Chalhuanca, we tried to perform our three tasks of the day. Stop at a pharmacy, a bank, and an internet cafe. None of these were able to be fulfilled in this little town, but we had fun here.

We perused an alpaca products store and then bought some food from a street vendor. The two ladies in charge of their restaurant on wheels took obvious interest as we asked what they had. We soon found ourselves seated and eating their traditional meal. Mom and I got some stir-fried dishes with rice and pasta while Kacie and dad enjoyed the more benign-looking potatoes and cream. Upon taking a closer look at my plate, I noticed, looped in and around the potatoes, onions, and tomatoes, these 4 inch long pieces of food. They were long, round, and smooth, except for the underside having short little tentacle-type entities protruding out, like caterpillar feet or something.

I couldn't take the suspense any longer, and I scooped a long dangling piece up with my fork and asked if it was from an animal. "Oh yes," they said. I put the piece of animal in my mouth. As I chewed it twice then swallowed, I concluded that its hard rubbery texture wasn't as bad as our previous concha experience back in El Salvador. Dad later expanded on how he thought it was brain due to its shape and size. The ladies who were eating at the same stand asked us the usual questions followed by a new one: "what do you eat to get so tall?" The Andean ladies are definitely a bit shorter than us. What a funny question though! Soon the whole plaza was buzzing with news about the gringos. As we watered the dogs behind the Land Cruiser, we heard "They're from the USA" and "They're going to Bolivia." Word sure travels fast!

Not far out of town, we stopped and hiked, or rather slid down to the beautiful mountain stream that flowed through the narrow valley. We wanted to wash up a bit just in case we would find a good spot to camp. The ice-cold water was really refreshing as we sat on the rocky bank. We washed our arms, feet, faces, and shoes. I love the land around here. The natives have their fields right next to the river on elevated fields about 12 feet up from the water. Everything around here is beautiful. We rolled into the big town of Abancay around 3:00. We eventually were able to accomplish our earlier tasks! After stopping at a few horrible excuses of internet cafes, we ultimately found a nice one.

We went to multiple pharmacies searching for Tabcin cold medicine. Tabcin is the third-world version of Alka-Seltzer. They didn't have any, so we settled for its expensive supposed distant relative in pill form. After finding our mistake of having $1.18 USD in our bank account, we were able to fix it and go back to the bank, this time with the dogs, and get money. From there, we walk to the plaza. Kacie and I couldn't resist going and petting a little white alpaca. Its young owner walked her little pet all along the street and told us her furry alpaca was named Blanca and was 5 years old.

We saw some men playing their beloved game of football and decided to sit down and watch. It was very entertaining. Mom bought some violin strings. Dad made his first hardware store purchase of a three-prong outlet adapter to charge our camera and computer tonight. They're really low on power. We were all thrilled to take hot showers and wash off the grime from our farm stay. Oh, it felt good. Enjoyed reading emails. I enjoyed today, but Kacie is being of utmost irritation right now. Dad is holding Kacie down and threatening to snake-bite her and not let go.

Kindra's Journal   10/28/2010

Woke up to still no reply from Levi Reed's. Thanks to Malachi, who sent lots of phone numbers, we finally got a hold of Levi's family and got directions. We creeped up the steep mountain road out of Abancay. We were surprised to see police in full riot gear, probably due to the lengthy and loud protest we witnessed last night in the plaza.

We curved around beautiful mountain roads for about an hour. We hardly made any forward progress but continued up. As we climbed, our view of the city made it look smaller and smaller. This scenery was different and perhaps one of the most amazing of our journey. The high altitude mountains were covered in trees and thick green pasture. Every person we passed was happy and either waved or whistled as we passed by.

Almost all of the houses we have seen today are made of thick adobe bricks with the common tile roof. After one and a half hours of driving, we were thrilled to come across some extraordinary Inkan ruins. It cost 30 Soles to get in but was well worth it. We first looked at the enormous boulder that the Indians had the entire village plan chiseled into. The tiny details were amazing. We had a good time walking through the main building, where chest-high stonewalls divided many little rooms. Further down the hill was an ancient waterway ruin that had to be about 50 feet tall, with terraced stairs going up the side.

We spent quite a bit of time on that tall structure taking in the panoramic view of the all surrounding peaceful farming community. It was one of those places you just don't want to leave. A man was splitting wood while a lady herded her cows down the creek, and a boy led his one little sheep out to the pasture. We saw many snow-capped mountains this morning and all along our drive. When we arrived at Levi Reed's house around 2:30, we were warmly welcomed into their house.

Their household was a bustle of activity since the missionary conference is going on right now. Fortunate for us, we were able to get in on the last of the sermons. We took the dogs out for a walk and listened in on the 4:00 sermon in Spanish. I think it may have been about kings and marriage? We were thrilled to meet all the people we missed along the way in this one place, and it's our last stop with a church family before we arrive at our new home in Bolivia. We visited, then had supper and visited some more until it was time for the final meeting. We sang in both Quechua and Spanish then listened to the sermon. I truly burnt my brain trying to concentrate on the Spanish. Still, I'm pretty sure he preached about our service, sacrifice, and offering for christ.

Mom shared her testimony while we visited. A very upbuilding evening and gathering. For being as hot as it was during the day, it has certainly cooled off tonight. Levi has a lovely family. I enjoyed visiting with his two daughters, one older and one younger than me. They have a super neat dairy farm out here in the mountains. This valley is beautifully green and surrounded by snow capped mountains. I think we're heading out in the morning, and it's well past 11:00 p.m., so I should go to bed. I'm all alone in this room. The rest of the family abandoned me to go to sleep.

Kindra's Journal   10/29/2010

Woke up with a grand total of 6 hours of sleep. We said goodbye to the clan here in Atabamba, then helped them get ready for the market. We left around 9:00, and the vehicle barely started due to the high elevation. We picked up one of the native Church brothers on the way out. We gave him a ride to the rental house Gordon's family was staying in. On my way there, we drove by a cattle market, and the whole road seemed to be in chaos. Farmer's were herding large droves of cattle and sheep on the road. Unfortunately, the animals didn't seem to have the same idea.

We traveled on through Cusco and, with Gordon's warning that there are no signs to guide you to the other side, did our best to guess which road to take. Although we ended up on a dirt road, we were going in the right direction, and ultimately we made it. An hour out of Cusco we stopped at some really tall ruins. A bit further down the road, we stopped at some more touristy ruins. We opted out of paying to see the ruins since dad suddenly realized that once again, we barely had enough money to make it to the next bank. We did find a plate and tablecloth for our new home and spent a small amount on the purchases. Kacie was thrilled to find two turtles to add to her collection.

At this point, the sickness I had been feeling all morning set in, and I felt terribly sick to my stomach. As we drove along, we found a sign for medicinal waters, and everyone got excited. We stopped to find a llama reserve and hot springs. Primitive but nice. We paid $2 per person, and we're soon bathing in our own private room with a 6x8 foot natural hot tub with water flowing through a hole in the wall to keep the pool super hot. Everyone else really enjoyed it, but it made me feel much sicker. The worker gave us permission to camp, so we set up our tent and crawled inside.

I layed on my bed for the rest of the evening, feeling so miserable. Right before everyone else went to bed, dad went out to get something from the vehicle. Bitty barked out into the thick darkness, and dad investigated what was out there. It turned out to be a man who had seen our tent all lit up. I woke up, and all of us girls shot up and poked our heads out of the tent door. In the darkness, we saw an old man and his dogs. He visited for a while and then talked about different languages, our beautiful tent, and the llamas on the hills. I tried to help dad with Spanish, but the man was not leaving.

Feeling a new wave of misery, I laid back on my mat, occasionally muttering a few phrases to help dad in his conversation. Finally, the man left, and we were all ready for bed. It started to get windy and rainy, so dad took the clothes off the nice ratchet strap line he had made. Earlier in the evening, while it was still light, one of the fuzzy medium-sized llamas came up to the fence and stuck its nose over. It looked so cute, and I wanted to pet it. I walked up to it and held out my hand for it to sniff with its soft little nose to sniff. All of a sudden, it put its ears back, puffed up its face, and spit on me. How rude! I guess their personality doesn't match their cute, innocent-looking faces. That llama just stood there with absolutely no look of remorse and just the same ignorant look they always have. It's super cold and hard to sleep. I'm shivering from the inside. I'm so cold and so sick. I feel terrible.

Trip Summary by Kristi VanderZon   Peru

Dear Family and Friends,

We had a reasonably easy border crossing into Peru this morning. There was a little confusion about where to get stamped out of Ecuador. After that, the process went smoothly. Evidently, there is no necessary paperwork for the dogs in Ecuador or Peru. This saved some time and made things easier.

After entering Peru, our first priority was to find a bank to get some Peruvian currency. In contrast to all the other borders, Peru had no money changers offering their services. This was a challenge, as the first town was reasonably large. We had to negotiate the Land Cruiser through downtown traffic and find both parking and a bank. We did accomplish this much but could not locate the ever-elusive road map we desired of Peru.

We enjoyed the coastal road for the first part of the day. Then the road turned into a curvy pattern between desert-looking cliffs, and we climbed higher and higher through canyon-type walls. We were treated to a good view of the ocean at the top.

There were long stretches with no sign of civilization, making it a peaceful, easy ride. We had a 215km stretch through the desert. That night we found a hotel in the town of Sullana for the night. We went to the hotel's restaurant for supper. After hardly eating anything all day, we were prepared for a complete meal in the hotel's formal dining room overlooking a nice pool. However, the only thing the waiter (who was the whole staff rolled into one) was prepared to offer us was ham and cheese sandwiches. We all agreed to this and waited a considerable amount of time for them to arrive. It was hard to hide our mixture of amusement and disappointment when a tiny sandwich on wonder bread arrived on a small teacup saucer. Although it was presented with great formality, it didn't go far to fill our hunger. We tried to stay good-humored through it all and talked about the big breakfast we'd treat ourselves with tomorrow. Hopefully…

That 215km stretch through the desert turned out to be 2 days through the desert. Some of it was flat, some of it was mountainous, but all was dusty and windy. We were missing signs of green, signs of life. The towns seemed almost deserted, and it was a challenge finding food.

You could see the ribbon of road many miles ahead

It was hard finding a hotel, and we were considering finding a gas station and just spending the night in the vehicle. But just when we were pulling out of the town of Chimbote, we spied a hotel. It wasn't glamorous, but it was the cheapest one yet, at $7.00 for the night. The neighborhood was a bit of a concern, but there was a gated parking lot, where we parked right outside the room. There was only one double bed, so the girls put their mats on the floor, and we all slept comfortably enough.

Pulling out of our Hotel Street

Among the sights was a stretch of "dump" where the garbage was deposited in the desert. All this alongside the road. It was a terrible sight to witness people actually digging in and making their home in the trash. There were little shelters erected in the rubble heap. People actually endured the harsh, windy conditions there among the garbage. Our hearts went out to the condition of their lives.

The road eventually ran along the coast again, and we found an ideal spot to pull over and take a break. David couldn't resist driving through the dunes, which we were all enjoying until the girls and I felt the vehicle was tipping too far. David finally gave in to our pleas to go back. He was only trying to see what the Land Cruiser was capable of, he said.

Some pictures from the coast

We found these boats neatly tucked into this cove

We arrived at Malachi & Rebecca Reeds Friday afternoon. They have an orange orchard near Huaral, which is about an hour north of Lima. The blossoms on the trees make the air smell sweet. They have four children, and Malachi works for Lamp & Light publishing. The weekend coincided with the Lamp & Lights student conference in Lima, so it was a busy weekend. Nevertheless, we enjoyed getting to know them. Rebecca cooked us some delicious hearty meals that made it feel like home.

Saturday morning, John, Malachi's younger brother visiting from Breckinridge, Kentucky, drove us to the market for the Reed Family's "moto-car." We enjoyed walking around and seeing the bounty of the area's fruits & vegetables. David & John spent an hour trying to wedge off a stuck-on oil filter in the Land Cruiser and eventually achieved success. Later in the afternoon, 2 other church sisters and 2 of the Reed children joined us for a hike up the surrounding hills. Our efforts rewarded us with a great view. We picked up a lot of dust running (and occasionally falling) back down the hills.

Our family at the peak of the hike

Enjoying some Inca Cola at the market

More sights at the market

The taxi used for family transportation here

Sunday, we had a restful day of worship with the believers here. After church, we enjoyed visiting with the Slater family during dinner on their farm.

We really appreciated our time here. We were able to do some much-needed cleaning in the vehicle and some maintenance on it. We got well-fed, well-rested, and well cleaned during our stay here. We were also fed spiritually as we spent time with these families and attended their worship service. It had seemed like a particularly long, lonely spell between Barranquilla and here.

We are planning on leaving here in the morning and heading for Pisco. We hope to meet Oliver Moore and spend some time on a farm there.

We had a good visit with Oliver Moore and spent the night at a farm near Pisco. Yesterday morning Oliver cooked us a good breakfast of pancakes, with a warm drink of fresh goat's milk and toasted barley. All of this compliments of Silvia, who graciously shared her farm with us. We had some visitors after breakfast. Ricardo & wife, who are newly converted believers, visited us before we had to leave.

Camping on the farm

Sylvia and some of her critters

On our way to Levi Reeds yesterday, we found some Incan ruins to explore.

We found a place to sit where we could view the expanse of a farming valley, and it was a beautiful sight. To see the simple, daily routine being carried out by the native farmers. With their colorful skirts, hats, and braids, the Andean women are a special treat to see. We refrain from taking pictures, as it can be offensive to them. We often see them walking along the road, maybe behind a cow, spinning their wool as they go. It's a beautiful culture. We've enjoyed the friendly little towns we've passed through.

Enjoying some ruins along the way

One of the andean women and her herd

Here at Levi's, we're about 45 minutes west of Cusco. There's a missionary conference going on here, so we were extremely blessed to meet many missionaries who serve all across South America. There were a few other families here, and we had a warm welcome with a refreshing night of fellowship. Dale Heisey spoke a message in the evening that inspired us to voluntary obedience to Jesus Christ. We certainly needed the spiritual encouragement, and praised God for this blessing!

We enjoyed the change of scenery as we left the coast and headed into the mountains. We enjoyed seeing the Alpacas in the pampas and in the mountains. Sometimes, we saw large herds grazing. Many times, they were crossing the road. Curiously, many wore ribbons on their ears.

These alpacas seemed delighted to pose for the picture.

Camping at the hot springs

Ready for a soak in the medical waters

Hot from the source

The temperature gets downright chilly in the mountains, but we were warm in our sleeping bags in the tent. We traveled on and came to the town of Chalhuanca, where we stopped and had lunch at a little vendor's wagon. We received a lot of attention from onlookers as we sat and ate lunch. I had trouble communicating with the lady serving us. I couldn't quite figure out what the squiggly, bumpy, noodle-like things were in my rice. We finally came to the conclusion they were cow brains. With so many looking on, I bravely ate as much as I could. It really wasn't all that bad.

We then drove on to Abancay and looked around for a bank, hotel, and internet café. It's our 92nd day of the journey. We wonder where day 100 will find us? Maybe home in Bolivia. Surely, it can't be much farther now. Thank you for your continued prayers. We are nearly shaking with excitement to be this close to Bolivia!

Love,

Kristi for the VanderZons

Some more ruins

CHAPTER 13

BOLIVIA

Kindra's Journal   10/30/2010

Oh, what a terrible night! My stomach hurts so bad, and there was a sizable lump beneath my mat. I had to make multiple excursions outside in the cold wind, but I'll spare you the details. We packed up, then the rest took another dip in the hot springs. I made multiple trips to the outhouse and then took a last look at the bubbling springs. I still feel awful, but we headed out.

The rest of the family was super hungry after not eating much yesterday, so they stopped in this little town and found a person selling lamb and potatoes. It cost 10 Soles per person, which seemed expensive. After watching dad and mom thinking and talking about the price, one of the vendors said she would sell it for 5 Soles a serving. Later, when we opened our bags further down the road, we found only bones with no meat and a few small potatoes. Dad was very disappointed.

We stopped and made a lady's first sale of the day by buying a super nice alpaca blanket. We got all mixed up in the thieving town of Juliaca that Gordon had warned us about. When we stopped to ask the police how to get to Puno, he told us, then said be very careful. I hate it when the police tell us that. We made it through town by following our usual well-proven method of going a few blocks down the best-looking road and asking the most trustworthy-looking man on the street for directions. We repeat this till we're out of the city.

Some police pulled us over on the way into the city for the usual, not having a license plate that matches the country. They kept repeating, "you need one from Peru." Finally, they asked for gas from our cans for their old pickup truck but let us go since we needed all our gas to drive to the Bolivian border. We stopped at a little store to get something for breakfast, but by then, it was noon. The lady was so paranoid we would take off with the glass soda bottles. She sat in the doorway and watched us as we swallowed the last sip of room temperature soda. As soon as the bottles were empty, there she was, reaching for the old scratched-up bottle.

We drove on for a few more hours along the beautiful shore of Lake Titicaca. With all of the sheep and colorful natives, we were almost in a complete state of awe as we rolled into the Bolivian border town. As we got our Peru papers canceled and exchanged our money for Bolivianos, I couldn't help but have a huge smile on my face. Here we are! We rolled the short distance over to the Bolivian immigration office. We found a bunch of interesting cultural pictures on the wall. When they saw we were from the states, they all almost shouted at us.

All of us were nervous, especially when the official guy took my passport. Just minutes before, I had filled in the missing information trying to match my handwriting to the consulate worker who filled in the rest of the visas beside mine. It wasn't a problem, praise the Lord! We soon found ourselves huddled around a little table filling in the little information sheet we had done so many times before. Mom always writes while I carefully read her the passport numbers, "4643... " and so on. Dad and Kacie finally returned with the necessary copies to complete the process.

One of the other workers behind a desk started to ask dad how long we wanted to stay and if we wanted to be permanent Bolivianos. I was over there helping dad fill out the papers in Spanish, and the man said, "it would be much easier if your daughter here marries a Bolivian. They are very hard workers." Of course, dad didn't understand, and it was so embarrassing for me. I really hated to translate what they had said. The man seemed to warm up to us, and we ended up talking about how we used to milk goats. He came up with this whole idea of having a milking competition in Rurrenabaque. All the while, the other workers stamped our passports. The ironic thing was that after they were all stamped, he went back to check all of the information! The stamp of Minneapolis, Minnesota, seemed to stump him along with the date 16th of July that our visas had.

All ended well, and as soon as we had our vehicle permit, we were off to our beloved Aduana. We were on our way. Finally, after 95 days of road travel, we're in the country of destination, Bolivia! Yay, we made it! We drove up on an overlook and found a great campsite on the top of a hill overlooking the lake Titicaca. We drove into town, where dad was happy to find a place that sold hamburgers, so we stopped there for supper. It took them so long we jokingly wondered if they had to go butcher a dog! We met a legless backpacker named Zack and talked to him for a while. We made our way back to the hilltop, where we fought the wind and intense cold to find a rockless flat spot for our tent. I mean, it was just so cold. I'm still not feeling well, and my stomach hurts terribly. We're all rejoicing to be here in Bolivia. I'm praying for protection for the rest of the trip. Good night.

Kindra's Journal   10/31/2010

What a night as I hardly slept at all. I spent a considerable amount of time freezing my bottom off while being sick atop that barren hill. We completed our wake-up process, picking up the tent in the below 30° temperatures with a crazy wind chill cutting through our sweaters. In all the bustle this morning, no one had empty hands to hold our new, cozy, and beloved alpaca blanket around them. We all worked with amazing speed to get ourselves in the Land Cruiser and out of the wind.

A crinkled old man happened to be passing by as we were pulling out of our spot. His voice sounded pitiful as he creaked out his plea of a ride in a barely audible tone. We girls crammed in the back, and he and his thin suit coat, warm pants, woolen top hat, cane, and backpack crawled into the front seat. He said nothing as we crept into the sleepy town of Copacabana. We stopped at the little plaza and let him out. He offered to pay but was thrilled when dad said no thank you. As mom helped his frail figure out of the Land Cruiser, he squeaked out multiple words of gratitude. We later found him on the street, his backpack full of beautiful flowers. I wonder what he was up to.

Dad was searching diligently for a coffee shop and was certain there had to be one in this town. Well, praise be, we happened upon a one of a kind cafè. Mom and dad were thrilled to find some strong organic Bolivian coffee. Kacie and I got some hot chocolate. The pain in my stomach was so intense I wondered if I would dare get on the road with no bathrooms. I passed on the opportunity to eat, but the rest enjoyed some eggs and toast. We got to use the internet and refill our water jugs. I tried to follow Roland's advice of "when you're sick, just drink coke." Despite my dislike of the unnatural beverage, I drank it in all forms: glass, plastic, warm, somewhat cold, fizzy, and flat.

We walked around the marketplace and the streets for a while, buying two sun hats for Kacie and me since we didn't have any. The natives are certainly not overly friendly and don't give us a welcome feel. We headed out of town past the crowded streets of tourists to wait in line at the only gas station in town. Finally, when it was our turn, they would only fill our tank and not our extra fuel cans. This was frustrating because as we waited on the one fuel pump for our turn, the vehicle in front of us filled up six extra cans. When they told us no, they said the other person was getting fuel for the boats. It was a relief to finally fuel up.

I was apprehensive about the car ferry, as we had been warned this morning on how precarious the whole setup was. Combined with my sickness, it made for quite the depressing feeling. However, when we got to the vehicle shipping station, I was relieved to find it was a very short distance from shore to shore. The wooden barges were nicer than I thought, and getting the Land cruiser on was no problem. We girls got on a launcha since only one person could go with the vehicle. It cost $1.50 Boliviano's, and we didn't have to wait long for it to fill up. Our load was complete with a bucket of trout, coca leaves, a propane tank, and 21 people crammed on board. Our guide attempted to start the almost antique motor. Finally, we were off. Slight waves rocked the boat, but I was glad to see many nice life jackets hanging there. We made it across, and we're glad to once again be with dad and the Land Cruiser.

We travel on to La Paz, but we're disappointed that we didn't get to see and reed on the lake that Titicaca is so famous for. However, we made some natives very happy by purchasing two toy reed boats and two reed llamas for our new house. My worst nightmare of having stomach sickness while traveling came into reality today. No bathrooms for hours forced me to forsake all shame and give in to being sick on the side of the road with no privacy.

Coming into la Paz wasn't too difficult, and thanks to an old man's direction, we got to the Autopista. Coming into La Paz had a different feel because it was our home capital, and we knew we'd be back here again. The Autopista highway was entertaining with all kinds of huge loads on undersized vehicles. It eventually spit us out on some city avenue. We drove by crowds of people in fancy festival costumes. People in Spanish moss, llamas, and cocoa leaves danced around along with some musicians in bright costumes. We were grateful to find an ATM, but finding a hotel with parking was not so easy.

After going to six different hotels, we finally learned that none were open because it was a Sunday. Finally, after exhausting all options, we found ourselves at a Radisson hotel for $140 USD, but it was the only one with parking. Cheap insurance, dad thought. We were way out of our element. Checking in took forever, and I felt so sick. We took the dogs for a walk and then got down our backpacks for the first time in days. The bellboy could hardly bear to see us carrying our backpacks, and ironically ended up carrying dad's while us girls struggled with ours. The vehicle barely fit into the parking lot. Since the food wasn't too expensive, we decided to splurge on room service. It was fun having a party since tomorrow we tackle the death road. The hot bath felt so good, but I'm still sick and tired.

Kindra's Journal   11/01/2010

What a day! When the alarm clock went off, I could hardly believe it was already 4:00 a.m. The bed was so comfy that I really didn't want to get up. I forced myself into the now automatic mode of throwing a dress on and making a mad dash to gather everything up and stuff it into the backpacks. Mom and dad took the dogs out to get some fresh air and discuss plans for the day. Finally, we had the vehicle packed and headed inside to have the complimentary breakfast. When dad went to open the door to the hotel entrance, he accidentally pulled it so hard that it almost snapped off its fancy little hinges. The doorman was quite amused at our best efforts. We were on our way out of town by 6:30 and convinced the gas station man to fill our extra fuel cans. Kacie had the great idea to just siphon the gas out of the tank into the containers and get back in line.

Believe it or not, we actually didn't get lost one time in La Paz. When we passed the huge bus station on the way out of town, we knew it had to be the right way. We reached an elevation of 15,500 ft before going back down on the rough road leading to the death road. All the while, mom seemed to get more worried even though she didn't say a thing. None of us wanted to disappoint dad and his obvious enthusiasm for this old road. For a while, no one said anything as we coasted on towards the death road. We passed two police checkpoints and continued down the already steep road. There was no mistaking our turn off when we saw a big yellow sign with the heading of precaution along with a rough gravel road.

We got a few pictures with the death road instructions, and we're off. It wasn't long until the road became one lane on the side of the mountain cliff. We all agreed it wasn't as scary as we thought, and with good brakes, steering, 4x4, and our beloved Land Cruiser, we knew it wouldn't let us down in this glorious moment. All that to say, about 20 minutes into the precarious roadway, a sound that made everyone in the vehicle dead silent came to our ears. It sounded like gears grinding on each other. It was a loud and ominous sound. After over 8,000 miles, we all knew the Land Cruiser's every sound and squeak considerably well. We drove on around another curve, and dad tried changing gears and disengaging the 4x4, to name a few things, but the grinding still continued. All of us were in disbelief. Dad found a good spot to pull over and, after checking the oil in the rear differential, found the level low. Of course, we all thought this was the problem. He filled it and jumped back in.

As soon as we started down again, the noise got more intense. It was obvious we still had not solved the problem. We pulled off again on a steeper grade this time, and dad put rocks under the tires just in case. After a few minutes of further investigation, he found another problem. It was a familiar one this time. The same problem we had over a month ago in Costa Rica. The driveshaft was coming apart. We girls waited in the fog and rain under an umbrella to assist with his wisely chosen tools. We could hardly believe it. We were on the death road in the fog with a broken vehicle in the rain. Even though it was all of the things we tried to avoid, we were in good spirits. About half an hour later, dad emerged from under the vehicle, covered in mud but ready to try again. His fix worked. Praise the Lord.

We drove on at a slow, cautious speed through the incredible yungas scenery. I was surprised to see the mountains covered in thick, almost jungle-like plants. Mom eventually warmed up to the whole drive and was really enjoying it, which was the answer to prayer for me. The thick fog obscured the road in the distance, as well as the deadly view below. I could see, as we traveled on that directly down from my window, the road disappeared altogether with not even a trace of a road. Occasionally a washout right at the edge of the road would protrude almost into our path. One of the many mind-boggling things of today had to do with these cliff edge ruts that the tire tracks continued right across. How odd.

I lost count of all the waterfalls, without a doubt some of the prettiest I have ever seen. Some flowed under the road, and quite a few shot right over the narrow track! One flowed smoothly down the straight cliff wall so flatly. Some falls cascaded down the mountains and were easy to spot by their fast-falling white streams of water. We were surrounded by absolutely magnificent views. Many crosses lined the road, continually keeping the deadly seriousness of the whole situation at the front of our minds. To our surprise, we dropped out of the cloudy fog after 2 hours and finished the rest of the drive to Coroico in the sunshine. We only passed two vehicles in that whole stretch since the rest of the traffic took the new and improved road. Accidentally got on the wrong road for an extra bonus hour of rocky roads but ended up connecting with the right road to Caranavi.

There was a little cluster of vendors where the roads met together, so we stopped to buy a few things, including a small bag of coca leaves. This provided much amusement to the owner, who did quite a thorough sharing of the chewing process. We set out thrilled with our big accomplishment of surviving the death road. Not far down the road, we had a half-hour delay as dad fixed the driveshaft again. Not surprisingly, it came loose from the roughest roads on the whole trip. Dad had no problem getting back in working order. We headed out again, this time on the left side of the road instead of the cliffside since we weren't on the death road anymore. As we rounded the curve, we almost crashed head-on with another vehicle! Back to driving on the left side of the road for us.

We thought Bolivians must just like to drive that way. As the road wound higher and grew to that same dreadful skinniness as this morning, we realized that the death road was indeed not even half over. For the rest of the day, we traveled on, now with two-way traffic. The road was super high, cliffed out, and curvy. There were more shacks and houses on this stretch of the road along with the ecological resort that cost as much as our hotel last night.

Who would have thought we would be coming up to another one of those thrilling outer edge cliffs. The curve was so sharp that we couldn't see the other side, so dad would honk his horn. This worked pretty well except when the oncoming traffic didn't hear, and we ended up almost bumper to bumper with a massive supply truck. Sometimes we could see a vehicle way in advance and maneuver off in one of the less precarious passing spots to let them pass. Often the oncoming vehicle would just barely have enough room to pass by.

We passed a car that was pulled off on the cliffside. Its passengers had piled out and stood solemnly around the edge where all of the trees, grass, and bushes had been torn away, leaving only bare scraped up dry soil. We had seen them pulling off before looking for the accident scene and happened to pass them as they found it.

Bumping along on that road and swerving for vehicles got old. After a while and we were all super tired and finally vibrated into Caranavi around 5:00. We found a hotel with parking for $25 Bolivianos a person. After walking the dogs around, we're ready to crash for the night.

The rest were feeling well enough to eat, so they got the typical plate of rice, potatoes, chickens, and platanos. When we got back to the room again, mom and dad fell asleep long before Kacie and me. We were busy with emails and journaling. The noise produced by people and music ascending from below was super loud. Tiredness eventually prevailed, and soon everyone was asleep. Everyone in that town stared and pointed at us so much. I really didn't care for the hostile feel of that town. My back, neck, and throat hurt so bad. All that bumping today was insanely painful for me in my sick state.

Kindra's Journal   11/02/2010

By the time we chased around for the seemingly elusive gasoline and internet connection that wasn't to be had, it was 9:00. We did a few laps around the unfriendly town before finding the right road to Rurrenabaque. The roads were so rough, and we still had to maneuver many death road style pull-offs and passings. We were driving on the right side of the road until, coming around a blind curve, we almost had a collision, and they told us we needed to drive on the left side of the road. So we did until about an hour later when the same incident occurred, and we were told to move to the right side again. How confusing!

Dad let 20 lb of air out of the tires to lessen the jolts that threaten to tear the vehicle apart. We finally made it to the lowlands, and from there, we drove on the long, straight, and flat, but still exponentially rough road. We reached a record-breaking speed of 35 miles an hour today. The battery kept coming disconnected, so we were having to stop every so often to fix it. At the gas station, it came disconnected and wouldn't start at the pump. We had to push it out of the way and fix it yet again in the blazing hot jungle sun.

The triumphant moment of the day came as we rolled into the beautiful and smooth cobblestone streets of Rurrenabaque at 4:00. Just a few streets into the amazing little tourist town, I happened to look to the side and see Don Wendy strolling down the street towards us. He immediately went into this hilarious slow-motion robotic walk when he saw us and rushed up to "see what condition our condition was in." How funny! We set up a tent at a hotel he took us to, took showers, and changed out of our dust-covered clothes. Don came back and then walked us through the town, introducing us to his friends and different shops.

Kindra's Journal   11/03/2010

Woke up early, got dressed, then went and found Don. We had breakfast with him and his son Mo. Dad went with Don to run around while we girls cleaned up our tent and living area. We tried to send some emails but had a problem. We tried seven different internet cafes before finding success. The bank had a super long line, so we headed home to make a new plan. While we walked around town, we would occasionally pass by Don, who waited with a dazed look for his taxi to the airport to arrive.

Spent a surprising amount of time at our tent, trying to decide what to get and what to do before heading out to Ixiamas. Finally, around 3:00, we went out and bought four mattresses, two pillows, a mop, broom, bucket, shorts for dad, and more tamarindo seeds. The load on the Land Cruiser's roof rack is outrageously high now. Spent some time by the river watching the bar just cross and their little canoes put up and down the river. We all took showers then went to a restaurant for something to eat.

Rurrenabaque is a very peaceful town with clean streets. It's surprisingly cool at night despite the bright sun and heat during the day. We put our mattresses in the tent for the night, so it's pretty tight in here. I wonder what tomorrow will be like. Hopefully, the vehicle will make it one more day. I'm so very ready to be home no matter what we find the house like.

Kindra's Journal   11/04/2010

This morning we packed up and headed for the bank to wait in line, which was easier said than done with the crowd. Mom and Kacie searched for orange juice while dad and I got shampoo, toothpaste, and a clock. We waited outside the door for 45 minutes before even being let in. We then had to wait some more, being careful not to let the other people cut in front like they have a way of doing. We had all of our missions accomplished, so we headed down to the barge to cross the Rio Beni. I couldn't believe it when I saw the pump that continually dumps the sizable amount of water that leaks into the boat. Perhaps if it failed, the whole barge would sink down into the murky brown waters. It was very uninviting. We loaded the Land Cruiser behind a huge truck and were thankful to make it across to the other side of the river.

We bumped, lurched, rattled, and splashed for 5 hours to Ixiamas. Our first river crossing was a disappointment as we splashed through without preparation. A broken piece in the Land cruiser allowed water into the distributor. A kind man who was also stuck working on his truck by the river helped us, and we were soon on our way. A few other problems arose over the rough roads caused on our route. The exhaust pipe was falling off of its holders, and the half working clutch and gears were making strange noises. When we would stop for repairs, the sun seemed so hot! It seemed like we would never get to the long talked of town of Ixiamas, but we did. Yay!

We asked some hideously dressed Russian Mennonites where the Millers were. We combined all of the directions we got and deciphered that we had to either go either 3 or 7 kilometers out of Ixiamas before turning onto our road. I thought it would be a no-brainer, but it wasn't. We ended up driving back and forth over the same stretch of road for 20 minutes until we found someone to ask for directions. We were told to go further down the road, and we finally found our street.

The house in the picture we saw looked significantly different and run down. I really don't think anything has been done to it since Leonna and Roland moved out. Honestly, I had imagined the worst scenario possible in my mind. That was good because I was neither shocked nor disappointed to find waist-high grass surrounding the house. There were dirty curtains, no furnishings, bugs everywhere, broken bed frames, and the list goes on. We are excited to reclaim this home and get the place in excellent working order once again. It's a good thing we got the mop room and buckets!

We drove down the road and met Amos and the Millers. It was good to meet the long talked of family and also to see Mervin again. We came home. That feels really good to finally say. We swept the porch then set up the tent on our freshly cleaned porch and unpacked the rest of the vehicle. We headed back up to the Millers for dinner. We had a great evening visiting, sharing travel stories, and hearing travel stories until 10:00 p.m. Came back to our home and made a speedy entrance into the tent. It is our haven of refuge from all of the bugs. A few unavoidable bugs managed to make their way in along with the dogs and us. Never ever have I seen such massive amounts of bugs. All kinds of bugs, both big and small, with some cockroaches reaching 5 inches long. Every type of bug imaginable must be down here. May God protect us. It's good to be here.

Trip Summary by Kristi VanderZon   **Bolivia**

Dear family and friends,

We arrived in La Paz and enjoyed an unusually luxurious night at hotel Radisson in the heart of the city. We always liked to see how cheap we could get a hotel room… that night took the prize for the most expensive. After pulling into La Paz and trying to get oriented with where we were, traffic got congested. I may have a Bolivian map, but no map for La Paz. The road was shut down in places due to a Halloween celebration in the streets, complete with costumes made out of moss and coca leaves. We tried many hotels, but none had guarded parking for our vehicle. Many parking lots were closed due to it being Sunday.

We stopped at the Radisson, and after hearing the price, kept looking. But we returned, as it was the only hotel with secure parking. We certainly are making the best out of the situation and ordered supper delivered by room service. We ate and enjoyed the spectacular view we had from the ninth floor. Here's the day in reverse...

Our view out our window at the Radison

Kindra and Kacie dancing around our spread

We were impressed by this load, which seemed commonplace: a couch and two chairs on top of a car.

The girls and I couldn't cross with David and the vehicle. So he was on his own. Well... almost.

Kindra and Kacie on the launcha crossing the lake. This ride only cost $1.50 Bolivianos (21 cents USD) each and even came with plenty of life jackets, unlike our other water crossing.

The Land Cruiser driving onto the barge.

The Yungas Highway, otherwise known as the death road, was the next big obstacle. We were excited as it marks the beginning of the end of our journey. We are a little nervous to finally experience the road we've heard so much about. Please pray for us to have peace and safety as we travel the road, despite the hazards.

We're glad we wound up in a nice hotel. A good night's sleep seems a prerequisite for the concentration and nerves it will take David to drive the road tomorrow. We've decided to take the old road. It has less traffic and will allow us to take our time and avoid some of the more dangerous vehicles that race down the other one. It's the day we've thought of since we decided to move to Bolivia. Part of the reason we drove here. We still have 3 days of travel and need your prayers as much as ever. We have appreciated all your notes of congratulations and encouragement as we near the end of our journey. Although the journey is drawing to a close, our adventure is just beginning. We look forward to keeping you posted on our beginnings in a new culture, a new land.

Well, our initiation into wild, primitive, Bolivia, ended with us all in one piece. We made it down the Death Road. Although there were times we didn't particularly enjoy being perched on a cliff with a big bus or truck squeezing by, in all, the road was an amazing experience! We'll let the pictures tell the story.

As we came to the spot where the old death road began, a dirt road dropped down into the fog. It felt lonely turning off the main road with all the traffic and committing to the foggy abyss. In a little while, it leveled out to a spot with a few leftover signs. We stopped there to take some pictures before going on. We were all a little nervous, but being on the old road with no traffic (we saw only one other vehicle) had its advantages, and we took our time and got some great pictures.

An ominous condor on the side of the road

Many memorials were on the side of the road, where vehicles had gone off the cliff.

David and I waving from this small bridge. Eventually, we dropped down under the fog and clouds and saw how beautiful the scenery was.

Passing was rather tight at times

277

This tunnel was a watery, muddy mess inside.

When we met back up with the regular route, we had to play the game of being on the cliffside while big vehicles go by. There's no room for two vehicles in many places, so at times, it's necessary to back up to a wider spot.

We made it to the town of Caranavi and found a hotel. We were all exhausted. Even the loud music and revelry going on somewhere below us in the night hardly mattered. We've made it this far, and either today or tomorrow, we'll be **HOME**! Thank you for all the prayers said on our behalf. Praise God for our safety thus far!

Love,

Kristi for the VanderZons

Author: 12 yr old Kacie

Since we are in Bolivia now, summarize our trip.

MEXICO

Mexico was a friendly place we all enjoyed very much. We met lots of lovely people there and had a pleasant surprise as it was our first Latin-American, Spanish-speaking country.

GUATEMALA

We had an enjoyable time in Guatemala too. I really enjoyed staying at a church family's house along the way and staying at the nature reserve on Lake Atitlan. The reserve featured monkeys, coatimundis, zip-lining, hiking, lovely little cabins, and swing bridges. The people were very friendly there.

EL SALVADOR

We enjoyed staying near the beach where there were lots of surfers.

HONDURAS

We had a horrible experience as we were at the border for 26 hours and only spent 1½ hours in the country, but I'm sure that Honduras has a nice side to it.

NICARAGUA

We enjoyed visiting a family in the capital city Managua, Nicaragua.

COSTA RICA

There was lots of coffee growing here. We stayed at a farm where we met a native Panamanian family working with the coffee.

PANAMA

Here we got to visit the Panama Canal, explore the San Blas – Islands, then ship the Land-Cruiser and ourselves.

COLOMBIA

It felt good to be on land again. Explored the port city of Cartagena and traveled through lots of beautiful countryside.

ECUADOR

We enjoyed seeing the Equator and being on Bolivia's side of the hemisphere.

PERU

Last country before Bolivia! We went through a big desert. Saw lots of the coast, went through the Andes mountains, and saw llamas.

BOLIVIA

Our new country! We finally made it home to Bolivia! Thankfully an easy border crossing. We got to cross Lake Titi-Kaka on a ferry on our way to the capital, La Paz. It did not seem so intimidating approaching this big city because I knew it would be a hometown. We're home after 100 days and enjoying every minute of it.

CHAPTER 14

JUNGLE LIFE IN IXIAMAS

Author: Kristi VanderZon   11/10/2010

Dear Family and Friends,

After 8,249 miles, 12 countries, and 100 days, our faithful beast of burden (the Land Cruiser) delivered us to our new home on November 4th. Praise God for his faithfulness!

It was rough going the last couple days of travel. We bumped along in a cloud of dust, not able to go very fast. At the same time, the vehicle practically rattled itself apart. We made a lot of stops while David fixed the parts that had rattled loose.

We made one final water crossing over the Beni River.

After leaving Rurrenabaque behind, where we crossed the river, there was a long desolate stretch for five hours. We realized some things we had always taken for granted weren't so easy to get anymore. Some gas stations were out of gas or closed. Road maintenance seems to be nonexistent, and sometimes large boulders are right in the road. Many creeks to cross and it seemed like an endless stretch of road.

Our first glimpse of the house.

Worth it All! We're finally home!

We explored the house and property, then went down the road to meet the Miller Family. They were glad to see us, and we ate some delicious meals there the first few days while we were settling in. We camped out under the porch at our house while we cleaned up the inside. The church came over Monday morning for a work bee to help clean up the yard. By the time they left, we had a lovely yard to look out at and could begin to envision starting a garden. We're surrounded by banana, mango, lime, and grapefruit trees.

Moving in and cleaning up a house that's been sitting vacant in the jungle for over two years had its challenges. The second night here, we had a small issue in the outhouse. The girls were nervous about using it in the dark, so I offered to go first. Kindra thought she had seen a nest of some kind down the hole, so with my headlamp on, I opened the lid to peek down there to see what I could see. Out flew about 10 bats right up over my head. More were hanging upside down under the seat, waiting for their chance for escape. For the next few days, the war was on to eradicate them from their territory. They kept wanting to get back in there. Eventually, they did reluctantly move out, and we can use the outhouse without fear and trembling.

We got our first glimpse of a tarantula when David moved some old boards in front of our porch. Underneath was a hollowed-out spot that seemed a favorite hideout for creepy crawly things. We found 2 snakes, one giant and hairy tarantula, and a scorpion. David was quite taken with the tarantula, and we had to convince him to kill it.

Some rodents had taken a liking to the upstairs, and at night would run up and down the rafters above our bed. We couldn't tell what they were. At first, we thought they were rats, but they had no tail. The closest I could describe them would be like a guinea pig, but more rat-like. We got home one night, and Mervin Miller was with us. I went up to the bedroom and immediately shined the light up to the ceiling, and sure enough, there was one of them. Mervin wanted to see it, and more than that, to kill it for us. He got a stick and went up to our bedroom. His efforts were applauded as he crawled in and out of our window, trying to strike it with the stick.

Finally, we formulated a plan. Mervin would hit it down, and David would wait on the ground with a shovel to kill it when it landed. Kacie was the flashlight holder, and Kindra and I were on the ground with David, fascinated to see what would happen. Mervin hit it square with his stick. The critter flew through the air with outstretched paws and hit the ground running. It met its end under Mervin's stick, who had somehow descended the stairs and beat David's shovel to the final death blow. Upon picking up the rodent for a close examination, Mervin had to admit he had never seen one before. It had thick hair like a deer and lots of whiskers. Its face looked like a rat, but its body was kind of like a guinea pig. Mervin asked a native about it the next day, who knew right away what we had killed, and informed Mervin that they're excellent to eat. That's one thing I don't plan on trying.

We really like it here in Bolivia, and the house looks more like home every day. The other families here have made us feel very welcome and have been an enormous help to us in these initial days of adjustment and challenges. We thank all of you for your prayers and thoughts during the journey here. It was such an encouragement to us during the long days of travel. We will continue to share our life with you through these emails and appreciate all of your emails as well.

Thank You!

Love,

Kristi, for the VanderZons

Author: Kristi VanderZon   12/03/2010

Dear Family & Friends,

I thought you might be interested in hearing what a typical trip to the nearest town with a post office and an immigration office to do our paperwork is like. It was our first experience traveling beyond our little bubble since we arrived here.

Monday was David & Kindra's trip to Rurre (that's what they call Rurrenabaque down here), and it was quite the adventure. It was their first trip on Bolivian public transportation: the bus. Kacie & I drove them into Ixiamas at the wee hour of 4:00 yesterday morning. They were supposed to be on the bus at 4:30, and it was supposed to leave promptly at 5:00. But this is Bolivia. They stood there for an hour waiting for the driver to show up, along with a gathering crowd. At 5:30, the bus showed up, and they were on their way 15 minutes later.

The bus was over packed with people standing or sitting in the isles for the four-hour journey to Rurre. But it wasn't that simple. Many stops along the way to pick up or let off more people really slowed down the trip. But the ultimate delay was a man waiting on the side of the road to get on with 50-60 huge bags of charcoal, 100 pounds each. People here produce charcoal in homemade big clay ovens to sell up in La Paz. Bag after bag was loaded by pushing and cramming them into the underside of the bus. The passenger & bus driver were bickering about the amount of charcoal and the poor quality of it the whole time. This took at least 45 minutes.

They finally arrived in Rurre at 11:30, 2 ½ hours later than the scheduled time. Knowing at 12pm, everything in town shuts down for siesta until 3:00 pm, which is when the return ride to Ixiamas was going to leave. This put a lot of pressure on Kindra and David to do some pretty fast walking. Their main goal was to find immigration and renew our visas, which expired the next day. They saw a friend on a moto who told them they were too late. Just about everyone drives motorcycles for transportation here, and they call them motos. Immigration had just closed its door for vacation and wouldn't open back up until Friday.

David could hardly believe this unfortunate turn of events. Before giving more thought to the matter, their one consolation was to go to the French bakery. We had become fond of it in our short time in Rurre on the way here. The little bakery is full of delicate French pastries. Our favorite being the chocolate-filled croissants. They had high hopes of bringing a bag home, but there was not one solitary crumb left of anything by the time they got there. Sadly they were all gone. In a state of frustration and mounting discouragement, they pursued their goal of getting the visas renewed, not willing to believe it couldn't be done till they tried.

They found the immigration office. To their surprise, it looked open. They went in, and David even remembered his Spanish courtesies, like saying good morning, and how are you, before blurting out his request. The girls and I have been lecturing him on his blunt, rude way of demanding things. He doesn't mean to be rude. He just doesn't know many words. All the politeness didn't help because the man sitting at the desk couldn't help them. He said the immigration official was indeed on vacation until Friday. Kindra then inserted herself, pleading on our behalf that it was imperative and necessary to get our visas renewed today, as tomorrow they run out. If you let them run out, they are non-renewable without leaving the country and coming back in. Pleading, begging, and whining are very effective here. The man said he would take them to some "house." We are still limited in our comprehension of Spanish, but this is what they thought he said.

He then escorted them out the door and shut it behind them. Where did he go? Had they misunderstood? In a few minutes, he came out and led them down the street a ways to a man's house. He called the man out and explained the situation. The man appeared to have lost no time starting his holiday, as he had no shirt on, and was quite a sight with his grand-sized belly proudly shining with sweat. Yes, this was the immigration official.

Nevertheless, he agreed to go down to the office and help us. Back at the office, he took the time to count the days on his calendar one by one, then made his stamp ready. He took the usual delight in creating a great show of stamping the visa.

Then he charged us double the regular price as this was his vacation. Not a problem, as we recognized the gravity of the favor. David handed him a 100 Boliviano bill for the total fee of 80. The man happily pocketed this, not even attempting to give David the change. This is typical. Here, it seems, no one has changed, and no one wants to provide change. This done, the race was on. Although they had already crossed the river once, they had to get on a boat to re-cross the Beni River and purchase the ticket for the return ride. They crossed the river again to get to the post office, where a special package from my mom could be waiting.

The post office was closed, but David would not be deterred. He called out "Hello" many times, and not getting a response, took his umbrella and started raking it up and down the ridged metal door. This eventually got the attention of the woman in charge, who was willing to let them in, and they were able to get the package. Hallelujah! They also mailed out some letters the girls and I had written. That done, they raced around purchasing the things we needed, then it was back across the river to get in a packed minibus. It was hot and cramped. As they sat there for 15 minutes, everyone started sweating. The impatient passengers began yelling out, "Vamos Maestro, es muy calor!" (let's go, driver, it's very hot). Finally, the driver got in, and they were on their way home.

The ride home was sweltering, cramped, noisy, and uncomfortable. David says there was not one square inch to spare in there. They were relieved to finally be back in Ixiamas. From there, they each got on a moto-taxi to get home. This was a first for Kindra, and it was a little out of her comfort zone to hop on the back of a motorcycle with all the bags she was holding for a half-hour, dangerous, muddy ride back home.

Shortly after 8:00pm, Kacie and I were overjoyed to see them pull up on the Motos. We sat around the table after hearing about their trip then opened the package. The other purchases included a block of cane sugar, some chewy fruit called tamarindo, a nice warm blanket for Kacie's bed, and five bags of coffee from the only known place to get coffee here.

That was our first trip outside of Ixiamas since we arrived here. It takes a lot of effort to get to Rurre. We'll have to return again in a month to extend the visas. Hopefully, we'll have what we need to extend it for a year.

With much love and thanks for your continued prayers,

Kristi, for the VanderZons

Author: Kristi VanderZon   12/16/2010

Dear Family & Friends,

"Paro" is the word used here for a blockade. We found out all about how it can make things difficult last week, as David & Kindra set out for the 24 hour trip to La Paz to do some paperwork. Kacie and I stayed behind to keep things running smoothly here on the home front. It really strengthens our trust and dependence on God when we have to separate from each other, as there is no easy way to communicate. Travel is dangerous and unpredictable. So while Kacie and I were at home, making frequent trips down to the Miller family so we wouldn't get too lonely, we thought we might have a week or two before we would see David & Kindra again. It was an incredibly lonely feeling with them gone. While we thought they were far away in La Paz, they were actually speeding down a dark, dusty, dirt road on a motorbike and surprised us by arriving home late one night.

I'll start at the beginning.....

Last Tuesday, David, Kindra, and some other American missionaries set off in a minivan to go to Rurrenabaque. From there, David & Kindra were going to go on to La Paz. Later that same day, they returned home after being informed that there was a "*paro*," or roadblock. No vehicles were allowed to leave Ixiamas. Here in Bolivia, it is common practice for towns to declare *paros* to get their way from the government for something they want. Maybe a new bridge, or other favor. It seems when one town declares one, the idea catches on. Even here, where the road ends, suddenly, no businesses were open in the little town of Ixiamas, and no vehicles could come or go. Even the sawmill at the end of our road was strangely quiet.

There are consequences if you try to get through in a vehicle. They will slash your tires. If you want to get through a blockade on foot, they might beat you with a stick. But depending on how important it is to get through, some people find it worth taking the beating. So, in this mindset, the little party returned home to wait out this *paro*. Later that same day, a family from Georgia stopped at our house on the way to Millers. They were in a minivan taxi and said there was no more *paro*. They came through with no problems. They all filed out of the minivan as the van could not get through the muddy road to get to Millers.

So there was the empty van, heading back towards Rurrenabaque. David and Kindra decided to take it. They hadn't even unpacked their backpacks and were all set to go. So unexpectedly, just like that, they disappeared down the road in the taxi. They made it all the way to Rurrenabaque that day. They wanted to take a flight from Rurrenabaque to La Paz, but no flights were leaving. The *paro* was still strong on the other side of the town going towards La Paz and had the main road and airport shut. No buses were being allowed to leave. Restless tourists who found themselves stranded there were preparing to take a 12-15 hour journey by boat down the Beni river to a little town, where the boat driver thought they might be able to get a ride to La Paz. This didn't sound too good to David, so they decided to get back home as soon as possible and forget trying to get to La Paz this time.

When they went to wait for a boat ride back across the Beni river, they thought it unusual to see a gathering crowd there. The ticket office was closed, and a man was walking around with a big stick, striking it against his hand, saying things like, "We're not going to let them get off the boat. We will beat them if they try!" The crowd seemed to appreciate his words and was getting excited. As the boat hauling people from the other side started approaching the shore, this crowd, led by their self-appointed "leader" with the big stick, started yelling at the boat that it wasn't welcome and couldn't come to shore. Still, the boat tried to get close enough to let the people off, but the crowd interfered. They physically blocked the people from getting off, except for a military man, who got off the boat and disappeared through the crowd. So, no help from the authorities. There were loud words and arguing, and the leader pushed the boat away from shore.

David and Kindra were hanging towards the back of the crowd. In a state of disbelief, their only way home was a boat that was now heading back across the river. They were considering the possibility that they would be "trapped" in the town of Rurre until this Paro was lifted. Sometimes these can go on for a month. Well, at this moment, God intervened. The mob leader looked back and looked at David & Kindra like he was just seeing them for the first time. He waved them towards the front and yelled at the boat to come back. When the boat got close enough to leap, they were on and thankful for getting the last boat across the river during this blockade. Thankful, too, that God opened up the way. On the other side, in the village of San Buena, the people were offended that Rurre wouldn't let them off the boat. This started loud protests and complaints from the people that "San Buena is good! We don't need Rurre! The name of San Buena will live on!" While this little drama was playing out, David wondered how to find a ride back to Ixiamas – still four hours away. People were saying, "No taxis to Ixiamas." David and Kindra found a bench to sit down on and wait.

A woman approached them and whispered secretively, "Do you want to go to Ixiamas?" Kindra excitedly answered, "Yes!" "Shhh!" the lady warned. "I know where a taxi is. Come with me, but don't act like we're together." They followed the lady, joined by six other people, who were silently "not" following her. They walked up to a group of waiting motorcycle taxis, and all got on. They sped off at once through little dusty side streets, which took them out of town. They stopped where a vehicle appeared to be waiting and paid their drivers, who sped away. A feeling of disappointment prevailed, as the vehicle was abandoned, with no driver in sight.

The group then flagged down a vehicle driving by on the road. They were pulling out their Bolivianos, offering to pay over twice the price for a ride. Still, the driver wanted no part and said, "No more taxis going out to the country." The group then dispersed and left David & Kindra standing alone on a hot, dusty road, with their heavy backpacks and a mop bucket they had purchased in town. Kacie had requested one. As they walked back towards town, they flagged down a few more vehicles. The answer remained, "No." No taxis are allowed to go to the country.

Just when they were about to give up, a motorcycle taxi stopped and asked where they needed to go. Generally, moto-taxis are for in-town travel, not for a long-distance trip on severely bumpy roads. When they told him their destination, he seemed agreeable to taking them for a reasonable price. He sped off for fuel (a commodity becoming rarer by the moment) and recruited another moto-taxi. As promised, he soon returned, and David & Kindra each got on one, thankful for a ride. Before they got too far, they stopped at a little wooden shack by the side of the road, which was something like a repair shop. The drivers tightened and oiled chains and aired up their tires, preparing for the rough, long trip ahead.

By now, it was late in the afternoon, and the trip took 5 ½ hours. There were many creeks, river crossings, and dangerous maneuvers. It was dark, and the trip seemed long. They were all grateful to see the town of Ixiamas come into view. People were waving and seemed excited to see anyone arrive during this time of "Paro". The fact that they arrived on motos really seemed to gain some attention and respect. It was 10:30 when their adventure came to an end in front of our quiet little house. Kacie and I were thrilled at their unexpected arrival, as we assumed they were all the way to La Paz by now. We're getting our Bolivian education by first-hand experience.

One other notable occurrence.... we had our first snake in the house dilemma. It started as quite a mystery. It was well into the evening, and we were downstairs in our home and heard something like water being poured out on the floor upstairs, above our heads. We then heard what sounded like marbles dropping on the floor. We thought it was very strange, but we didn't go check on the source of the noise. Later, Kacie went upstairs to get ready for bed and said, "Something's weird up here. It looks like something puked." Strange words to hear.

So we all went up to check it out, and right beside her bed, on the floor, was a wet puddle with white-looking egg stuff in it and some pellets around it. We were genuinely stumped as to the source of this mess. We were all offering our ideas of what could have made this mess. A monkey who dropped an egg? A snake? Surely not a snake. Well, David went outside and shined his flashlight around the house, and up outside our window was the culprit. A four-foot-long snake. We formulated a plan. David went up and leaned outside our window with a hoe, and Kacie was shining the light and making sure the snake didn't come back inside. Kindra and I were down below on the ground to watch where the snake would land and make sure it didn't get away. David didn't want to be unnerved by my scream (he knows me well), so I held one hand over my mouth and held the flashlight with the other. Just in case I forgot and screamed when the snake hit the ground. It worked, and the snake hit the ground and just stayed there. David then killed it, and the excitement was over.

The snake minus its head.

In other snake news... David & Mervin found a coral snake. They are very poisonous. A couple of nights ago, Kacie and some others were walking down the Miller's lane in the dark and barely missed stepping on a coiled-up, very poisonous viper called a *Yoperojabobo*. The snakes are out, probably due to a lot of rain lately.

Kindra and Kacie bring back lots of bounty of a banana plantation

Kristi playing her violin

David has green beans, squash, onions, beets, kohlrabi, and tomatoes growing in the garden. We will have a hearty appetite for fresh produce by the time they're producing. I've been asked questions about our diet. It's rough right now, except when we're eating down at the Miller's home or the hearty meal served after church on Sundays. We don't have dairy, meat, or vegetables. So it's usually rice and beans, or noodles.

We have oatmeal for breakfast, and we've learned how to steam bake a cake or bread by putting the batter in a bowl in a steaming pot of water with the lid on. Thank the Lord for the fruit! Bananas are in abundance to snack on all day long. Right now, it's raining mangoes all around the house. Our brothers & sisters in the Lord here have been faithful to drop off a hunk of cheese, a quart of milk, or even a leg of wild pig every now and again.

It means so much, I can hardly convey a big enough thank you to them. Starting up is the hardest part, and we need to have patience while we get established. It's very hopeful to see green plants in the garden now, and we want to get a cow. We have plans to build a brick oven to bake in. Until then, we're thankful that our needs are met and that we have an opportunity to learn contentment authentically. Many people experience true hunger, and all we lack is variety. This isn't exactly a hardship.

Thank you all for your prayers. The Lord has been so good to us! We often reminisce about our trip and what a great experience it was. It was a lot of fun sharing it with all of you.

May God bless each one.

In His love, Kristi, for the VanderZons

Author: Kristi VanderZon   01/05/2011

Greetings to all our Family & Friends. May God bless this New Year!

Time has been passing quickly here in our new home. We recently enjoyed picking corn and making tamales with some friends at a neighbor, Dona Hilda's house.

First, we picked the corn...

Then after cutting all the kernels off the cob, we ground it.

After mixing the ground corn with some cheese, sugar, cinnamon, and salt, the girls filled the corn husks with the soft mixture.

We then turned them over to Hilda and her clay oven.

Here, Delilah is cooking lunch for us all. Above her is hanging wild pig "charque", the dried meat that is popular here.

At Dona's Hilda's

We really enjoyed our day at Dona Hilda's learning to make tamales.

Kacie washing dishes with her little friend

Almost ready to pop them in the oven...

Dona Hilda working her clay oven

Other things of interest... We brought home a cow from the Miller's named Tulip. The first night, she ran away, but we found her the next morning back at the Miller's. We're very thankful to have fresh milk again.

Kindra milking Tulip, the cow.

We know many of you are praying for us daily, and we want to say a huge "Thank You" and "Praise God", as we believe his hand of protection has been over us. The other night, I was up in the middle of the night, and as is my usual custom, I shone my flashlight over the girls to make sure all was well. I was surprised to see a scorpion right there on Kacie's side, easily identifiable against her pale blue nightgown. She was in a deep sleep, so I woke David up to help me. We both looked down on her peaceful sleeping form, wondering how to best get the scorpion off her without waking her up or causing it to sting her. We decided Duct tape might work best. David took a strip and quickly pressed it on the scorpion and peeled it off her nightgown, and there we had it. A tribute to the many uses of Duct Tape. Kacie never even woke up! So our hearts were very thankful to God for his mercy and protection.

A beautiful jungle sunset

A beautiful jungle moon

The weather here has been pleasant. Although it's the rainy season, in between the rains, it's often sunny and breezy. David's been working in the garden, and things look hopeful, with green beans in the near future and squash plants blossoming. The tomatoes are underway and are growing well.

We love you all and appreciate each one. We're looking forward to walking with the Lord through another new year and whatever it may hold.

Love, Kristi, for the VanderZons in Bolivia

Author: Kristi VanderZon   01/11//2011

A warm greeting to all our family & friends!

For some time now, we've wanted to write about our church here. We feel very blessed to be among the believers here. The church is led by Ryan Hershberger of Muddy Pond, TN. There are a few American families here, and also some Native Bolivians that attend.

Here is a group photo.

This is the church house.

Inside

The church house is built on Diana Kardona's place. This is her house.

We're doing well, and when the rains aren't too heavy, and we can safely cross the river between us & church, we go. We enjoy worshipping together with this group of believers. After the service, we have a meal together and usually stay late into the afternoon visiting.

With Love from Bolivia,

Kristi for the VanderZons

Author: Kristi VanderZon   04/18/2011

Dear family & friends,

It seems that our time in Bolivia is coming to an end, at least for now. We have learned much and have enjoyed sweet fellowship with some very dear friends after six months here. However, after much prayer and discussion, we feel it is in the best interest of our family to return to the States. This time traveling by air, not by land. Many factors led to this decision. Difficulty obtaining the correct documents for our visas and my mom's health on the top of the list. She is being treated for cancer.

We would greatly appreciate your prayers as we begin the journey home. There are some uncertainties about traveling here in Bolivia. We will leave Sunday for Rurrenabaque, and from there, try to find a flight or ride to Santa Cruz, and from there, fly home to the USA. We could be facing a lot of travel time to get to Santa Cruz. There is political unrest here in Bolivia, causing many inconvenient roadblocks. The road to Santa Cruz is partly underwater. The other option, the road to La Paz, the "Death Road", is plagued by landslides, and recent travelers report 60 hours to 6 days for the usual 20-hour trip. We're trusting the Lord for his timing and protection on the way.

We have been very encouraged by everyone who took an interest in our journey here and have faithfully kept in contact with us during our time here. We look forward to seeing many of you upon our return. As we know more specific dates, we will let you know.

Praying for His will to be done,

In Love, Kristi for the VanderZons

CHAPTER 15

RURRE LIFE

Author: Kristi VanderZon   11/27/2010

Dear Friends and Family,

It was strange to write the subject of this email "Pilgrims Leaving Bolivia."
When we came here, we didn't know how long our stay would be. We
really didn't envision it being as short as a six-month stay. In those six
months, we became very close to the Miller family and a few extraordinary
Bolivian friends from the sawmill down the road from our house.

Our family in the house

Kacie swimming in the creek. We did our laundry in the creek and cooled off many times here.

Kindra weaving baskets with natural local materials

Kindra and Biddy enjoying some hammock time

Kristi hanging up laundry by the house. You had to be careful and take the
clothes down before nightfall so borros wouldn't lay eggs in your clothes
and then burrow into your skin.

307

A few of our special friends.

Friday, we set out on a beautiful hike with our friends and some of the Miller's to a waterfall about 2 ½ hours behind the Miller's home. It was a wonderful day full of the beauty of God's creation. We enjoyed being together with loved ones, knowing our time with them was growing short.

The girls and walter at the base of a gigantic walking tree

The girls on top of a boulder in the creek

Kindra and Kristi cooling off in the water

We saw a pretty green snake on the way, which was very poisonous despite all its beauty.

Sunday morning, the Miller family brought us down a special Bolivian breakfast of fresh fried fish caught from the river by their son, Dylan, and roasted wild pig, captured the night before by their son-in-law, Eduardo. They paired it with the typical Bolivian foods that we've come to appreciate, like yucca, papaya, and fried bananas. They sent us with food for the journey. Not the usual picnic type food we might have traveled with in the States, like sandwiches and chips, but a whole, roasted, leg of pig, yucca, rolls, and some of Laura Miller's good fresh cheese. The parting farewell was a heartbreak for all. Never have we had such a sorrowful parting. It was almost enough to call off our plans to go. We persevered, and with a tearful parting prayer, pulled away in the Land Cruiser. We were unsure when or if we would ever return to these dear people that have been like family to us.

On the road again.... It sure felt different to set out traveling again. Very lonely. The buses weren't running Sunday due to muddy road conditions, so we were the only vehicle on the road for a while. The conditions were terrible, the worst we've seen. But our faithful vehicle pulled through the worst of it. We were delayed when we came to a swollen river, where we had to wait 4 ½ hours for the water to go down so we could cross.

Waiting to cross the river. It was chest-deep in the middle with a powerful current. When the level went down to waist-deep, a vehicle crossed. It was swept sideways a bit due to the current but pulled out on the other side. We decided to go next, successful, though shadows of uncertainty hovered over us as we plunged through the deepest part.

We traveled well past dark, and one of the headlights went out. We finally came to the Beni River, but the barge to take the vehicle across was closed. We found a hotel for the night and crossed early the following morning. A remarkable new friend and brother in the Lord, Pastor Alfred, kindly offered that we stay in his church house during our stay in Rurrenabaque. We are grateful for a place to stay that accommodates us, our dogs, and our pile of belongings so well.

Kacie & Biddy in front of the church house.

We spent some time waiting by the Beni River for Pastor Alfred to meet us.
Kindra faithfully records our travels in her journal.

Our friend and brother in the Lord, Don Wendy, came from Ixiamas to Rurrenabaque yesterday to help us sell the vehicle. He's been a big help taking us around and helping us with little details. It's going to be a hard thing to see the Land Cruiser go. It's been more than just a vehicle on this trip; it's been like home. It's going to be a sad feeling to be without it.

We got our email last night and were very touched by the response we've gotten from many of you. Truly, we've never been alone, even on desolate roads. God is an ever-present help in times of trouble. Your emails and assurance of prayers make it clear we're not forgotten by our friends and family either. Thank you to everyone who has been faithful to remember us.

After we sell the vehicle, we'll be traveling either to Santa Cruz or La Paz to find a flight home. We'll then fly into Miami or Orlando and then be visiting the brethren in Tennessee. After that, we plan to spend some time in Michigan with my family. We will be prayerfully seeking the Lord's will and direction from there.

We'll keep you all posted on our traveling progress out of Bolivia.

Love, Kristi for the VanderZon family

Author: Kristi VanderZon   11/09/2010

Dear Friends and Family,

A dear pastor here in Rurrenabaque has taken us under his wing and is letting us stay in his humble church house for as long as we need to be here. It's a great help to have a place to stay, store all our things, and allow the dogs. We have an American friend who traveled yesterday from Ixiamas to help us sell the vehicle.

Our pile of possessions

Kacie snoozing with the dogs on our mats

The toilet/shower area

Yesterday, the weather was beautiful. So was Rurrenabaque. We walked around town, got some repairs done on the vehicle, and shopped around. Kacie purchased a Bolivian turtle to add to her collection. Today, we're going to get the vehicle all cleaned up and meet a man who wants to buy it. It's going to seem strange to part with our Land Cruiser. It's been more than a vehicle, it's been like a home to us on this trip. Without it, it's going to be much more challenging to get to Santa Cruz to get a flight. But…still easier than driving it all the way back…right?

Enjoying breakfast pastry at the amazing French Chef's booth

An anteater up in a coconut tree

Love, Kristi for the VanderZons

Author: Kristi VanderZon   7/23/2011

Dear Friends and Loved ones,

Our apologies for the lack of timely communication. We have unexpectedly changed our plans of returning to the States. We instead opened a breakfast café here in the beautiful riverside town of Rurrenabaque, Bolivia.

Time sure flew by as we began to prepare, and then opened up the café. We left behind the early days of drinking coffee and waiting for people to come. Now, there's not much time to drink coffee, and we're busy serving the tourists that come in looking for an excellent homemade breakfast.

Some French Backpackers eating at our café.

The girls initially did well selling our baked goods on the street, but now we're focusing more on the café itself, as it takes all four of us to run it well.

We were blessed to find a house to rent in a peaceful area just a ten-minute walk from the café. We "said goodbye" to a faithful friend. We sold our Land Cruiser to a local man who is using it to take tourists out on jungle tours.

We're enjoying the unique opportunity to run the café and meet people from all over the world. May the Lord use our service to others for his kingdom as people are curiously observing our family. We have many opportunities to share our belief in God's word and let them know, "We weren't always this way…the Lord changed our lives…"

Krist the cook, proudly displaying a fresh plate of crepes

David washing the dishes. He was the kitchen support

Kacie, the DJ and Shopper

Kindra the waitress

Biddy mingling with her street dog friends

We appreciate all of you who have sent concerned emails to us, proving we are still thought of and prayed for. Thank you for your love even when my correspondence was temporarily delayed due to the new schedule we are keeping. We also lost our computer charging cord (which we just got replaced). I appreciate all of you and continue to look forward to reading your emails out loud to the family.

Our house in Rurrenabaque made out of natural local materials

Our view of the town from the thatched loft

Having some fun with the food

Kindra and Kacie crafting in the outdoor living room

Kindra soaking up some sun

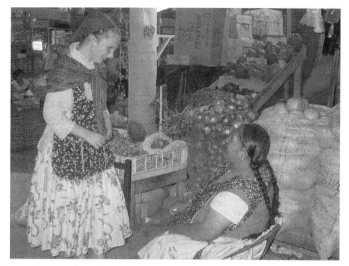

Kacie on her market shopping rounds. She made good friends with the vendors through her friendly personality and dressing in their native styles.

The ladies having fun with Kacie's doll, Timoteo

If there's one thing that grieves us where we are, it's the lack of spiritual fellowship. We feel it is only for a season, but at times it is hard to be "alone" here. The people we meet daily are very kind. We're getting to know the locals along with the transient backpackers. Many times they are here for a week or two and come for breakfast every morning. It's been a blessing to make many friends around the world this way, and some, I'm sure, we will continue to be in contact with.

We also have made good friends with our neighbors at the cafe, and we are very grateful that the Lord always seems to put people in our lives to encourage us on the way.

We continue to press on and grow as a family, working together. Our girls enjoy this opportunity immensely. Their comprehension and use of the Spanish language continue to soar high above David's and my own.

Love, from Bolivia

David, Kristi, Kindra & Kacie VanderZon

Author: Kristi VanderZon   11/09/2010

Dear Friends,

We apologize for the delay in sending out the news that we're back in Michigan. I suppose many of you have already heard and know the circumstances. But for all of you who haven't...

We've had a busy, emotional time these past weeks as we decided to travel back to Michigan. Although many things in Bolivia were going well for us, we began to feel a longing to be back in Michigan. Coupled with the news that my mom's health was rapidly deteriorating, we decided to leave as soon as possible. Still, all in all, it took about three weeks to actually execute the plan. We closed down the café, packed up, and worked on arranging flights, etc. It was tough to pack up and leave. When we finally made it to the Bolivia/Peru border, immigration took our passports and wouldn't let us leave due to a fine. After working throughout the year to obtain our one-year visa, we never did accomplish it, and our fine was rather large.

We had understood that they would let us leave by land and give us a "'no return" stamp in our passports, but that wasn't true. Instead, we got sent back to the capital city of La Paz. This caused a huge inconvenience, as we already had flights booked out of Lima, Peru. We spent the next day

324

in Immigration being told various things. Everything from "come back tomorrow" to "we're going to deport you". The deportation thing would have been great, but it would have taken too long. We went back and forth all day and reached a compromise with our fine and agreed to leave that very night. American Airlines was able to accommodate us, but we barely had time to reach the airport. We were finally able to fly out of La Paz on the 22nd of August.

Despite our best efforts, the airline refused to take the crate that our dog, Walter, was in. This was very sad for us, as he was nine years old and very special to us. He had made the trip to Bolivia with us, and we didn't want to leave him behind. A friend came and got him, but we still are trying to arrange to get him back. Our other dog was in a crate they would take, so at least she came home with us. When we came into Miami, we couldn't get a rental vehicle, as the agencies all want credit cards, not cash. This started a very stressful leg of the journey, where we thankfully got a flight right to Traverse City, Michigan. We had to split up, and each of our groups of "2" missed the connecting flight in Chicago. We had 48 hours of catching flights and missing flights before Kacie and I finally arrived in Traverse City on the 24th of August. My family met us at the airport with an enthusiastic welcome and took me straight home to see my mom.

The girls and the dogs waiting for our flights

Finally back in the USA. Waiting in the sweltering Florida heat

Kindra and biddy stretching their legs

We spent a precious day together, which took about the last of her strength. The next day, she was exhausted, and the next, she was in a semi-coma. She died that night. I praise the Lord for his sustaining grace, which allowed me precious time with my mom before she died. All six of us children were able to be home for her passing, and I know us all being there brought her great peace. But her greatest peace was faith in Jesus Christ and God the Father.

So, for a time, we're living in Traverse City, Michigan, sharing a house with my Dad. Our Bolivian experience is still bright in our minds and alive in our hearts. It's something we will never forget.

Thank you, everyone, for your prayers, concern, and interest in our journey. It was a highlight of the trip, sharing it with all of you and getting your emails and encouragement. All the families we stayed with on our journey were a blessing and hold a special place in our hearts. It gave us a sense of the blessings that come from the ministry of hospitality. It is a gift.

For now, we are content to wait and pray for direction in the next phase of life for our family.

With Love,

The VanderZons

Obituary Tribute to Carol Ellen Stevens

Carol Ellen Stevens, 72, of Traverse City, went to heaven on Saturday, Aug. 27, 2011, at her home, surrounded by her loving family.

Carol was born Oct. 8, 1938, in Muskegon, to the late Eino Jacob and Bernice May (McClain) Wiitala.

On Oct.12, 1956, she married Gerald Lee Stevens at Kaleva Baptist Church. They made their home in Traverse City and lovingly raised six children.

Carol was a kind, loving Christian mother redeemed by the blood of the Lamb of God, Jesus her Savior. She enjoyed serving the Lord at Immanuel Baptist Church in Traverse City.

Carol was a natural musician. She loved to play the organ and had an amazing gift for harmonizing with the special different groups of people with whom she sang, including the Honey Harmonizers from Mesick High School class of 1956.

In her spare time she loved to play and listen to the piano, sew, read to her grandchildren, and cook for her family. She had an incredible gift of hospitality. Recently she achieved KOPS status and was named queen of her Tops Club.

Carol was dearly loved and cherished by her family and we will always be grateful for the godly heritage she provided for us.

Surviving Carol is her husband, Gerald; children Matthew (Sandra) Stevens, Jeff (Terry) Stevens, Terry (Tricia) Stevens, Leeanne (Michael) Lane, Linda (David) Livermore, Kristi (David) VanderZon; daughter in-law Jackie Stevens; grandchildren Clay (Alicia) Stevens, Lucas and Jacob McClure, Benjamin (Cayla) Lane, Isaac Boyer, Alaina Stevens, Kindra VanderZon, Zachary Lane, Carolyn Lane, Emily Livermore, Elizabeth Lane, Kacie VanderZon, Grace Livermore and Peter Lane; great-grandchildren Brylie and Caylie Stevens; brother Don (Joan) Wiitala and Marilee (Richard) Duncan; and many nieces, nephews and cousins.

Carol is preceded in death by her parents, and grandson Aaron Stevens.

Carol, with the love of her life

CHAPTER 16

EPILOGUE

Author: Kacie Molina

After grandma's passing, we lived with our grandpa "Poppy" while we got back on our feet. It was an extraordinarily special time getting to support each other through the pain of life without grandma. Life was tough in the first months back in the states. I remember struggling with the shift in culture and language. I would often catch myself speaking Spanish during normal conversation. I wouldn't notice until I saw the questioning face of whom I was speaking with. Our small town routines were very abruptly replaced. Walking everywhere established a comfortable sense of community. Shopping at the market was a very personal and social experience. That was all replaced with the hustle and bustle of fast cars, crowded traffic, and a disconnection from the people around us.

We were all grateful to be home in the states. Still, transitioning from such a vastly different culture was especially hard on Kindra and me since we were young. We eagerly sought a new place to call home, and I think our shared craving drew us into homesteading in the Northwoods of Michigan. There we could live off the land, tending vegetables and animals. We relied on our horses for work and pleasure. Long rides through the peaceful lush woods allowed me to notice everything in the environment again. From the wildlife to the landscape and every flower in between. We would plow over a mile to maintain our dirt road on long winter days after heavy snow. It seemed to bring us all an irreplaceable peace and connection to the land again. My sister settled in and dug new roots.

The rest of us felt satisfied with the experience of creating a new homestead. We planned to settle down and stay put, leaving adventures and traveling behind to embrace a simple life. Almost like a cool glass of water after a long run, we enjoyed the moments of refreshment. After the glass was empty, the fleeting feeling left us renewed and rejuvenated, and we learned about a place called Jackson Hole.

Dad and mom wanted both of our girls to pursue our dreams. Kindra wanted to get married and have a family, so after meeting Christopher, they built a quaint little Log cabin on our homestead. Kindra gave birth to little Chloe Ellen in their cabin. It was a cold, snowy day, and with the midwife and mom there to assist, she was a lively and healthy little girl.

On the other hand, I claimed I never wanted to get married and wanted to go explore the world of skiing and competing. We had started watching ski movies and shredding our local hill. We began to pursue a more modern lifestyle and embraced exercise and athletics. So much for settling down since that idea didn't stick for long. Now, just the three of us, we set our sights on a new adventure. One filled with mountains, snow, and a quest to find where I belonged apart from the church and in a modern world.

I could only squeeze a fraction of the pictures I wanted to share in this book, so here's the link to our website where you can check out extra pictures and videos! https://welcometothejourney.us/

If you would like to hear more adventures from before or after our Bolivia trip, feel free to drop us a line and let us know here. Mom has over 10 years of daily journal entries that recorded our life in the Amish and homesteading. I'm sure before she shares them she'd love to hear some encouragement from her readers! https://welcometothejourney.us/?page_id=7

If you have any questions feel free to post them here and I will do my best to personally answer them!

https://welcometothejourney.us/?page_id=16

Kacie Molina was born in the big city of Milwaukee, WI. She was raised in an Amish community riding horses, playing with baby dolls, and reading. Kacie has since grown up and developed a passion for business, life abroad, and enjoying every moment with her husband, Tony, to the fullest.

Kindra Gillette currently enjoys life with her little farm family in northern Michigan. She has learned to go with the flow of a farming, homeschooling family, a herd of sheep, a hundred plus chickens, and dogs. When she isn't moving pasture fences, doing dishes, transplanting veggies, or teaching math, she loves drinking coffee, teaching essential oil classes, and learning wilderness survival skills with her 3 little kiddos. She is the proud wife of a fun, hard-working, handsome metal roofing contractor.

Kristi VanderZon was born and raised in Traverse City, MI. She was the youngest of 6 and had a lively and loving family. Kristi enjoys waking up early to work out, loving her family, cooking tasty meals, enjoying the fresh mountain air, wearing stylish clothes everyday, and drinking craft whiskey.

Made in the USA
Middletown, DE
16 September 2021

47866428R00192